1974

Readings for Social Work Practice

Volume I

Edited by
The Social Work Practice
 Area Faculty
Fordham University
 School of Social Service

Everett Busby

Helen E. Dermody

Mary Harm

Rev. John McCarthy, S.J.

Miriam Olson

Harold W. Robbins

Albert C. Tricomi

Ann Hartman, Chairman

MSS Information Corporation
655 Madison Avenue, New York, N.Y. 10021

Library of Congress Cataloging in Publication Data

Main entry under title.

Readings for social work practice.

    1. Social service--Addresses, essays,
    lectures.
I. Busby, Everett, comp.
HV37.R4   361   72-8103
ISBN 0-8422-5056-5
ISBN 0-8422-0250-1 (pbk)

CONTENTS

VALUE ISSUES AND SOCIAL WORK PRACTICE

This collection of readings has been gathered by the faculty of the Social Work Practice Area of Fordham University School of Social Service to make readily available to students in the first semester of the generic social work practice course some basic and supplemental materials. Although collected as an aid to the study of generic practice, many of these articles do not deal with generic practice per se, but with specific areas in a conceptual framework which allows for integration and comparison.

In order to give some guidelines to the reader in integrating this varied collection of readings, it is perhaps useful to introduce this volume with a discussion of the meanings of the word "generic" as applied to social work and a view of how generic practice might look. It is particularly important to differentiate the two major ways the word is used. The word "generic" is used to describe the common base that underlies all practice and is also used to denote a "general practice" of social work.

The Generic Base

The generic base of social work practice consists of that body of knowledge, skills and values that underly all social work practice with any size system. This common base is considerable and has perhaps been obscured by the fact that the three major methods have developed separate terminologies and are often really utilizing similar concepts under different names. Out of the development of the generic base has come a heightened awareness of what is specific to practice with different size systems. It would appear, however, that frequently specific differences arise, not out of the size of the client system but out of the nature of the need, purpose, and sanction.

The Generic Social Work Practitioner

The term generic has also been used to describe a "generalist" worker, a general practitioner of social work. This "general practitioner" is able to intervene with a broad range of client and systems, to utilize a wide variety of interventive measures, to approach different target systems. As practice is currently defined by the nature of the service delivery system, general social work practice is likely to develop in two different ways, depending on the worker's point of entry and the nature of the unit of attention.

A. An "Extended Action System" Model

This is the generalist practice model or a generic "stance" whereby the worker, as a part of a flexible agency, may follow the needs of the client system and utilize a variety of interventive methods. The original point of entry may be via an individual, a small group, a family, but the worker conceptualizes the "client-system-in-situation" in the broadest possible terms. The assessment process is approached with a sophisticated view of multiple transacting variables and in relation to this assessment, a wide variety of interventive measures may be utilized in behalf of the client system.

To illustrate: In a school social work situation, a ten year old boy is referred to the social worker because of acting out behavior in the classroom. The unit of attention includes this youngster and all of the social, economic, psychological, and cultural variables that may be transacting in the person-situation complex. Out of a sophisticated assessment, the worker may intervene with the child, the teacher, the peer group, the school administration, the family, the welfare department, the school board, the leaders of the community served by the school, etc. Thus the worker may work with an individual, a family, a group, a community group or organization, and the professional roles may well include supporter, enabler, catalyst, mediator, educator, therapist, negotiator, advocate, organizer, among others. We have called this the extended action system model because, although the entry point is via a specific client system, a wide variety of action systems could be mobilized to meet the specific need.

B. An Extended Client System Model

In this model of generalist practice, the worker's entry into the situation is not via a specific individual, family, or small group. On the contrary, the boundaries of the client system may be defined geographically, or in terms of a shared problem, or perhaps by other variables. For example, the client system could be defined as the tenants in a tenement building, or a particular service in a hospital, the third grades of a particular school,

6

or the pre-school children living in an area
served by a particular health center who are potentially malnourished. In approaching this extended client system, it is the task of the generalist to gather and assess data, to engage the
client system, to work with the client system to
develop a plan of intervention, and to mobilize
action systems in the service of these plans.

Selection of the Readings

The first semester of the Social Work Practice Course
introduces the student to the breadth of social work practice within the context of the major value issues, historical development, and Fordham's major concern with institutional racism and poverty. Also in this semester, the
beginning phases of social work practice are studied in
depth with emphasis on identification and engagement of
the client system, and on data collection, analysis, and
assessment. The readings have been selected in relation
to these areas of content, but as they are supplemental to
other required readings they do not cover the range nor do
they necessarily represent the emphasis of the course.

Other factors also entered in to selection. There
were limitations on what could be made available for inclusion. Furthermore, because of the greater availability
of materials dealing with work with individuals, there is
some greater emphasis on readings of particular relevance
to practice with larger client systems.

Finally, in this rapidly changing world, the above
discussion and the selection of readings can only be a
reflection of where we are now. New experiences, knowledge, and demands will lead to continued development and
revision.

AN INTRODUCTION TO SOCIAL WORK PRACTICE

BY PRANAB CHATTERJEE AND RAYMOND A. KOLESKI

The Concepts of Community and Community Organization: A Review

THE WORD COMMUNITY is charged with ambiguity, carrying different connotations in different situations. But as Ruopp writes, to abandon the word will lead to departure from the "concept of community."[1] He adds that the "chief virtue of the concept of community is that it emphasizes the qualitative aspects of human development rather than quantitative."[2] He seems to define community as follows:

> ... [It is] not only the attribute of every group brought together by the fusion of certain integrative forces such as shared locality and shared interactions. It is also something to be achieved ... for it is at the same time a descriptive and a normative concept.[3]

Ruopp's concept thus embraces two focal points: (1) interactive and ecological boundary and (2) normative and aspirational conjuration.

The problem for social workers and social scientists is manifest in Ruopp's definition —it is the difficulty of separating the interactive aspect of community from its aspirational one. The interactive part calls for an analysis of the present structure of community and of the purpose this structure currently serves; the aspirational part signifies the possibilities for the future. Analytically, then, it is possible to see the former as the means and the latter as goals. Subsequently a working definition of community may be offered as *the aggregate of all the institutional means available to some given groups in interaction toward the accomplishment of an aggregate of all the institutional ends*. It is to be noted that the notion of a shared locality has deliberately been avoided here and the locus is delineated in terms of "some given groups in interaction." Before discussing this working definition of community, it is necessary to review the past approaches toward it.

PRANAB CHATTERJEE, Ph.D., *and* RAYMOND A. KOLESKI, MSW, *are Assistant Professors, School of Applied Social Sciences, Case Western Reserve University, Cleveland, Ohio.*

[1] Phillips Ruopp, "Approaches to Community Development," in Ruopp, ed., *Approaches to Community Development* (The Hague: Theltague W. Van Hoeve Ltd., 1953), p. 5.
[2] Ibid., p. 4.
[3] Ibid.

Reprinted with permission of the National Association of Social Workers, from SOCIAL WORK, Vol. 15, No. 3, (July 1970), pp. 82-92.

10

Various authorities place different degrees of emphasis on the primary variables contained in a concept of community. Some tend to focus on the spatial or ecological aspect, some on the various institutional structures and cultural systems, still others on the interactional components only. While all tend to emphasize that a community is to be viewed as a whole, during the years it has nevertheless been clear that there are different "schools" of approach to the community. A fivefold typology summarizes these various approaches: (1) regulatory, (2) integrative and structural-functional, (3) ecological, (4) monographical, and (5) political-stratificational. The political-stratificational approach has two varieties, the reputational and the pluralistic models.

Regulative versus integrative. An examination of the historical perspective of the concept of community shows that both classic and modern authors have leaned more on the regulative forces than on the integrative as key variables in defining community. For instance, Maine's "status" and "contract," Tonnies's *"Gemeinschaft"* and *"Gesellschaft,"* Spencer's "military" and "industrial," Pareto's "circulation of elites," Cooley's "primary and secondary groups," Durkheim's "mechanical society" and "organic society," Redfield's "folk and urban continuum," Becker's "sacred and secular society," and the like are differentiated by their regulative forces, which, depending on the author, are identified as a product of either the polity or the economy.[4] All of these approaches may be classified as regulatory, since they delineate community in terms of the principal institutions themselves. It is imperative in this approach

that the principal institutions regulate the character of the community.

Weber, however, differentiated between class and status on the basis of their integrative forces, and Parsons in turn, following the "action paradigm," analyzed the concept of community as an "integrative agent."[5] Sanders's analysis of community is actually an elaborate analysis from the premises of the functional paradigm.[6] This type of approach may be termed integrative since the conceptual premises are derived from the way the institutions in the community are integrated. The essential difference between the regulatory and integrative approaches is that the first delineates community only in terms of its principal institutions, whereas the latter focuses on the nature of integration among the institutions.

Ecological approach. Analysis of community on the basis of either its regulative or integrative forces really describes the type of social organization in it rather than defining it as a whole. Some specific variables in a community were extensively studied by the ecological school of sociology. These variables included delinquency and its relationship to community (Clifford Shaw and Henry McKay), crime rate and urban community (Marshall Clinard and David Eastman), urban community and organization of the social welfare system (Arthur Hillman), participation in voluntary organizations in an urban community (Herbert Goldhammer), the small ethnic community within the urban community and the function of ethnic voluntary asso-

---

[4] *See* C. Wright Mills, *The Sociological Imagination* (New York: Oxford University Press, 1959), pp. 152–153. *See also* Ferdinand Tonnies, *Community and Society*, Charles P. Loomis, trans. (New York: Harper & Row, 1957), pp. 12–29.

[5] Compare Max Weber, *From Max Weber*, H. H. Gerth and C. Wright Mills, trans. (New York: Oxford University Press, 1958); and Parsons: ". . . community as that aspect of the structure of social systems which is referable to the territorial location of persons (i.e., human individuals as organisms) and their activities." Talcott Parsons, *Structure and Process in Modern Societies* (New York: Free Press of Glencoe, 1960), p. 250.

[6] Irwin Sanders, *The Community: An Introduction to a Social System* (New York: Ronald Press, 1958).

ciations in it (Helena Znaniecki Lopata), participation of migrants in urban associations (Basil Zimmer), and so on.[7]

Monographical approaches to community primarily document specific communities in a descriptive manner. Such descriptive or case studies of community border on an anthropological approach. Examples are the Lynds' classic works on Middletown and Redfield's descriptive generalization.[8]

The essential problem in all four approaches outlined is the fact that definition of the community as a unit is still lacking. Greer observed:

> Those who emphasize the dissolution of the community to the growth of mass society, Spengler, Ortega, Durkheim, Tonnies, and others, forecast an increasingly complex and heterogeneous society in which order results from the functional interdependence of organized groups and solidarity within groups leads to dynamic relations among them. . . . The analyses by Georg Simmel and Lewis Wirth emphasize these social aspects of the city (a) its heterogeneity, (b) its impersonality, (c) its anonymity, (d) the consequent social fragmentation of the individuals who make up the urban world. In this view the primary group structure of society is in a process of rapid dissolution, and with it, the primary community.[9]

Perhaps the association with the word community—the association of the social scientists included—is synonymous with primary group relations and active participation in all community institutions. Only recently have social scientists been intro-ducing new concepts into the realm of community research. Some of these include the formal organization as a functional community (MacIver, Komarovsky, and Lipset), the local area as community (Janowitz), areas of participation (Axelrod, Bell and Greer), and so on. Janowitz, for instance, introduced the term "the community of limited liability." [10] These, however, do not contribute to a single concept of community and really indicate that there are many implications in the idea.

The political-stratificational approach is an effort by urban sociologists, social workers, and political scientists to evaluate the concept of community in terms of distribution of power without regard to the problem of what units constitute the community. Here one finds oneself in the dilemma of having to decide whether the community embraces a monolithic power structure or various decision-making processes at a pluralistic level.[11] Based on their methodology and findings, the political-stratificational approach is subdivided into two sections: the "reputational" approach of Hunter, leading to the support of Mills's theory of economic-elite dominance, and the studies of decision-making and levels of influence by Dahl and Banfield leading to the conclusion of the pluralistic model of community.

DEFINING AND DELINEATING UNITS

The problem is essentially a matter of definition and delineation of units. It lies in the fact that the recent growth of any metropolitan center, which tends to become a megalopolis (Lewis Mumford and Jean Gottman), does not really facilitate the con-

[7] For an overview of the relationship between the variables in an urban community, *see* Ernest Burgess and Donald Bogue, eds., *Contributions to Urban Sociology* (Chicago: University of Chicago Press, 1964); and Basil Zimmer, "Participation of Migrants in Urban Structures," *American Sociological Review*, Vol. 20, No. 1 (April 1955), pp. 218–227.

[8] Robert S. Lynd and Helen M. Lynd, *Middletown* and *Middletown in Transition* (New York: Harcourt, Brace & Co., 1929 and 1937 respectively); and Robert Redfield, *The Little Community* (Chicago: University of Chicago Press, 1955).

[9] Scott Greer, *The Emerging City* (New York: Free Press, 1962), pp. 87–88.

[10] Morris Janowitz, *The Community Press in an Urban Setting* (Glencoe, Ill.: Free Press, 1952).

[11] Compare Floyd Hunter, *Community Power Structure* (New York: Doubleday & Co., 1953); Robert Dahl, *Who Governs?* (New Haven: Yale University Press, 1961); Edward Banfield, *Political Influence* (New York: Free Press, 1961); Banfield, *Big City Politics* (New York: Random House, 1965); and Roscoe C. Martin et al., *Decisions in Syracuse* (Indianapolis: Indiana University Press, 1961).

ventional understanding of community. Charles Adrian et al., for instance, observed:

> The term, community, is confusing and inconsistent, both as it is generally used in social science writing and as it exists in the minds of citizens when they discuss their own problems. Although the word, community, will appear often . . . and although empirical studies are still being made by sociologists who seek to delineate the community in geographical terms, it has not been defined adequately except operationally for specific purposes. But because of the rapid means of transportation and communication that exist today, the community, for most purposes, has become a *functional* concept rather than a geographic one.[12]

It is to be remembered that Adrian has in mind large metropolitan centers where it is difficult for all the individuals to have a common sense of territoriality and participation in all institutions. It is perhaps necessary, therefore, to distinguish between small community, large community, and large metropolitan centers.[13] Considerable writing has been done on the existence of small ethnic communities within large metropolitan centers.[14] However, it is the large metropolitan center as a whole to which the concept of community is often vaguely attributed and that in turn poses further problems for a precise definition.

Hillery found ninety-four definitions of the term community and arrived at the conclusion that "beyond the concept that people are involved in community, there is no complete agreement as to the nature of community."[15] Sjoberg comments:

Although the term has been variously employed as a synonym for *society, social organization,* or *social system,* many writers agree that it has a specific territorial locus, often limited in character. And this appears to be the way it is most commonly used by researchers.[16]

If one leaves aside that part of the sociological concept of community that is defined in terms of symbiotic and commensalistic relations, then one is faced with the sometimes overlapping and sometimes contradictory definitions that have been examined so far. This problem in sociology and other related social sciences is essentially heightened by the high rate of technological and industrial growth in the economic sector and an immense degree of bureaucratization in the social organization sector. As a result a comprehensive analysis of the urban community is still lacking, since it is hard to switch the mode of thought from a primary group-oriented small community to a formal organization-oriented urban community.

INTEREST GROUPS

A key point that ought to be introduced at this time is that with the decline of the primary community and the subsequent growth of the urban community there has been a consistent growth in a varied number of interest groups. These can be seen in various levels of business and commerce, in civic groups and voluntary associations, and in many other similar institutions. In the primary community of the past there was at least a shared membership in all the institutions that all the community residents more or less had in common. Added to this was the common territoriality, and such a community, in Giddings's words, could have had a feeling of "we-group."

[12] Charles R. Adrian et al., *Social Science and Community Action* (East Lansing: Michigan State University Press, 1960), p. 3.

[13] Compare Arthur Vidich and Joseph Bensman, *Small Town in Mass Society* (Garden City, N.Y.: Doubleday & Co., 1960); and Robert S. and Helen M. Lynd, op. cit.

[14] Compare Herbert J. Gans, *The Urban Villagers* (New York: Free Press, 1962); St. Clair Drake and Horace R. Cayton, *Black Metropolis* (New York: Harper & Row, 1945).

[15] G. A. Hillery, "Definitions of Community: Areas of Agreement," *Rural Sociology,* Vol. 20, No. 2 (January 1955), p. 119.

[16] Gideon Sjoberg, "Community," in Julius Gould and William L. Kolb, eds., *A Dictionary of the Social Sciences* (New York: Free Press of Glencoe, 1964), p. 114.

At that point other communities could have been seen as "they-groups." [17] With the loss of territoriality in today's urban community and the emergence of functional communities, such a concept of we-group has become somewhat diffuse. As a result it can perhaps be hypothesized that what was intercommunity conflict yesterday—for instance in feudal societies—has been replaced by both intra- and intercommunity conflict today. Conflict in such cases, however, is usually limited to either highly committed activists or to people who fear their interests or advantage are threatened. [18]

It is possible to see today's urban community in terms of conflicting interest groups rather than in terms of extensive citizen participation in a primary community. From the viewpoint of one author on the urban community, it is possible to see that it is a complex capitalistic social organization (as opposed to economic organization) vis-à-vis both its beneficiaries and nonbeneficiaries. [19] Dahrendorf attempts to start the theory of conflict where Marx had left it and proposes that it is the network of various levels of class conflict that leads to the perennial change in an urban community. [20] If the concept of class can be used

interchangeably with the term "interest group" (since allegedly different classes have different interests and the distribution of resources is constantly shifting), then it is possible to maintain that an urban community is a network of conflicting interest groups.

Dahrendorf actually had gone beyond describing the process of conflicting interest groups in an urban community. He also advances the following:

> The social system, like utopia, has grown out of familiar reality . . . consensus on values is one of the prime features of the social system. Some of its advocates make a slight concession to reality and speak of "relative consensus," (in the models of which there is no place for "relatives" or "almosts") and the observable facts of reality (which show little evidence of any more than highly formal—and tautological—consensus). That societies are held together by some kind of value consensus seems to me either a definition of societies or a statement clearly contradicted by empirical evidence. . . .
>
> . . . . .
>
> It is hard to see how a social system based on ("almost") universal consensus can allow for structurally generated conflicts. . . .
>
> . . . . .
>
> In talking about change, most sociologists today accept the entirely spurious distinction between "change within" and "change of societies," which make sense only if we recognize the system as our ultimate and only reference point. [21]

According to Dahrendorf, then, today's urban community with its industrial base is a large nexus of self-generated change.

LACK OF A COMPREHENSIVE THEORY

Now, to return to the structure of the large metropolitan community, one finds that no comprehensive theory exists that can explain all the phenomena in it; what exists

[17] See Franklin H. Giddings, Studies in the Theory of Human Society (New York: Scribner & Son, 1922); and W. G. Sumner, Folkways (New York: New American Library, 1960).

[18] "Communities differ widely in the degree to which community life is important and enough to argue about. Within large cities, for example, there is usually considerably less to involve the residents in civic affairs than there is in a small, self-sufficient town. In a large city a man's work is outside his neighborhood; often his children go to school outside that neighborhood and in the extreme case the neighborhood itself is hardly distinguishable as a unit. Thus, in the large cities, involvement in controversy is usually least widespread, often confined to a few activists." James S. Coleman, Community Conflict (New York: Free Press, 1957), p. 3.

[19] Ralf Dahrendorf, Class and Class Conflict in Industrial Society (Stanford, Calif.: Stanford University Press, 1964).

[20] Ibid., pp. 3–12.

[21] Ralf Dahrendorf, "Out of Utopia," American Journal of Sociology, Vol. 64, No. 2 (September 1958), pp. 115–127.

are bits and pieces, only some of which can really be put together. For instance, if one accepts the views of mass society theorists and those of the early Chicago school, then one finds a large territoriality based on contractual relations, diminishing primary groups, dominant secondary control, increase of private interest groups and voluntary associations, and atomized social life. The newer generation of sociologists has found that primary group ties do exist in metropolitan centers in much greater degree than previously thought, membership in various voluntary associations tends to create a functional community rather than a geographic one, and a new type of family life has emerged. Coleman suggests that the number of active participants in community conflict is rather low. Dahrendorf suggests that conflict is inherent in the industrially based metropolitan structure.

Thus the central problem is that of delineating the community as a unit that would encompass such elements as (1) the ascriptive norms, (2) the goals generated by the ascriptive norms (the institutional goals) and the available institutional means toward their fulfillment, (3) the structural conflict inherent in the means-ends continuum, and (4) the nature of boundaries, regardless of whether they are geographic or functional. In view of these problems of delineating the community as a unit, the rationale for the working definition of community offered at the beginning of this paper becomes evident. This being the state of affairs with the concept of community in sociology (and related social sciences), it is now possible to turn to the concept of community organization as a social work method and examine its past and present form.

COMMUNITY ORGANIZATION AS A METHOD

Community organization as a concept has also been fraught with ambiguity. It has eluded attempts at definitive description since both in practice and in conceptualization it has been marked by evolution. This unfolding process has been tied over nearly half a century to shifting emphases in practice as associated with the larger society plus an increasing degree of academic interest as the preparation of community organization professionals has moved into the university. Although little noticed at first, community organization as a social work method has rapidly emerged in the last quarter century as a full partner in the social work design.

Richmond's pioneering book, published in 1922, described four essential social work methods but did not include community organization.[22] However, probably the first textbook on community organization was Hart's volume, published two years before Richmond's book.[23] Yet community organization as a recognized social work method does not appear in the *Social Work Year Book* until as late as 1941.[24] Prior to 1941 work at the community level was referred to in the Year Book as "social welfare planning," which in many ways resembles administration and coordination of welfare services.

During this period, however, quite a number of publications on community organization appeared. For instance, Steiner's 1925 work uses the terms "community organization" and "community development" rather interchangeably and both terms are treated as synonymous with "community improvement."[25] The work of Woods, which was also published at this time, con-

[22] Mary E. Richmond, *What is Social Casework?* (New York: Russell Sage Foundation, 1922).
[23] Joseph K. Hart, *Community Organization* (New York: Macmillan Co., 1920).
[24] *See* Fred S. Hall, ed., *Social Work Year Book 1929* (New York: Russell Sage Foundation, 1930), pp. 100–101; Fred S. Hall, ed., *Social Work Year Book 1933* (New York: Russell Sage Foundation, 1933), p. 100; Fred S. Hall, ed., *Social Work Year Book 1935* (New York: Russell Sage Foundation, 1935), p. 86; Russell H. Kurtz, *Social Work Year Book 1937* (New York: Russell Sage Foundation, 1937), p. 94; and Russell H. Kurtz, ed., *Social Work Year Book 1941* (New York: Russell Sage Foundation, 1941), pp. 128–133.
[25] Jesse F. Steiner, *Community Organization* (New York: Century Co., 1925), pp. 70–87.

sisted more of sociological variables and proposed ways and means of community improvement.[26] In these cases the concept of community improvement seems to have meant arousing concern on the part of citizens' groups for different needs and issues. In these works, however, the unit for improvement was never defined quite consistently, and it is not clear exactly what was meant by "community." Taking the concept from Zorbaugh, in 1926 sociologist Burgess proposed the "natural area" of metropolitan centers as a unit for community work.[27] Actually, long before this proposal, the "natural area" of the city was already the unit for many community improvement programs.[28]

During the thirties and early forties sociologists and social workers were in many ways still working together whenever community organization was being discussed. The Chicago Area Project was still fresh in the minds of all concerned. Sanderson, a sociologist, became one of the pioneer authors in the community organization method and constructed typologies of "unorganized," "underorganized," "overorganized," and "disorganized" communities.[29]

[26] Arthur E. Woods, *The Philosophy of Community Organization* (New York: American Sociological Society, 1923).

[27] Ernest W. Burgess, "The Natural Area as the Unit for Social Work in the Large City," *Proceedings of the National Conference of Social Work, 1926* (Chicago: University of Chicago Press, 1926), pp. 504–510. *See also* Harvey W. Zorbaugh, "The Natural Areas of the City," in Ernest W. Burgess, ed., *The Urban Community* (Chicago: University of Chicago Press, 1926), p. 223.

[28] "Community organization practice is not a new development; it is indeed the earliest stage in the history of modern social work. The creation of 'Charity Organization Societies' and 'Settlement Houses' were the result of community organization effort; they predated the definitions of casework and group work practice by several decades." Harry L. Lurie, *The Community Organization Method in Social Work Education*, Vol. IV of the Social Work Curriculum Study (New York: Council on Social Work Education, 1959), p. 12.

[29] Dwight Sanderson and Robert Polson, *Rural Community Organization* (New York: John Wiley & Sons, 1939).

Saul Alinsky, a sociologist by training, had started his work in the Back of the Yards area of Chicago. (Concern with the ethics of Alinsky-style community organization is rather recent among social work professionals.) In 1945 Johnson stated that "the community organization worker draws heavily upon sociology for an understanding of forms of human association in groups. She finds illuminating the theories relating to culture, social change, and cultural lag." [30] Johnson also settled the ambiguity around the term community by saying:

"community" is used as a convenient term to refer to a group of people gathered together in any geographical area, large or small, who have common interests, actually or potentially recognized, in the social welfare field . . . the meaning of community is unimportant except for working purposes—it can be defined and redefined as new projects are undertaken.[31]

CHARACTERISTICS OF COMMUNITY ORGANIZATION

During the late thirties and the forties, distinct and different opinions were offered as to the definition of community organization. The Lane Committee Report of 1939 was one of the landmarks in the identification of characteristics of community organization. Among its more significant observations were the following: community organization was identified as both a process and a field, terms used comparably to describe medicine, law, and teaching; the general aim of community organization was concerned with continuing adjustment of social welfare resources and social welfare needs.[32] To this day questions raised by

[30] Arlien Johnson, "Community Organization in Social Work," in Russell H. Kurtz, ed., *Social Work Year Book 1945* (New York: Russell Sage Foundation, 1945), p. 94.

[31] Ibid.

[32] Robert P. Lane, "Report of Groups Studying the Community Organization Process," *Proceedings of the National Conference of Social Work, 1940* (New York: Columbia University Press, 1940), pp. 456–473.

the Lane Committee Report have tended to evoke single-gauge answers too narrow to account for a variety of circumstances. The report questions center around issues such as these: the indistinctness of the term "community" in "community organization" as an indicator of differential actors and levels of effort involved in the processes, the activities of the action sequence of the community organization processes, and, perhaps most crucial, the principle and hypotheses for guiding the practitioner that emerge from underlying theories derived from systematic analysis of human behavior, especially community organization activity.

In 1945 McMillen noted:

> The interests of students of community organization tend to separate them into two schools. One group is primarily concerned to evaluate the concrete methods used in the day-to-day job of those engaged in community organization. The other group is primarily interested in analyzing group behavior and in identifying the determinants that influence its course.[33]

It is obvious that McMillen was identifying the second group as the followers of Newstetter, and Newstetter produced a formal statement of his viewpoint (which he called intergroup process) two years later.[34] Dunham had already declared that community organization as a process "is directed toward bringing about and maintaining adjustment between resources and needs in a geographical area or a special field of service."[35] It is perhaps fair to comment that

Dunham's mode of thought—along with others in agreement with Dunham—is responsible for the school of community organization that proposes coordination of all community-wide services at the council level as the essence of community organization.[36] Pray added the concept of the role of "enabler" when he observed:

> The objective is not to make over either the environment or the people involved in it, but rather to introduce and sustain a process of dealing with problems of social relationship and social adjustment, which will enable and assist those involved in the problems to find solutions satisfying to themselves and acceptable to the society of which they are a part.[37]

One thing is clear—that by this time social workers had added a body of professional knowledge and gained professional experience in various specialized forms of community organization and community organization had increasingly come to mean coordination of community welfare services.[38] As a result it was assumed that community improvement would result from better coordination of services, and the earlier notion of mobilizing citizens' groups around community issues became rather secondary.

---

[33] Wayne McMillen, *Community Organization for Social Welfare* (Chicago: University of Chicago Press, 1945), p. 8.

[34] Wilbur I. Newstetter, "The Social Inter-Group Process: How Does it Differ from Social Group Work Process?" *Proceedings of the National Conference of Social Work, 1947* (New York: Columbia University Press, 1948).

[35] Arthur Dunham, "Community Organization for Social Work," in Russell H. Kurtz, ed., *Social Work Year Book 1943* (New York: Russell Sage Foundation, 1943), p. 138.

[36] "The need for broad participation in interagency planning has indeed become so generally recognized that the council device has become part of the social machinery of every sizable community in the United States, and exists in several forms at the national level. Increasingly citizen activity is being reemphasized as vital to these agencies in joint planning in order that the product which results may be truly community organization for social welfare." Russell H. Kurtz, "Community Organization for Social Welfare," in Kurtz, ed., *Social Work Year Book 1949* (New York: Russell Sage Foundation, 1949), p. 130.

[37] Kenneth L. M. Pray, "When Is Community Organization Social Work Practice?" *Proceedings, National Conference of Social Work, San Francisco, 1947* (New York: Columbia University Press, 1948), p. 277.

[38] *Neighbors United for Better Communities* (New York: Community Chests & Councils of America, 1956).

DIFFERENTIATION OF COMMUNITY ORGANIZATION AND SOCIAL ACTION

After this period certain texts were clearly differentiating between the three basic methods of social work (casework, group work, and community organization) and the three auxiliary methods of social work (administration, research, and social action).[39] Thus community organization had become differentiated from social action and the two methods by this time meant two different orientations.[40]

Approximately fifteen years ago Ross provided a definition that was more general in its objectives and in the same work he specified various settings in which the implementation differs. By community organization Ross means

a process by which a community identifies its needs or objectives, orders (or ranks) these needs or objectives, develops the confidence and will to work at these needs or objectives, finds the resources (internal and/or external) to deal with these needs or objectives, takes action in respect to them, and in so doing extends and develops cooperative and collaborative attitudes and practices in the community.[41]

Ross actually further analyzes the structural differences and similarities between *geographic* and *functional* communities and suggests five basic approaches for community organization: exploitive, reform, planning, process, and therapy orientations.[42] However, he ignores the polar positions and states that "most of our current conceptions of community organization fall [in the]

three midpositions identified." [43] In this approach, then, it becomes apparent that community organization is not reform alone; neither is it singularly a process of planning and coordination at a council level. Ross does not limit community organization to welfare services alone and contends that it is useful in many other facets of community life, e.g., agriculture, education, and so on.

USE OF THE SOCIAL SCIENCES

Sieder provided a further indication of the maturation of community organization when she described it as a service to both local and nonlocal groups with the necessity for use of special knowledge derived from the social sciences.[44] The suggested goal by the Council on Social Work Education for a sequence in community organization in a school of social work, however, is as follows:

The aim of a sequence of courses in community organization should be to prepare students by giving them an understanding of and concern for, plus an ability to promote, social well-being by means of the organization, maintenance and improvement of community welfare programs and services, considered as integral parts of the overall structure of community life.[45]

A statement on community organization by the National Association of Social Workers, however, is far more comprehensive and includes broader goals than the one recommended for social work students by the

[39] Herbert H. Stroup, *Community Welfare Organization* (New York: Harper & Bros., 1952).

[40] Mary Richmond described social casework, social group work, social research, and social action as the four basic methods of social work, and it seems that she did not make the differentiation between community organization and social action. *See* Richmond, op. cit.

[41] Murray G. Ross, *Community Organization: Theory and Principles* (New York: Harper & Bros., 1955), p. 39.

[42] Murray G. Ross, *Case Histories in Community Organization* (New York: Harper & Bros., 1958), pp. 4–5.

[43] Ibid.

[44] Violet M. Sieder, "What is Community Organization Practice in Social Work?" *Social Welfare Forum*, 1956 (New York: Columbia University Press, 1956), pp. 160–166. The reference to the importance of social science was perhaps made in recognition of the important research of Floyd Hunter, a social worker turned sociologist, in *Community Power Structure* (Chapel Hill: University of North Carolina Press, 1963), and of Ruth C. Schaffer and Cecil G. Scheps, *Community Organization: Action and Inaction* (Chapel Hill: University of North Carolina Press, 1956).

[45] Lurie, op. cit., p. 24.

Council on Social Work Education. For instance:

> The practice of community organization is rooted in the values traditionally associated with the practice of social work. . . .
>
> • • • •
>
> The community organization practitioner works with representatives of the community or segments of the community for the purpose of intervening in the community process with a problem-solving approach. . . .
>
> • • • •
>
> The roots of sanction for community organization practice are not only derived from the values and purpose (of social work), but also from the social conditions particular to our time. . . .
>
> • • • •
>
> Community organization is concerned primarily with the community as a system of behavior. The practitioner must have special knowledge of the ways through which the community as a social system can be helped to change. . . . In addition to knowledge about the community, community organization practice must draw from knowledge about group and individual systems of behavior and their interrelationships. The practice of community organization requires knowledge of function as well as dysfunction of these systems and the resultant social consequences and social problems. . . .
>
> • • • •
>
> Method in community organization practice is the orderly application of a relevant body of knowledge, guided by social work values. The worker applies systematically and sequentially this coherent body of knowledge employing practice-wisdom and learned behavior through characteristic, distinctive and describable procedures to help the community engage in a process of planned change toward community improvement.[46]

Paralleling the development and circulation of the NASW statement was a strong trend toward use of social science theory and research in education for community organization. The works of social scientists such as Warren, Sanders, Rossi, Banfield, Lippitt, Meyerson, Dahl, Coleman, Lindblam, Seeley, Form, Miller, Adrian, Long, Gans, and Zald became part of community organization conceptualization. But perhaps even more important were the reports and theoretical papers that flowed from the research of specialists in community organization analysis themselves. Morris on organizational interaction, Morris and Binstock on planned change, Rein and Morris on differential organizational use of strategies in pursuit of goals, and Rothman on professional roles as related to goals, to name a few, carried those interested in the development of community organization away from the global, clinical models of prescription toward the more middle-range models of description, analysis, and prediction.[47]

CURRENT EVENTS

The current pace of events in the action world of community organization and planning has been almost too swift for contemplation and documentation. Social movements have evolved. Legislation concerning citizen participation has appeared, been modified, and has reappeared in different shapes and forms. Ideas centering on social reform and power have been resurrected. New concepts of theory related to action

[46] "Defining Community Organization Practice" (New York: National Association of Social Workers, 1962), pp. 5–15. (Mimeographed.) See also summary statement by Meyer Schwartz, "Community Organization," Encyclopedia of Social Work (New York: National Association of Social Workers, 1965).

[47] Robert Morris, "Basic Factors in Planning for the Coordination of Health Services," American Journal of Public Health, Vol. 53, Nos. 2 and 3 (February and March 1963), pp. 248–259 and 462–472; Robert Morris and Robert H. Binstock, Feasible Planning for Social Change (New York: Columbia University Press, 1966); Martin Rein and Robert Morris, "Goals, Structures and Strategies for Community Change," Social Work Practice, 1962 (New York: Columbia University Press, 1962), pp. 127–145; Jack Rothman, "An Analysis of Goals and Roles in Community Organization Practice," Social Work, Vol. 9, No. 2 (April 1964), pp. 24–31.

have been proposed. Most of these concepts have been formulated to reflect what is transpiring in the world of action. Others have been directed toward a reconceptualization of behavior to guide action.

New authors have become a part of the community organization literature, thereby reflecting an expanding interest in planning, protest, power, and program. Expressing their concern with new institutional arrangements are such diverse activists and theorists as Martin Luther King, Jr., Malcolm X, Whitney Young, Jr., Stokely Carmichael and Charles V. Hamilton, James M. Gavin and Arthur Hadley, Richard A. Cloward and Frances Fox Piven, Milton Kotler, Bernard J. Frieden and Robert Morris, Nicholas van Hoffman, Paul Davidoff, Harvey S. Perloff, Peter Marris and Martin Rein, Wilber Thompson, John Gardner, Lee Rainwater, Warren Haggstrom, C. A. Doxiadis, and George Brager, as well as the operations research planners and the writers of the new radicalism.[48]

These—and many more—are documenting thoughts that guide action or are attempting to record behavior in the world of action. Their efforts as well as those of equally significant but lesser known theorists and activists help to shape the basic ideas in the quest to conceptualize the evolving and multiformed area of community organization and planning.

---

[48] For an example of current thinking on community organization at the neighborhood level, *see* John B. Turner, ed., *Neighborhood Organization for Community Action* (New York: National Association of Social Workers, 1968). For examples of work by operations research planners, *see* the series of papers by Arthur Blum, Raymond A. Koleski, Bernard Olshansky, Ralph Gregory, Elliot Marcus, Judah Rubinstein, Burton V. Dean, Arnold Reisman, Norman C. Eisenberg, Alan Beckman, Samuel J. Mantel, Jr., Allan L. Service, and Richard Ronis in *Journal of Jewish Communal Service*, Vol. 46, No. 1 (Fall 1969), pp. 70–92. For a continued effort to examine the relevance of five approaches to the concept of community as developed in this paper, *see* Pranab Chatterjee, "Community in Social Science and Social Work," to be published in the July 1970 issue of the *Indian Journal of Social Work*.

TOWARD A STRATEGY OF GROUP WORK PRACTICE

WILLIAM SCHWARTZ

The author is a member of the faculty of the New York School of Social Work of Columbia University. This article is based on a paper read at the Problem-finding Conference, Research Institute for Group Work in Jewish Agencies, Arden House, New York, April 28, 1961.

IN THE long history of the helping professions, it has been only recently that the working processes of the practitioner have been accepted as an appropriate field for scientific study. Once it has defined its body of knowledge, its social aspirations, and its goal-commitments, a profession must say something equally precise about the ways in which these entities are put to use in the working relationship between the practitioner and his clients.

In the group work segment of the social work profession the methodological problem had not yet become apparent when, in 1948, a committee of the American Association of Group Workers issued the now classical "Definition of the Function of the Group Worker."[1] This statement, used as a basis for teaching and interpreting group work practice during the past decade, has until recently served as an excellent model of the state of professional thinking. In its time, it served to formulate social goals, define the field of operations, stake a claim to certain kinds of expertness, and reveal some basic assumptions about people and groups in a democratic society.

What it did not do was to make the necessary distinctions between means

and ends which could have helped to dissipate the strong teleological emphasis and to challenge the intrenched assumption that professional skill was somehow inherent in the worker's goals, his knowledge, his feeling for the client, his value-commitments, and certain of his personal attributes. The gap between the worker's intent and his effect was bridged with terms like "enables," "provides for," "functions in such a way that," "aims to," and other phrases that produced closure without coming to grips with the theoretical problems involved in designing a strategy of professional practice.[2] The difficulty was aptly summed up by Louis Towley, who pointed out in 1957 that "this specialized field is rich in democratic concepts; it has a wealth of examples; but in professionally unique concepts, 'method theory,' it has been curiously poor."[3]

The newer interest in the systematic study of professional practice is part of a similar impetus in social work as a whole. Although there are those who see

[1] Dorothea F. Sullivan (ed.), *Readings in Group Work* (New York: Association Press, 1952), pp. 421–22.

[2] For a more extended historical treatment of the means-ends relationship in group work, see William Schwartz, "Group Work and the Social Scene," *Issues in American Social Work*, ed. Alfred J. Kahn (New York: Columbia University Press, 1959), pp. 110–37.

[3] Frank J. Bruno (with chapters by Louis Towley), *Trends in Social Work, 1874–1956* (New York: Columbia University Press, 1957), p. 422.

SOCIAL SERVICE REVIEW, September 1962, pp. 268–279.

21

this development as a "retreat into technique" and as a distraction from the "real" purposes of the profession, practitioners and teachers are gradually becoming excited by the possibility of finding out, after many years, what the exact nature of group work skill is, what it looks like in action, and how it can be conceptualized and taught.

How does a profession proceed to develop and systematize its concepts of practice? To say that it needs to build a more intimate working relationship with science is only the beginning of an answer. Certainly the liaison of science and practice is a historic one; professions that do not keep pace with new knowledge soon cease to be professions. But it is also true that an orientation to scientific inquiry does not provide a simple method of converting facts into acts, scientific findings into appropriate professional behavior. The transition from knowing to doing is more complex.

The complexity arises from two major problems faced by all the human-relations professions as they survey their appropriate fields of knowledge. One is that the body of potentially useful information is encyclopedic, encompassing every conceivable aspect of human development and organization; the other is that action cannot be deduced directly from knowledge, no matter how vast that knowledge may be.

In relation to the first problem—the overwhelming array of pertinent information—Max Millikan has pointed out that the Bavelas-Perlmutter experiments at the Center for International Studies suggest that "an individual's capacity for making sound judgment about a complex situation may be seriously impaired by supplying him with a lot of information which he believes should be relevant but whose influence on the situation is not clear to him."[4] Harold Lasswell comments that "the idea of strategy does not depend upon omniscience."[5] The dilemma Millikan describes, a familiar one to group workers, seems to stem directly from the fact that the worker finds himself burdened with a great many answers for which he has no questions. He can make little use of such information until he has ordered his experience into some coherent frame of reference from which he can develop his questions and focus his inquiry into the undifferentiated mass of scientific data. Thus the search for significant problems—for the questions that will draw forth the kinds of information most needed to throw light on the practical tasks of the group worker—calls for a theoretical effort designed to develop a system of interconnected concepts drawn from the experience of practice.[6]

It is when we question what these concepts shall be about that we come to the second difficulty mentioned above —that action is not deducible from knowledge. Those who assume that scientific evidence carries within it its own implications for behavior make the same mistake made by those in an earlier time who believed that action flowed inevitably and appropriately

[4] Max F. Millikan, "Inquiry and Policy: The Relation of Knowledge to Action," *The Human Meaning of the Social Sciences*, ed. Daniel Lerner (New York: Meridian Books, 1959), p. 160.

[5] Harold D. Lasswell, "Strategies of Inquiry: The Rational Use of Observation," *The Human Meaning of the Social Sciences*, p. 89.

[6] For a discussion of theory-building and empiricism, see James B. Conant, *Modern Science and Modern Man* (New York: Doubleday Anchor Books, 1953).

from one's convictions about values and goals. It is what Millikan refers to as the "inductive fallacy—the assumption that the solution of any problem will be advanced by the simple collection of fact."[7] The fact is that the gap between what is known and what should be done is invariably bridged by value-goal orientations, often implicit and unformulated. When knowledge is converted into action on the basis of subtle and unstated values, the principle is unverifiable, except by those who unconsciously share the same assumptions. When creeds and valued outcomes are made explicit, practice principles are verifiable by all, on the basis of whether, given the first two variables—a fact and a valued outcome—the third will provide the implementing force. Practice cannot be "testable" in any other sense.

It is, therefore, suggested that practice theory, or method theory, can be defined as a system of concepts integrating three conceptual subsystems: one which organizes the appropriate aspects of social reality, as drawn from the findings of science; one which defines and conceptualizes specific values and goals, which we might call the problems of policy; and one which deals with the formulation of interrelated principles of action. Each of these constitutes a major area of investigation, each has its own conceptual problems, and each is related to the others within a total scheme. The purpose of this paper is to point up some of the major conceptual problems in each of these areas and to show how each area depends upon the others for its own clarity and coherence.

[7] *Op. cit.*, p. 163.

As we turn to the social sciences for information about human behavior and social organization, our task is to establish those lines of inquiry which emerge most directly from our experiences with people. Gordon Hearn has suggested some proposals to focus the study of social work practice in general[8] and Robert Vinter has discussed some lines of work within the context of his frame of reference for group work.[9] From my own orientation to the tasks of the group work practitioner,[10] the following are suggested as some of the central themes around which the struggles of practice have taken place.

The individual and the social.—Probably the most enduring and pervasive methodological problems have stemmed from an inability to develop an integrative conception of the relationship between individual need and social demand. This is the difficulty that gives birth to the issue of "content versus process"—the dilemma wherein the practitioner is forced to make impossible choices between the functional necessities of individual growth and the social requirements of the culture in which he operates. The early efforts of

[8] Gordon Hearn, *Theory Building in Social Work* (Toronto: University of Toronto Press, 1958), p. 25.

[9] Robert D. Vinter, "Group Work with Children and Youth: Research Problems and Possibilities," *Social Service Review*, XXX (September, 1956), 310–21. See also his "Small-Group Theory and Research: Implications for Group Work Practice Theory and Research," *Social Science Theory and Social Work Research*, ed. Leonard S. Kogan (New York: National Association of Social Workers, 1960), pp. 123–34.

[10] William Schwartz, "The Social Worker in the Group," *Social Welfare Forum, 1961* (New York: Columbia University Press, 1961), pp. 146–71.

Sherif,[11] Mead,[12] Kropotkin,[13] and others to effect a workable synthesis were significant, but group workers were not yet in a position to formulate their problems so that these concepts could be used. In recent years, social scientists have come alive to the issue. Alex Inkeles' attempt to analyze this work without regard to internal professional boundaries has been helpful.[14] For practitioners, the present problem is that much scientific work is pegged either at a very high level of abstraction or at empirical laboratory efforts with artificial groupings that are difficult to translate into terms relevant to group work experience. As in so many other problem areas, the need is to break down the general question into some middle-range propositions that can be tested in our own situational field. Lippitt, Watson, and Westley have suggested work on the "forces toward innovation" through which people attempt to use, control, and change the people and things around them.[15] Another more specific line of inquiry might consist in the effort to develop motivational typologies with which to ascertain elements of consensus among group members and agency personnel.

[11] Muzafer Sherif, *The Psychology of Social Norms* (New York: Harper, 1936).

[12] George Herbert Mead, *Mind, Self, and Society* (Chicago: University of Chicago Press, 1934).

[13] Peter Alekseevich Kropotkin, *Mutual Aid: A Factor of Evolution* (New York: Alfred A. Knopf, 1917).

[14] Alex Inkeles, "Personality and Social Structure," *Sociology Today: Problems and Prospects,* ed. Robert K. Merton, Leonard Broom, and Leonard S. Cottrell, Jr. (New York: Basic Books, 1959), pp. 249–75.

[15] Ronald Lippitt, Jeanne Watson, and Bruce Westley, *The Dynamics of Planned Change* (New York: Harcourt, Brace, 1958), pp. 4–5.

From my own frame of reference, which assumes a symbiotic interdependence between the individual and his culture and which conceives the agency as a special case of the individual-social engagement, my prediction would be that mutually perceived "success" would take place primarily in these areas of motivational consensus.

The group work setting—as a living laboratory of the individual-social encounter—has failed conspicuously to produce its own research and add to the systematic study of this relationship in action. The field was so completely captured, early in its development, by the character-building, social-conformity pressures of the group work "movement" that the need to change people far outweighed the need to understand them and to examine carefully the ways in which their natural tendencies carry them into the society in which they develop. Thus, the move was made from socialization as a process—which needed to be analyzed and understood—to socialization as a demand. From that point, the road was a short one to the dilemma of "content versus process" and, ultimately, to the individual versus the group.

The structural and the dynamic.— Our historic tendency has been to rely heavily on structural descriptions— "diagnostic" typologies—to describe the people with whom we work. The study-diagnosis-treatment model— based partly on the physician's detection and cure of disease and partly on the methods of research—is built from the assumption that these structural characteristics are stable enough for workers to base predictions, referrals, and "treatment" decisions upon them. However, it has been difficult to show that this model bears any practical relation to the moment-to-moment, situationally fluid realities of the helping process in action. Hubert Bonner reports that "research has shown that it is difficult to predict the behavior of persons in a group from pre-measures of personality variables,"[16] and Gordon Allport has scored the "faddism" involved in the "overemphasis on diagnosis." "It is simply not true," he states, "that successful treatment invariably presupposes accurate diagnosis."[17]

Interest is mounting in elaborations of a newer approach, which has particular implications for the situational field in which the group worker operates. This approach points up the "circular, reciprocal relations . . . through which the component members of the field participate in and thereby create the field of the whole, which field in turn regulates and patterns their individual activities."[18] This model calls attention to the interdependent transactions within a functional system—an organic whole "within which the relations determine the properties of its parts."[19] The emphasis on relational determinants of behavior, while at the same time subjecting structural determinants to more critical scrutiny, has a strong potential impact on all group work practice conceptions. It may provide the stimulus for closer analysis of the differential forms of stress, social demand, and social opportunity offered by the various settings of group work practice.[20] It may also stimulate the development of terminology—and perhaps new typologies—that will help us to express relations as well as structure and to distinguish more clearly between the two.

The group as "it" and as "they."—We have not yet developed a working conception of the group as a whole which might help the group worker to implement his traditional claim that group work skills are directed to the group as well as to the individuals within it. If the small group is a system which—like society itself—both integrates and differentiates its parts,[21] group workers remain far more perceptive about the attributes of individuals than they are about the activity of the group as a whole. Familiar evidence is found in recorded anthropomorphisms like "the group laughed," in references to the group as "they," and in models of confusion, like "the group looked at each other." This failure to distinguish between the attributes of members and those of the collective has made it difficult to isolate and describe those professional skills which are designed to affect the system itself rather than any of its component parts.[22] Efforts have been made to use the wealth of em-

[16] Hubert Bonner, *Group Dynamics: Principles and Applications* (New York: Ronald Press Co., 1959), p. 20.

[17] Gordon W. Allport, *Personality and Social Encounter* (Boston: Beacon Press, 1960), p. 283. Discussed in chapter entitled "Social Service in Perspective."

[18] Lawrence K. Frank, "Research for What?" *Journal of Social Issues,* Supplement Series, X (1957), 12.

[19] Talcott Parsons, *The Structure of Social Action* (Glencoe, Ill.: Free Press, 1949), p. 32.

[20] For a limited attempt of this type, see William Schwartz, "Characteristics of the Group Experience in Resident Camping," *Social Work,* V (April, 1960), 91–96.

[21] See A. Paul Hare, Edgar F. Borgatta, and Robert F. Bales, *Small Groups: Studies in Social Interaction* (New York: Alfred A. Knopf, 1955), pp. 345–47.

[22] Robert D. Vinter's conception of "indirect means of influence" is an effort in this direction. See his "Small-Group Theory and Research . . . ," *op. cit.,* p. 128.

pirical research on group dimensions, but again the lack of theoretical models has been a barrier. Much energy has been devoted to building longer inventories of group traits, but there is little knowledge of how these traits may be related to each other in the life of the group.

The recent work of the organizational theorists,[23] the developing insight into the interdisciplinary implications of the system construct,[24] and other integrative attempts now offer group workers the opportunity to analyze the group work experience in a new way. In the process they may begin to make their own unique contribution to this field of inquiry. The growing diversity of small-group systems in which they operate gives group workers the chance to observe both similarities and differences in the ways in which different kinds of groups integrate and differentiate their human components and relate themselves to the larger systems in which they operate.

Internal and external determinants of change.—Much of the discussion on "self-determination versus manipulation" has been carried on in a high moral tone, while a great deal of work needs to be done in studying the specific conditions under which people enlist the aid of others in their attempts to solve problems. The group worker is in a unique position to study the uses of help and the nature of influence, since he works within a system the essence of which is that people create many helping relationships in addition to, and

concurrent with, the one formed with the worker. The problems of the group members in using each other are co-existent with their problems in using the worker. The group worker has an opportunity to examine in microcosm a very old idea, long since forgotten in a highly specialized civilization. This is the idea that the client-worker relationship is simply a special case of what Kropotkin described as the evolutionary theme of mutual aid[25]—that is, the social devices through which human beings establish conditions of mutual support in the struggle for survival. More specifically, the group work situation offers the conditions for studying peer help and professional help within the same dynamic system, guided by the strong possibility that these two sets of movements have much in common and that, in fact, the latter may be a stylized, intensified version of the former.[26]

PROBLEMS OF POLICY

The relationship between science and policy is reciprocal. Science takes its cues from human problems and yields its best answers to those who are disciplined and urgent in their search for solutions. The contribution of science to policy is to define boundaries, limit expectations, and clarify the range of alternatives.[27] This idea of knowledge as a disciplining, limiting force is important in each of the problems to be discussed briefly below. It should be remembered that we are still in the

[23] See, for example, Mason Haire (ed.), *Modern Organization Theory* (New York: John Wiley & Sons, 1959).

[24] See Roy R. Grinker, M.D., *Toward a Unified Theory of Human Behavior* (New York: Basic Books, 1956).

[25] Kropotkin, *op. cit.*

[26] Bertha Capen Reynolds' *Social Work and Social Living* (New York: Citadel Press, 1951) explores this basic proposition in detail.

[27] For a detailed discussion of the science-policy relationship, see Millikan, *loc. cit.,* and Lasswell, *loc. cit.*

context of the study of practice, and these problems are viewed from that perspective.

Functional definition.—Much of the difficulty in understanding the nature of group work skill stems from the lack of a clear and limited statement about the unique, operative function of the worker in his group. Such a statement, made in terms of action rather than intent, of function rather than purpose,[28] would provide a focal point for a general strategy of practice. The strategic lines of action would be appropriate to the worker's ascribed function, would be directed to certain tasks and not to others, would be related to the functional performance of the members, and would be directed to the specific and limited factors over which the worker exercises some influence.[29]

The components of the functional statement would be drawn from three main areas of investigation: the specific problems faced by group members as they move to relate their own sense of need to the social demands implicit in the collective tasks of the group; the functional assignment of the agency within its own dynamic system of neighborhood and community; and the social function of the profession itself as it lends itself to the agencies in which it works.[30] This general orientation to the operational problem offers many questions for study: In what precise ways does the practice of group workers reflect the degree of conflict—and consensus—about the proper function of the worker within the group, as viewed by group members, agency administrators, and the worker himself? What are the conditions under which certain kinds of group behavior may be functional to the members and dysfunctional to the requirements of the agency, or vice versa? Under what conditions is it desirable to convert latent functions into manifest ones?

Structural ordering.—The task here is to study the circumstances under which the group establishes and maintains its position within the agency, for these circumstances create the framework within which the worker interprets and performs his tasks. If the structure is unclear and ambiguous—as in situations in which the agency secretly aspires to build character while it teaches clay-modeling—the worker's function becomes diffuse and unmanageable.

Several aspects of the relationship between the client group and its host system seem profitable for study. One is the process through which the stage of group formation or group intake establishes conditions of consensus or conflict about the nature of the "contract" between the group and its agency —what each may expect from the other, the normative requirements to which each may be held, and other factors which bind them together. Another important structural aspect lies in the complex of prepared events, activities, and ethical commitments which agency

[28] The distinction between purpose and function is helpfully discussed in Robert K. Merton, *Social Theory and Social Structure* (Glencoe, Ill.: Free Press, 1957), chap. i.

[29] These criteria are elaborated in Schwartz, "Group Work and the Social Scene," *op. cit.,* pp. 130–32.

[30] Cf. Everett Cherrington Hughes, "The Study of Occupations," *Sociology Today: Problems and Prospects,* pp. 442–58: "The composition of an occupation can be understood only in the frame of the pertinent social and institutional complex (which must in turn be discovered, not merely assumed). The allocating and grouping of activities is itself a fundamental social process" (p. 455).

administrations perceive as integral to their function and as substantial elements in their contributions to group life. Under what conditions do these prepared events and prestructured experiences become functional or dysfunctional for the groups for which they are intended?

Much of this problem of structural ordering lies in the relationship between what George C. Homans calls the "external" and the "internal" systems of the group—between "group behavior that enables the group to survive in its environment" and "group behavior that is an expression of the sentiments towards one another developed by the members of the group in the course of their life together."[31] The tension between these two systems of group behavior sets up some of the central methodological problems of the group worker.

Value orientation.—A great deal has been said and written about the worker's obligation to acknowledge values and to profess them openly. But these injunctions are hard to obey, because they suffer from the same shortcomings as do the value formulations themselves—that is, they are too global, internally inconsistent, and unrelated to the specific conditions of group life. The professional commandments to stand for absolute and overgeneralized themes like "Jewish belongingness" or "social maturity," to "bear" values but not to "impose" them, to uphold both religious and secular-humanistic values at the same time,[32] to extol modesty and thrift to children whose family modes are prevailingly those of conspicuous consumption—these are very complex materials from which to compose a ra-

tionale for the position of values in the strategy of practice. At this stage what is needed is more exact information about the value themes which merge or conflict within the lives of different groups and about the conditions under which these circumstances vary from group to group and from setting to setting—the religious and the secular, the sectarian and the non-sectarian, the therapeutic and the recreational. Content analyses of group work recording may help uncover some of the conflicts and inconsistencies which have made it difficult to break up the problem of value orientation without seeming to attack value systems themselves. Most important would be an attempt to isolate and formulate value items of limited scope which apply directly to the life of the group itself, which are drawn from its own history, and which represent normative guides without which the worker actually could not function.

Goal setting.—What kinds of knowledge would be best designed to help "place limits on the range of possible outcomes"?[33] Here, as in the value question, the first requirement is that we begin with a willingness to drop exorbitant claims.[34] Caught up early in the social promise of the small-group experience, it has been hard for group workers to give up the claim that the

[31] George C. Homans, *The Human Group* (New York: Harcourt, Brace, 1950), p. 110.

[32] For a thorough discussion of this point, see Alfred J. Kutzik, *Social Work and Jewish Values* (Washington, D.C.: Public Affairs Press, 1959). Also see Herbert Bisno, *The Philosophy of Social Work* (Washington, D.C.: Public Affairs Press, 1952).

[33] Millikan, *op. cit.*, p. 166.

[34] Barbara Wooton, *Social Science and Social Pathology* (London: George Allen & Unwin, 1959). Chapter ix, entitled "Contemporary Attitudes in Social Work," makes particular reference to the American scene. Here the author characterizes some claims of American group workers as "arrogant" and "self-deceptive."

club group in the leisure-time agency alters personality, creates new value systems, and effects other profound changes in people's lives. This abstract and totalistic way of framing its objectives has prevented the field from examining the real, if limited, influence that skilful group work practice probably has, and the kinds of specific help that people in groups are actually able to use.

There are several lines of study that may help to bring practice goals closer to reality. There is, for example, the problem of separating worker goals from member goals, so that one can distinguish between the process of teaching and the process of learning— or, in social work terms, the dynamics of giving help and those of taking help. Study of the moment-to-moment interaction of these two processes should help clarify the means-ends structures of each and relate the desired outcomes more closely to possible ones.

A second line of inquiry may be directed toward the definition of outcomes that may reasonably be expected. If, for example, a worker aspires to help a group develop a wider variety of problem-solving devices, he may then create instruments to measure his degree of success. This is what Martin Wolins calls "a single, readily ascertainable development."[35] By contrast, a change-objective like "achieving socially desirable goals" is both unmeasurable and unachievable since the behavioral indexes are undefined and, even if they were defined, they would

[35] Martin Wolins, "Measuring the Effect of Social Work Intervention," *Social Work Research*, ed. Norman A. Polansky (Chicago: University of Chicago Press, 1960), p. 263.

still remain far beyond any conceivable range of influence to be expected of a single worker operating in a small sector of people's lives.

PROBLEMS OF ACTION

Given a body of knowledge about the social realities of group experience, and given a use of this knowledge to work out a realistic function and achievable value-goal objectives, one must next lay out a plan of action. Such a plan is essentially a way of breaking down a broad functional assignment into its component classes of activity.

At this point an organizing construct is needed from which to create the categories in which to gather up the various acts that the worker performs as he goes about his job. This is the point at which there might be advantages in using the "role" construct, an action-oriented idea designed to relate the worker's movements to those of others in a dynamic system. However, the term is so overladen with ambiguities and special uses that one experiences difficulty in using it without developing a specialized rationale for its meaning in this context. For the present, the term "task" may serve. Any function can be divided into a number of tasks necessary to perform it, and any specific act may be understood as related to one or another of these task headings.

Once having determined what these implementing tasks are, one must define and describe the skills necessary to carry them out. In this framework, then, the problems of action which climax the methodological study are those of task definition and skill definition.

Task definition.—The problems of task analysis revolve around three main points. Each task (*a*) must emerge from the theoretical scheme to which it is related, (*b*) must be directed to the tasks of the group members themselves, and (*c*) must be broad enough to encompass a number of helping activities, which should be specifiable in concrete terms.

For example, if "the general functional assignment of the social work profession is to mediate the process through which the individual and his society reach out for each other through a mutual need for self-fulfilment,"[36] we may then conceive of five implementing tasks: (1) to search out the common ground between the client's need-perception and the social demands with which he is faced; (2) to detect and challenge the obstacles that obscure this common ground; (3) to contribute otherwise unavailable and potentially useful data; (4) to reveal and project the worker's own feeling for the client and his problem; and (5) to define the limits and requirements of the situation in which the client-worker relationship is set.[37] The analytic process in examining the second of these tasks, for example, would proceed as follows. It would begin by describing the ways in which this task is designed to implement the functional statement. It would then proceed to describe and document some of the specific social realities involved—the origin of obstacles, what they look like in action, and the forms in which they are perceived by the members. Finally, it would describe the worker's activities—revealing impediments to action, supporting the mem-

bers as they enter the area of taboo, and protecting the focus of work, lest it be lost in the preoccupation with obstacles. This is of course a highly condensed account but it may serve to give some inkling of the possibilities offered in carving out limited areas for intensive study.

Skill definition.—The difficulty in defining skill in human relations is the problem of describing an act in its own terms, rather than in terms of its results. One may jibe at the notion that "the operation was a success, but the patient died," but the fact remains that it is impossible to develop a communicable art of surgery until we are willing to admit that it is possible for an operation to be well performed and for the patient to die. All this means is that the human material has a dynamic of its own and that the process of helping consists of two interdependent processes—the offer of help (the worker's act) and the use of it (the client's response). To say that the skill of an act is to be measured by its effect is to equate skill with predictive certainty and to leave out the client entirely. Social work cannot use a model borrowed from those who work with completely controllable materials—that is, inanimate objects.

It is true, of course, that the concern with skill is designed to help us narrow the range of uncertainty—that is, to find those acts which go most directly toward their purpose. Such acts must reflect "the greatest degree of consideration for and utilization of the quality and capacity of the material,"[38]

[36] Schwartz, "The Social Worker in the Group," *op. cit.,* pp. 154–55.

[37] *Ibid.,* pp. 157–58.

[38] Virginia P. Robinson, "The Meaning of Skill," *Training for Skill in Social Casework* (Philadelphia: University of Pennsylvania Press, 1942), p. 12.

but unless we can develop some descriptions of skilful activity, independent of effect, we cannot judge skill or order its "levels," or teach it; we certainly cannot, as we have often complained, interpret it to the general public.

This is a difficult job, but there are some indications that it is not an impossible one. We know, for example, that skill is an action concept. Skill is observable behavior of an actor-with-a-purpose toward others in a relational system. There are, of course, a number of mental acts—expressed mainly in the concept of "diagnosis"—but these have no value until they are translated into overt behavior guided by purpose. We know, too, that the factor of immediacy is important—that is, the further we move from the idea of present purpose, the "next step," the more difficult it is to define an act in its own terms. Thus, the ability to read a hidden message and to show the client his problem in a new form is a response to an immediate problem in helping. As such, it is definable, teachable, perhaps even measurable. By contrast, the attempt to formulate skills designed to "make the client more self-sufficient" is an impossible task.

A major contribution can be made in this area by those whose responsibility it is to educate for professional skill— social work teachers, agency supervisors, administrators of in-training programs. In this connection, an interesting attempt has been made by a group of field instructors to develop some models of group work skill, to make some determinations about levels of practice, and to describe the specific teaching and learning problems associated with the various models.

A NOTE ON RESEARCH

Despite the impatience of those who would like to move as quickly as possible into studies of outcome and effectiveness, our main progress for a time will probably be in studies of process and of limited effects.[39] In the course of what Bartlett has called "learning to ask better questions,"[40] our important devices are still descriptive, exploratory, and theory-developing; our major tools are still the group record, the life-history, the critical incident, and other techniques for codifying and conceptualizing the experience of practice. Perhaps our most critical problem is that so much of this experience is unavailable to us, since so little systematic and analytic work has been emerging from our potentially richest sources of information—the leisure-time agencies and their practitioners.

This is a period in which the social scientists are increasingly aware that the study of social systems—small and large—presents new challenges to the partnership of science and practice. Lawrence Frank put it this way to an assemblage of psychologists:

Perhaps we can devise new and appropriate methods if we will focus on the situation or difficulty, as in operations research, instead of relying so much on the assumptions and formulations of our discipline, especially since these offer little help in approaching organized complexities.

What the practitioner seeks is not merely a presentation of what exists or is occurring, or what trends may be revealed, no matter how

[39] See Wolins, op. cit., for his distinction between "effectiveness" and "effect."

[40] Harriet M. Bartlett, "Ways of Analyzing Social Work Practice," Social Welfare Forum, 1960 (New York: Columbia University Press, 1960), p. 205.

precisely these are measured or correlated. Rather, he needs a plan of action, a strategy for dealing with situations so that desired ends may be attained through a kind of action research which will help people to change their ideas, expectations, and behavior.[41]

It is this development of a "plan of action"—a strategy of helping people in groups—that represents the next major task of the group worker in social work.

[41] Frank, "Research for What?" *op. cit.*, p. 19.

*BEULAH ROTHMAN, D.S.W., is an Associate Professor
and CATHERINE P. PAPELL, M.S.W., is an
Associate Professor at the School of Social Work,
Adelphi University, New York, New York.
This paper was presented at the Faculty Day Conference
on Group Work, January 28, 1966, at the
CSWE Fourteenth Annual Program Meeting
in New York, New York.*

Social Group Work Models:
Possession and Heritage

by CATHERINE P. PAPELL and BEULAH ROTHMAN

THE SOCIAL GROUP WORK METHOD, like all social work methods, has developed largely experientially. Yet it has done so within a framework of some kind of guiding consensus about its essential elements. Persistently, social group workers have sought to formulate a logical relationship between these elements and pragmatic solutions to the tasks that have confronted them in practice. The evolutionary efforts of group workers to describe repeated patterns of phenomena and to define practice, in the language of science, has resulted in the emergence of several different theoretical models of social group work method. We have arrived at that stage of theory construction that can now be identified as model building.

A theoretical model is described by Kogan as "a scheme or map for 'making sense' out of the portion of the real world" in relation to which the worker is seeking to act.[1]

A model is a conceptual design to solve a problem that exists in reality. A model orders those elements in a given universe that are relevant to solve the problem. Higher levels of generalization or theory can be formulated when relationships hypothesized from a model are found to apply to a multitude of problems involving similar elements.

In our opinion, three models for social group work method can now be identified. The sequence of emergence of these models is elusive. Rudiments of these models are found scattered historically throughout the development of group work. Each has had periods of ascendent or waning commitment as practitioners have responded to the social scene and innovative calls for our professional services.

1 Leonard S. Kogan, "Principles of Measurement," in Norman A. Polansky, ed., *Social Work Research* (Chicago: University of Chicago Press, 1960), p. 90.

EDUCATION FOR SOCIAL WORK, Fall 1966, Vol. 5, pp. 66–77.

33

A core problem to which each model is addressed is concerned in some way with the central search of all of social work to identify its societal functions. One model tells us that our first priority is provision and prevention. A second model prefers restoration and rehabilitation. A third model attempts to encompass and reconcile these two historical streams. Thus our present state of theory building is but one of the several efforts within the broader arena of the professional struggle to establish a relationship between our methods and our service to society.

The question of function is intertwined with a second problem of major import. Historically in group work theory and in its practice there has existed the eternal triangle of the individual, the small group, and the larger society. These three have presented themselves as significant ingredients to be considered in any theoretical formulation, but the appropriate balance of each to the others has never been resolved. Thus, when one theoretical formulation tends to stress the individual, professional criticism is raised loudly from many quarters. When a formulation emerges that gives precedence to either of the other two factors, a similar reaction can be observed. The writers are not free of bias in regards to this triad. In our conjecture of the models that have emerged, a review of each will call attention to the gap or emphasis given these three integral parts.

It is perhaps the determination to resolve these two central problems, function and focus, that has deterred the development of a unified model for social group work, but has at the same time reaffirmed the common threads of our history. The three models that we describe and examine in this paper we shall henceforth identify by the following designations:

1. The social goals model
2. The remedial model
3. The reciprocal model

In order to grasp the attributes and characteristics distinguishing these three models, we shall address ourselves to the following three levels of inquiry:[2]

First: How does the model define the function of social group work? Who is the client to be served by the method? How does the model view the group as the unit of service? What is the image of the professional role? What is the nature of the agency auspice through which the group work service is rendered?

Second: What are the knowledge sources that serve as theoretical foundations for the model?

Third: What practice principles are generated by the model? Since it is necessary to limit the scope of this paper, we shall be concerned primarily with practice principles that pertain to assessment and implementation.

THE SOCIAL GOALS MODEL

Before proceeding with discussions of the social goals model, it must be understood that this model does not exist as a single formulation in our literature. It is not identified with a central theoretician who has systematically set forth all its elements. It is, in fact, a model that has its origins in the earliest traditions of professional group work practice. The central problems with which the social goals model attempts to deal are those related to the social order and the social value orientation in small groups. Historically, youth serving organizations, settlements, and Jewish community centers relied heavily on this model in developing and promoting group work services.

The early writings of such foremost thinkers as Coyle, Kaiser, Phillips, Konopka,

2 The formulation of this analytical frame borrows heavily from Robert D. Vinter, "Problems and Processes in Developing Group Work Practice Principles," *Theory Building in Social Work*, Workshop Report, CSWE 1960 Annual Program Meeting (New York: Council on Social Work Education, 1960).

Cohen, Miller, Ginsberg, Wilson, and Klein provide essential concepts and connecting propositions which, when combined, can be said to have produced this model. None of these writers would subscribe to this model in its entirety. In fact, several are clearly identified with the other two. However, each could find in the social goals model some piece that could be identified as his contribution and commitment.

The social goals model, although emerging from our past, has not been discarded. Interestingly, the model has been reaffirmed as critical strains have developed in the larger society. During the war era, the McCarthy era, and now during the period of struggle for integration, world peace and economic opportunity, this model has been presenting itself for use. Rooted as it is in the value system of our profession, every new effort at theoretical formulation of group work method either incorporates something of this model or is subjected to criticism in relation to it. Since 1962 a striking revival of interest in this model is evident. The University of Pittsburgh's recent position paper challenges the strains in the profession that seem to be abandoning this model.[3] Hyman J. Wiener's, work has produced a new level of theoretical sophistication in restatement of the model.[4]

Key concepts in the social goals model are "social consciousness" and "social responsibility." The function of social group work is to create a broader base of knowledgeable and skilled citizenry. "It is our role and function," state Ginsberg and Goldberg, to bring about "discussions of social issues . . . to help define action alternatives which in turn, hopefully result in informed political and social action."[5]

The model assumes that there is a unity between social action and individual psychological health. Every individual is seen as potentially capable of some form of meaningful participation in the mainstream of society. Thus the social goals model regards the individual as being in need of opportunity and assistance in revitalizing his drive toward others in a common cause and in converting self-seeking into social contribution. The therapeutic implications of social participation makes the application of this model available to group work practice with groups of varying illness and health. In describing a social action project at Camarillo State Hospital, Joseph D. Jacobs illustrates the use of the social goals model in a treatment setting.[6]

Consistent with its view of the individual, the social goals model approaches every group as possessing a potential for affecting social change. Program development moves toward uncovering this strength in the group, with social action as the desired outcome. This potential derives from the assumption that collective group action represents individual social competence.

The social goals model views the worker as an "influence"[7] person with responsibility, according to Wiener, for "the cultivation of social consciousness in groups . . . elevated to the same priority as . . . developing closer interpersonal relations."[8] Wiener speaks of this as the "political man approach."[9] He goes on to say, however, that the group worker "does not attempt to dictate a particular political view but does seek to inculcate a value system."[10] The group worker personifies the values of social responsibility and serves as a role model for the client, stimulating and rein-

3 Mildred Sirls *et al, Social Group Practice Elaborated: A Statement of Position* (Pittsburgh: University of Pittsburgh Graduate School of Social Work, April, 1964). (Mimeographed.)

4 Hyman, J. Wiener, "Social Change and Social Group Work Practice," *Social Work*, Vol. 9, No. 3 (July, 1964).

5 Mitchell I. Ginsberg and Jack R. Goldberg, "The Impact of the Current Scene on Group Work Policy and Practice," *Summary Presentations: Group Work Section Meetings, 1961-1962*, p. 30.

6 Joseph D. Jacobs, "Social Action as Therapy in a Mental Hospital," *Social Work*, Vol. 9, No. 1 (January, 1964).

7 Wiener, *op. cit.*, p. 109.

8 *Ibid.*

9 *Ibid.*

10 *Ibid.*

forcing modes of conduct appropriate to citizenship responsibility directed toward social change.

The social goals model primarily envisions group work services at a community level and agency as an integral part of the neighborhood. The setting is accessible and flexible in offering institutional auspices for a variety of collective efforts. It responds to the interests of various segments of the community and is willing to initiate and recruit for social action. The agency then becomes the vehicle through which members may acquire instrumental skills in social action and institutional support for communal change. The social goals model does not set up priorities for services but insists that such priorities develop out of the particular needs of the community at a given moment in time. Grappling with agency policies or agency limitations is not regarded as a deterrent to client strength. Rather it is the fabric from which practitioners and their clients learn to "test the limits of authority and sanction, demonstrating that sanction is the product of an ongoing process—constantly evolving and often susceptible to more influence than we think."[11]

Furthermore, the agency conveys the value that increased leisure time shall be harnessed for the common good and not solely for individual enrichment.

Since the social goals model in the past has been reliant more on ideology than on science, its theoretical underpinnings have only recently become more apparent. It would appear that neo-Freudian personality theories have been utilized in attaching importance to cultural differences and to the significance of interpersonal relations. A significant degree of individual and group malfunctioning is attributable to the malfunctioning of the social system. From the newer body of sociological theory the model picks up on opportunity theory and on theories of powerlessness, cultural

deprivation and inter-generational alienation. Current treatment theories of crisis and primary prevention are congenial to this model. The theories still to be seen exerting most influence on the model are theories of economic and political democracy and the educational philosophies of Dewey, Kilpatrick and Lindeman, particularly with regard to conceptions of leadership, communal responsibility and forms of group interaction.

To deal with the external environment of the group, the social goals model has generated a large body of principles designed to activate the group in relation to agency and community. Clarification of agency policy, positive use of limitations, identification with agency goals, determination of appropriate issues for collective action and the weighting of alternatives for action and their consequences, are all familiar principles heavily relied on in the social goals model. Furthermore, assessment and implementation with regard to the individual do not have to await intensive study of each member. The worker's assessment is first directed toward understanding normative behaviors manifested in the group as representative of the life style of the community and its sub-cultures. It is against this background that individual assessment can be formulated with respect to self-image, identity, social skill, knowledge of environmental resources and leadership potential. Principles related to the group emphasize participation, consensus and group task.

It is understandable that considerable explication of practice principles is to be found in recent writings pertaining to intergroup relations. We cite the work of Eleanor Ryder[12] and Jack Wiener.[13] In their papers they set forth principles which tell us

11 *Ibid.*

12 Eleanor L. Ryder, "Some Principles of Intergroup Relations as Applied to Group Work," *Social Work With Groups 1960* (New York: National Association of Social Workers, 1960), pp. 52-61.

13 Jack Wiener, "Reducing Racial and Religious Discrimination," *Social Work With Groups 1960* (New York: National Association of Social Workers, 1960), pp. 62-73.

how and when to make use of supra-ordinate goals to bring groups together, how to reduce the threat to individuals in heterogeneous groups, and how to engage members in inter-racial activities through a sequence of orderly and manageable steps. On a somewhat different level, but of major importance in this model, are those principles related to self-awareness and professional discipline particularly with regard to the value system and life style of the worker. It is interesting to note that the transfer of leadership from the professional to the indigenous leadership is implied in this model. Yet specific practice principles dealing with this aspect are noticeably absent in the literature.

A serious shortcoming of the social goals model is that it has not produced a theoretical design that is adequate to meet the problems facing practitioners in all areas of service. Its under-emphasis on individual dynamics and its lack of attention to a wide range of individual need leave the practitioner without guidelines for carrying out a social work function with client groups where individual problems take precedence over societal problems. It is difficult to see how this model would serve (except by distortion) to provide a basis for social group work practice with "admission" or "discharge" groups in a mental hospital.

Each of the models places the social group work method in some relationship to the other social work methods. The social goals model tends to move group work toward community organization method, but in so doing further obscures the boundaries between them. Ambiguity is particularly evident when group-serving agencies increasingly call upon grass roots membership to solve community problems sometimes in the name of the group work method and other times in the name of community organization method.

One last comment must be made about the social goals model. The principles of democratic group process that are fundamental to this model have become the hall-mark of all social group work practice. Every practitioner, regardless of his theoretical loyalty, tends to work toward the adoption and institutionalization of democratic procedures in small groups.

In summary, the essence of the social goals model is embodied in the words of the late Grace Coyle:

> It is not enough . . . for man to seek enjoyment in isolation from others. Because of his essentially social nature his fullest growth comes only as he uses his expanding powers in conjunction with and for the benefit of others. For his own deepest growth he must be socialized . . . we . . . mean by this his ability to establish mutual relations with others and the capacity to identify himself with the good of the social whole however he conceives it, to use his capacities in part at least for social ends beyond himself. Each must find for himself his social objects of devotion, but to discover them is as essential to fulfillment as to find the objects of his more personal loves. To hope for such attainment in however small a measure is no doubt the common goal of all who sincerely wish to work in some capacity with people.[14]

THE REMEDIAL MODEL

Placed in historical context the remedial model further facilitated the integration of the group work method in the profession of social work. It offered a congenial base for the linkage of the social group work method with the method of social casework. As in casework, the remedial model established the treatment of individuals as the central function of group work. Through the remedial model the social group work method offered another means by which the profession could restore or rehabilitate individuals.

Early development of the remedial model was conspicuously influenced by the work of Redl in the institutional group treatment of children. Later the model was elaborated by social group workers such as Konopka, Sloan, Fisher and Gantner. A

14 Grace L. Coyle, *Group Work with American Youth* (New York: Harper & Brothers, 1948).

systematic formulation of the model has been presented in the writings of Robert Vinter, now identified as its major theoretician.

The problems of adjustment in personal and social relations that can be treated through the use of the group are considered within the special competence of the social group worker. Attention to such problems reaffirms "the profession's historic mission of service to those most in need."[15] In this manner, the concept of priority is introduced in the remedial model. Criticism is directed towards the deployment of limited personnel to those services which are categorized as "socialization and consumption" services.[16] It follows logically, then, that the image of the client is that of an individual who is suffering from some form of social maladaptation or deficiency. In this sense, the remedial model is clearly a clinical model focused upon helping the malperforming individual to achieve a more desirable state of social functioning.

The group is viewed as a tool or context for treatment of the individual. Diagnostic goals for each individual as established by the worker, supersede group goals. ". . . changes in the group structure and the group process," states Arthur Blum, "are the means to the end goal of individual change. . . ."[17] Group development is not conceived in the interest of collective growth that has meaning unto itself. There is no idealized image of a healthy group per se. A conception of group health transcends the particular needs of the therapeutic situation. Blum continues:

> A "good" group is the group which permits and fosters the growth of its members. This does not presuppose any fixed structure or

level of function as being desirable except as it affects the members. . . . Evaluation of the desirability of its (the group's) structure and processes can only be made in relation to the desirability of its effects upon the members and the potential it provides for the worker's interventions.[18]

The treatment group primarily envisioned by the remedial model is the "formed" group, wherein membership is pre-determined and diagnostically selected by the worker.[19] Natural or friendship ties are not considered essential unless they meet the therapeutic prescription, or where there are no other bases of group formation open to the worker. Group composition is considered a significant factor in the potential of the group to serve as an effective treatment vehicle.

Processes within the group which help members to help each other are given recognition in this model but the limit of the self-help system is contained within the boundaries of the diagnostic plan. The remedial model deals only peripherally with a full range of collective associations such as are to be found in spontaneous groupings, informal lounges, and mass activities. Moreover, the preventive use of the group in relation to normal developmental needs is of secondary importance. The group program is primarily evaluated for its therapeutic potential rather than for its creative and expressive qualities.

The worker is viewed as a "change agent" rather than an "enabler" facilitating self-direction of the group. He uses a problem-solving approach, sequentially phasing his activities in the tradition of study, diagnosis and treatment. He is characteristically directive, and assumes a position of clinical preeminence and authority. He exercises this authority through such ways as the assigning of task and role, and the screening of activity against his own pro-

---

15 Robert D. Vinter, "Group Work: Perspectives and Prospects," *Social Work With Groups 1959* (New York: National Association of Social Workers, 1959), p. 135.

16 *Ibid.*, p. 136.

17 Arthur Blum, "The Social Group Work Method: One View." *A Conceptual Framework for the Teaching of the Social Group Work Method in the Classroom* (New York: Council on Social Work Education, 1964), p. 12.

18 *Ibid.*, p. 12.

19 For further amplification see Rosemary Sarri *et al, Diagnosis In Social Group Work* (Ann Arbor: University of Michigan School of Social Work, October, 1964). (Mimeographed.)

fessional objectives. His authority derives from the mandate given to him by the profession and the agency. While his authority must be confirmed by the group, it is not fundamentally established by the group. From this position of authority his intervention may be designed to do *for* the client as well as *with* the client. The model does not require the worker to give priority to the establishment of group autonomy[20] nor to the perpetuation of the group as a self-help system.

With regard to setting, the remedial model seems to require a structured institutional context. It assumes clearly defined agency policy in support of treatment goals. When these are not available, it suggests professional efforts to develop them. The remedial model makes less provision for adapting service to the informal life style of the client. It appears to depart from the tradition that the group worker engages with people where he finds them as they go about the business of daily living.

From the earliest development of the remedial model it was necessary to draw upon individual psychological theories in support of its individualizing focus. The model relied heavily upon traditional sources of individual theory utilized by social casework. For example, psychoanalytic theory provided a set of concepts that sensitized the group worker to "resistance" and "transference" phenomena and the "symbolic" representation of the group as a family. More recently the utility of ego psychology to explain behavior in relation to internal and external forces is being recognized and explored.

Whereas social group work has had more difficulty operationalizing psychoanalytical concepts, social role theory has lent itself to a simpler and more direct application for understanding and treating the individual in the group. The significance of this theory lies in its power to provide conceptualizations that define and describe the "presenting" social problems more in harmony with the method of treatment to be used. Social role theory as an interactional theory, therefore, is congruent to the unit of service employed by the social group worker. It is this theory that has been employed prominently in the writings of Vinter and his colleagues at the University of Michigan School of Social Work.[21]

Since the remedial model assumes that "group development can be controlled and influenced by the worker's actions,"[22] it must draw heavily from theories of small group dynamics. These theories help to account for changes in the group and suggest opportunities for professional interventions in carrying out the "change agent" role.

In the remedial model the central and most powerful concept is "treatment goal." Emphasis on this concept is . intersticed throughout most of its practice principles. The influence of the "treatment goal" is to be noted in the following selected practice principles:

1. "Specific treatment goals must be established for each member of the client group."[23]

2. The worker "attempts to define group purposes so that they are consistent with the several treatment goals established for the individual members."[24]

3. The worker helps "the group to develop that system of norms and values which is in accord with the worker's treatment goals."[25]

---

20 This same observation was made by Mildred Sirls *et al., op. cit.,* p. 6.

21 For elaboration on the use of social role theory in group work practice, see Paul H. Glasser, "Social Role, Personality, and Group Work Practice," *Social Work Practice* (New York: Columbia University Press, 1962), pp. 60-74.

22 Rosemary C. Sarri and Maeda J. Galinsky, "A Conceptual Framework for Teaching Group Development in Social Group Work," *A Conceptual Framework for the Teaching of the Social Group Work Method in the Classroom* (New York: Council on Social Work Education, 1964), p. 21.

23 Robert D. Vinter, "The Essential Components of Social Group Work Practice" (Ann Arbor: University of Michigan School of Social Work, 1959), p. 4. (Mimeographed.)

24 *Ibid.,* p. 6.

25 *Ibid.,* p. 12.

4. The worker prestructures "the content for group sessions based on the worker's knowledge of individuals expressed through his treatment goals as well as his knowledge of structural characteristics and processes that take place within the group."[26]

These principles state clearly that assessment begins with the needs of individual members. Knowledge of these needs is derived from information secured prior to the individual's participation in the group. It is assumed that with such knowledge the group worker can integrate individual needs into a needs-satisfying system through the formation of a group. Thus it is the group worker who diagnoses the needs and who formulates treatment goals *for the client*. The lesser emphasis on the concept *with the client* sharply differentiates the remedial model from the other two models.

The model places considerable import on possession of knowledge by the group worker as a key to diagnosis and treatment. The model assumes that (1) such knowledge is available, and (2) given the appropriate knowledge the group worker will know precisely how to act in relation to it. This is far removed from the realities of both theory and practice. Appropriate knowledge may not always be available. More often we know better from knowledge what *not* to do than what should be done. There is, in fact, a limit to prescriptiveness in the real world that is not taken into account in this model. There is a mechanistic quality about the remedial model which precludes the creative and dynamic aspects of human interaction.

A sense of unreality prevails in the demands that are made upon the group worker in the early contact with the group. In actual practice most of the group worker's initial efforts are directed toward problems of group management and maintenance in the external environment. Individual therapeutic goals are subject to the

reality stress of group formation and may themselves be modified. Treatment goals during this phase provide less of an anchorage for professional activity than is implied in the model.

Further analysis of the remedial model reveals insufficient provision for a group to contribute to its environment. Actually the model constrains the group worker from viewing the group as a system to be sustained and utilized for the purpose of enhancing the milieu. "Obviously," says Vinter, "the aim of group work is not to help persons to become good members of successfully operating client groups."[27] In the remedial model the human group has little claim to existence except for what it can give to the individual. In the light of this, it is difficult to determine from this model the specificity of the group work function in contrast to the general function of group therapy. Moreover, the model leaves unanswered what is the special contribution of group work in the full spectrum of social work with groups.

Within its circumscribed boundaries, the remedial model has made several theoretical advances. It has systematically set forth (1) guidelines for diagnostic considerations of individual functioning in the group, (2) criteria for group formation, (3) foundations for clinical team participation, and (4) diagnostic utilization of the group where other treatment modalities coexist. Thus the model has greatly facilitated the functioning of group work practitioners in clinical settings, and has drawn upon the learnings from these settings for incorporation in a general framework of social group work method.

THE RECIPROCAL MODEL

This model advances a helping process that is intended to serve both the individual and society. It proceeds on the assump-

26 Paul H. Glasser and Jane Costabile, "Social Group Work Practice in a Public Welfare Setting" (Ann Arbor: University of Michigan School of Social Work, November, 1963), p. 4. (Mimeographed.)

27 Robert D. Vinter, "The Essential Components of Social Group Work Practice" (Ann Arbor: University of Michigan School of Social Work, 1959), p. 6. (Mimeographed.)

tion that social group work is a special case of a general social work method which is addressed to the human condition whether it be presented in a single or collective context. Whereas the reciprocal model has been specifically organized by one author, William Schwartz, it reflects the influence of many contributors. It opens the way for providing a larger theoretical umbrella to more adequately encompass the whole of the social group work method.

The duality of its focus suggests Kaiser's early conceptualization[28] in this regard. The strong emphasis on process, enabling, and on quality of engagement is reminiscent of Phillips.[29] More recently the work of Emanuel Tropp[30] illustrates possibilities of further developing several aspects of the model in greater theoretical depth.

The reciprocal model presupposes an organic, systemic relationship between the individual and society. The interdependence is described as "symbiotic," of basic urgency to both, and normally subject to crisis and stress. This interdependence is the "focus" for social work and the small group is the field in which individual and societal functioning can be nourished and mediated. The range of social work function can include prevention, provision, as well as restoration. Breakdown in the interdependence between systems may occur at any point on the continuum between health and pathology.

Within the logic of this model the group is in a position of preeminence. Since the group is accorded such central status in the model, it can be said that it is, in fact, the client of the group worker. It follows that key concepts in this model largely pertain to the group. The most striking concept of the reciprocal model is "mutual aid system."

Unlike the remedial model, the reciprocal model does not begin with a priori prescriptions or desired outcomes. However, it does conceive of an ideal group state, namely a system in mutual aid. Such a system is not dependent upon the specific problem to be resolved by the group but is a necessary condition for problem solving. To state it in still another way, the reciprocal model has no therapeutic ends, no political or social change programs, to which it is addressed. It is only from the encounter of individuals that compose a reciprocal group system that direction or problem is determined. Emphasis is placed on *engagement* in the process of interpersonal relations. It is from this state of involvement that members may call upon each other in their own or a common cause.

Group members, states Schwartz, "move to relate their own sense of need to the social demand implicit in the collective tasks of the group."[31] Tropp takes this further by insisting that it is the "common goals group . . . with shared authority . . . pursuing common decisions"[32] that is the core group at the center of attention of the social group work method.

The concept of shared authority derives from the assumption "that people create many helping relationships in addition to and concurrent with the one formed with the worker."[33]

The reciprocal model views the individual primarily in terms of his motivation and capacity for reciprocity. The model, therefore, focuses on the relational aspects of behavior as determined by the present reality of the group system. Understanding of the individual is bounded by the social context in which he, the group, and the worker interact. Diagnostic considerations or structural descriptions of the individual are not regarded as significant predictors of

[28] Clara Kaiser, "The Social Group Work Process," *Journal of Social Work* (April, 1958), pp. 67-75.

[29] Helen Phillips, *Essentials of Social Group Work Skill* (New York: Association Press, 1957).

[30] Emanuel Tropp, "Group Intent and Group Structure: Essential Criteria for Group Work Practice," *Journal of Jewish Communal Service*, Vol. XLI, No. 3 (Spring, 1965).

[31] William Schwartz, "Toward a Strategy of Group Work Practice," *Social Service Review* (September, 1962), p. 274.

[32] Tropp, *op. cit.*, p. 234.

[33] Schwartz, *op. cit.*, p. 273.

behavior in the group. Therefore they do not serve as a basis for selection of members for a group or assessment by the worker.

The image of the worker projected by this model is that of a mediator or enabler to the needs system converging in the group. The worker is viewed as a part of the worker-client system both influencing and being influenced by it. In the terminology of social work, he neither does *to* the client nor *for* him, but *with* him. The relationship between worker and client in this model involves deep investment and emotional commitment in which the worker reveals and makes available his aspirations, knowledge and effect within the boundaries of the "contract" between himself, the group, and the agency.

The reciprocal model makes no reference to a type of agency auspice, but it does assume that, whatever the agency, it will engage in the mutual establishment of a "contract." Thus the agency also accepts a place in a reciprocal system with inherent limitations. The authority of the agency is not emphasized in this model.

The knowledge base of the reciprocal model primarily originates in sociological systems theory and field theory. In analyzing group work and constructing a formulation of group work method, a structural-functional approach is employed. However, it is to be noted that while Schwartz posits the parts-whole concept, he chooses to focus on the relationship of parts to whole, paying scant attention to the specificity or autonomy of parts themselves.

A second theoretical source, although not directly acknowledged, is inferred by the reciprocal model. This theoretical source is known under the general rubric of social psychological theories of personality. Shades of Adler, Fromm, and Sullivan are to be found in the assumptions that underlie the individual's motivation and capacity for reaching out to collectivities.

In turning to the practice principles generated by the reciprocal model, they are found to be first developed as generic methodology for social work as a whole and subsequently transformed for ultilization in a worker-group system.

Schwartz has conceptualized five major tasks to be carried out by the social work practitioner. In very brief form they are as follows:

> 1. The task of searching out the common ground between the client's perception of his own need and the aspects of social demand with which he is faced.
> 2. The task of detecting and challenging the obstacles which obscure the common ground. . . .
> 3. The task of contributing data—ideas, facts, value concepts—which are not available to the client. . . .
> 4. The task of "lending a vision." . . .
> 5. The task of defining the requirements and the limits of the situation in which the client-worker system is set.[34]

Each of the these generic tasks has been operationalized through a series of principles that specifically guides social group workers.

To illustrate, we will take task #1, that of "searching out common ground." The model suggests three primary principles as follows: (1) The worker helps the group to strengthen its goals through a consideration of what it is in common that the members are seeking. (2) The worker interprets his role through clarifying with the group what it is they wish from him that he has available to give from which a clear "contractual" agreement can be drawn. (3) The worker acts to protect the focus of work against attempts to evade or subvert it.

Pervading this model is a series of practice principles that are devoted to worker honesty and directness and the avoidance of withholding knowledge and effect. These principles seem to reflect as much the author's determination to dispel a "mystique of professionalism" as to relate to the functional tasks.

---

34 William Schwartz, "The Social Worker in the Group," *New Perspectives on Services to Groups* (New York: National Association of Social Workers, 1961), p. 17.

42

The contribution of the reciprocal model lies in its unifying abstractions. Intensive individualizing and social focusing within the small group are rendered in a conceptual balance, providing a coherent footing for further theoretical development.

The limitation of Schwartz's formulation lies more in theoretical *gaps* than in inconsistencies. Middle range supporting theories are insufficiently developed in several areas. For example, interest in the individual system is strikingly sparse. Schwartz does not make allowance for the latitude of human personality which may be necessary to explain the manner in which the individual coheres in any system in aid of others. There is a sense of unreality in the notion that the motivation toward collectivity is always productive of individual and/or social good. Without guidelines in relation to individual dynamics and normative expectations, there is no basis for assessing the impact of change upon individuals. There is produced a tendency toward permissiveness and abdication of worker's authority. Process itself is elevated to an unreal superordinance.

It is to be noted that ego-psychological concepts increasingly being utilized by social group workers may fill the gap regarding individual dynamics without violating the central logic of the reciprocal model.[35]

Group system theory is likewise underdeveloped. Schwartz does not sufficiently take into account similarities or differences in a variety of group systems. Moreover, while his conceptualization is useful in beginning with a group, it does not offer a framework for dealing with changes that may occur in the group over time. Thus the model ignores what has been observed experientially by group workers and is known from scientific study of small groups. Group development is perceived simplistically, without conceptually accounting for new

levels realizable as a result of group experience and achievement.

Schwartz's formulation is distressingly lacking in any clarification of group program. One might deduce that discussion as a channel for communication overshadows all others.

It seems appropriate now to recall Irving Miller's comments on an earlier form of this paper. He addressed himself to the level of abstraction of a theoretical model. He raised the possibility that "the concrete solutions and specific applications which may be eventually deduced from a broad and generalized model may be so attenuated as to suggest that the specific applications do not necessarily flow from or require the original abstraction."[36]

Despite limitations of the reciprocal model, its outstanding contribution is the construct of a mutual aid system with professional interventions flowing from it. What has been vaguely referred to in the past as "helping members to help themselves" has acquired a higher level of theoretical statement. It is possible now to systematically consider the attributes and culture of such a specialized system and to transmit the skills necessary to support its realization. This is probably the single most important contribution that group work method can make to the social work profession at large.

In conclusion, we submit that the significant movement of social group work in theory building lies in the production of models systematic designs by which the elements of social group work practice have begun to be ordered and problems in practice rendered more solvable. We have found three models to be clearly in existence. Each independently pursues lines of inquiry relating historical tradition to present societal requirements. The foremost contribution of each is not made by the other

---

35 A most current example is to be found in Baruch Levine, "Principles for Developing an Ego Supportive Group Treatment Service," *Social Service Review*, Vol. XXXIV, No. 4 (December, 1965).

36 The original form of this paper was presented at Columbia University School of Social Work Alumni Conference, April, 1962. Irving Miller served as a discussant.

two. Each falls short in encompassing the totality of social group work method. This suggests that new models will emerge either parallel or in a subsuming relationship to those that presently exist.

Even as the kinship of all social group workers to each of these models insists itself upon us, so also the continued authorship of our theory lies with each of us. Regardless of the particular bias of practice or educational institution, it is essential that all new practitioners enter the profession with a knowledge of the state of its theoretical development and with ability to relate their thinking to the models that exist.

Furthermore, all practitioners and educators writing today about social group work practice should in some manner take into account where their work falls in relation to these patternings that have developed. Thus each of these models will be moved ahead in order, fullness and complexity or will be replaced by more useful theoretical structures. The possession of models provides a baseline for further elaborating the utility of the social group work method in the profession's service to mankind.

Ann Hartman

But what is social casework?

Ann Hartman is associate professor, School of
Social Service, Fordham University,
New York, New York.

With what we now know was considerable optimism, Helen Harris Perlman made
the following statement in the April 1970 issue of this journal:

I think we are past the peak of the battle against
casework. If I am not being made myopic by
excesses of weariness or hope, I think we may
speak of it in the past tense. It was a battle,
waged with lethal accusations and crusader ban-
ners whose mottoes spoke to massive need for
massive social action programs.[1]

Nearly one year after we read this welcome
reassurance, the following headline appeared
in the *New York Times:* "Community Service Society Changing Tactics: Will Drop
Casework."[2] Could it be that casework was
finally dead, killed at last by a blow from an
institution that figured prominently in its
birth and nurturance?[3]

Rumors had been circulating for some time

about program changes being considered at
that venerable agency, but few anticipated
what James G. Emerson, Jr., its general director, called "this 'complete turnaround.'"
The agency planned to end its "123 years of
family casework and individual counseling.
. . . The techniques . . . had proved inadequate for the poor who face overwhelming
problems in the slums." In this turnaround,
the community would be the client. "If the
individual is to be helped, someone has to deal
with the complex of social ills that bears on
the individual, not just on the individual himself."[4]

Several examples of preferred or more effective services were used to illustrate
Emerson's argument. One study was reported
to have concluded that "'the development of
a learn-to-read program . . . would make a far
greater impact per dollar spent than intensive
therapy with X families.'" Another program
cited found that "training homemakers had
'far more effectiveness than if they put 10
caseworkers in there, because the need was
not for therapy, but for someone home so the

[1]Helen Harris Perlman, Casework and 'the
Diminished Man,' SOCIAL CASEWORK, 51:216
(April 1970).

[2]*New York Times,* January 29, 1971, p. 1.

[3]In the *Social Work Year Book, 1945,* Charlotte
Towle dates the beginning of modern casework as
1898, when the Charity Organization Society of New
York, now the Community Service Society, started
a summer training program that led to the founding
of the New York School of Philanthropy, now the
Columbia University School of Social Work. See
Charlotte Towle, Social Case Work, in *Social
Work Year Book, 1945* (New York: Russell Sage
Foundation, 1945), p. 417.

[4]*NewYork Times,* January 29, 1971, p. 1.

SOCIAL CASEWORK, July 1971, Vol. 52, pp. 411–419.

father could get a job.' " One final comment, "Casework may be done if community groups ask for it,"[5] calls to mind these words from the Perlman article: "[Casework] is not a 'thing' that can be 'given' to anyone."[6]

Defining casework

Thus, we are led to the basic question, What is social casework? Should we not—as in any good eulogy—describe, define, and capture the basic identity of the deceased? I would like to suggest that when we talk about casework, dead or alive, effective or ineffective, we seem to think that we are all talking about the same thing. Is Emerson's casework the same as Perlman's casework, or Florence Hollis's casework, or Lydia Rapoport's, or Carol Meyer's, or Louise Bandler's, or even—to move back to our original expositor—Mary Richmond's?

Mary Richmond made the first attempt to define casework practice, and the difficult task has been with us since. Many social workers still consider her famous definition from *What is Social Casework?* as the most adequate. She defined casework as *"those processes which develop personality through adjustments consciously effected, individual by individual, between men and their social environment."*[7] This definition includes three major points: (1) the objective of casework is people changing or, in Richmond's words, "personality development"; (2) the approach is to the individual; and (3) the area of concern lies in the relationship between man and his environment. Richmond operationalized this definition through a simple classification scheme: direct treatment, or "the action of mind upon mind," and indirect treatment, or action through the environment.[8]

The next major effort to define social casework was made by participants at the famous

Milford Conference of 1929. Although an attempt was made to distinguish the generic aspects of social casework, "The group were not able at that time to define social case work itself so as to distinguish it sharply from other forms of professional work."[9] The Milford Conference continued to meet in the early 1930s after the publication of its first report. Bertha C. Reynolds, a member of the group, was active in continuing attempts to define or redefine social casework in the light of the impact of the depression and of psychoanalytic knowledge. In an article growing out of her work with the conference, she wrote:

The essential point seems to be that the function of social case work is not to treat the individual alone nor his environment alone, but *the process of adaptation which is a dynamic interaction between the two.*[10]

Describing just that professional role that Abraham Flexner had defined as not professional,[11] Reynolds described social caseworkers as concerned with the whole person, and thus, "Among the specialists, social case work may find its function as co-ordinator of services."[12] In a later article she added, "Social case work is essentially a mediating function ... [it] finds its function in dealing with difficulties in the relationship between individuals or groups and their physical or social environment."[13] Reynolds also described a crisis or

[5]Ibid.

[6]Perlman, Casework and 'the Diminished Man,' p. 217.

[7]Mary E. Richmond, *What Is Social Case Work? An Introductory Description* (New York: Russell Sage Foundation, 1922), pp. 98–99.

[8]Ibid., p. 102.

[9]American Association of Social Workers, Studies in the Practice of Social Work No. 2, *Social Case Work: Generic and Specific* (New York: American Association of Social Workers, 1929), p. 3.

[10]Bertha Capen Reynolds, Can Social Case Work Be Interpreted to a Community as a Basic Approach to Human Problems?, *The Family*, 13:337 (February 1933).

[11]Abraham Flexner, Is Social Work a Profession?, *Proceedings of the National Conference of Charities and Correction* (Chicago: National Conference of Charities and Correction, 1915), pp. 576–90.

[12]Reynolds, Can Social Case Work be Interpreted, p. 337.

[13]Bertha Capen Reynolds, Whom Do Social Workers Serve?, *Social Work Today,* 2:8 (May 1935).

public health model of practice in the belief that caseworkers could be helpful in aiding people to deal with the:

. . . inevitable hazards of living, the disasters wrought by sudden changes in natural surroundings such as floods and climatic irregularities, to changes in the life cycle, infancy, adolescence, middle life, and old age, to new experiences, migration, to the death of loved ones and unavoidable loss.[14]

She looked forward to the day when social casework could be truly "institutional," the day when the total population would be properly served by a variety of social provisions.

Auxiliary to a rational system of distribution, and to the community services of public health, safety and education, social case work can provide the indispensible touch with individuals which no mass program can do without. Perhaps social case work will be the "personnel department" of the community of the future.[15]

As the defining and developing process continued, it was perhaps Fern Lowry, delivering the opening paper at the American Association of Psychiatric Social Workers meeting on differential diagnosis in 1936, who made the next major addition to the definition of casework practice. The scope of possible interventions was broadening, and the client's needs, she believed, should be the polestar that guided all the worker's activities.

To elucidate this concept, Lowry developed a diagnostic and treatment classification based on differential assessment of client need. The first form of treatment described in the classification was that "primarily directed toward the enrichment of environment for the individual, toward helping him make more profitable use of his environment, or toward the modification of environment." She illustrates this treatment approach by

describing a situation in which "the worker's activities were almost wholly related to assisting the man in his search for employment, helping his wife get adequate medical care, and providing camp care and scholarship help for the two children." The second form of treatment involved a dual approach to the individual and the environment or to the individual via the environment, "for example, in the case of a boy with whom the worker discusses his school difficulties, helping him to express his resentments and bringing about some release in tension, *at the same time* that she is working directly with the school, making arrangements for special classes, interpreting his needs to the teacher, and so on."[16] This middle range definition of casework was later explicated in more transactional terms by Lucille Austin, who called it "experiential treatment."[17]

The third form of treatment, which Lowry called "personal or psychological,"

. . . is that in which the worker's activities are primarily related to the client's subjective realities, his emotional conflicts, feelings, and so on —the primary purpose being to effect a better adjustment to his environment through effecting a better adjustment to himself. This type of treatment is carried out largely through the medium of the relationship between client and worker with the interview as the primary technic.[18]

Range of casework objectives

If in our search for the elusive identity of social casework it is important to find historical precedents, then we find in the words of these creative leaders in casework—written thirty-five to forty years ago—a broad range of objectives and measures included as a part of casework practice. Casework can be institu-

[14]Ibid., p. 6.

[15]Bertha Capen Reynolds, Between Client and Community: A Study of Responsibility in Social Case Work, *Smith College Studies in Social Work,* 5:124 (September 1934).

[16]Fern Lowry, The Client's Needs as the Basis for Differential Approach in Treatment, in *Differential Approach in Case Work Treatment* (New York: Family Welfare Association of America, 1936), pp. 5–6.

[17]Lucille N. Austin, Trends in Differential Treatment in Social Casework, *Journal of Social Casework,* 29:203–11 (June 1948).

[18]Lowry, Client's Needs, p. 6.

tional or residual; it can have as its change objective the environment or the individual or the individual via the environment; the caseworker can function as mediator, advocate, social broker, counselor, or psychotherapist.

Richmond's definition has not only been expanded in these definitions of the thirties; it has been altered. In Reynold's institutional view and in Lowry's first form of treatment, people-changing objectives are no longer required as an essential and necessary part of a definition of casework practice. Further, on the other end of the definitional spectrum, a form of treatment exclusively focused on the psychological aspects of the person-in-situation complex is also included under the umbrella of casework.

Throughout the ensuing years, there appears to have been general agreement that the middle-range, dual-focus practice was indeed social casework. It was around the two poles of pure psychotherapy, on the one hand, and simple provision, on the other, that confusion and controversy developed. The profession struggled with the question of whether the individualized and appropriate administration of a concrete service without any people-changing objectives was, in and of itself, casework practice or whether such tasks were a meaningful part of casework only when used as a tool in treatment, as an instrument to bring about individual change or growth. The literature is replete with discussions of the use of a variety of concrete services as tools in treatment, that is, for rehabilitation rather than for simple provision. Homemaker service has been a favorite for this rehabilitative use and, at times, abuse. For example, if we believe what we say about self-determination, then it is an abuse to utilize a homemaker as a rehabilitative tool while the client accepts the service as a social provision.

The social workers of the Pennsylvania School took yet another position in regard to the relationship between the delivery of concrete service and casework. Calling such service delivery the "administrative backbone" of casework practice, the functionalists repudiated the concept of concrete service as a tool in treatment as coercive and manipulative. However, although they believed that the concrete service as defined by the function of the agency had basic value in and of itself, their view was that the process through which the service was delivered offered the client an opportunity for growth.

Emphasis on psychotherapy

There has been even greater interest, controversy, and discussion around attempts to define, describe, and differentiate casework at the other pole. "Somehow, social casework has come to be equated with psychotherapy,"[19] Rapoport said at the fiftieth anniversary of the Smith College School for Social Work. The reasons for this equation and the influences that led social casework practitioners to an overemphasis on psychotherapeutic functions and neglect of environment-changing functions have been discussed at length. Certainly status considerations, the impact of psychoanalytic knowledge and methods, feelings of impotence in the face of apparently intractable and destructive environmental forces, and the marriage of puritan and Freudian individualism and absolutism all played their parts.

One additional factor appears to have been underplayed as we search—primarily within ourselves as a profession—for the reasons for this emphasis on the psychological. (We are so consistent in our inner focus that when we try to discover why we have persisted in looking inward, we look inward for the answers.) Social work is a socially sanctioned, publicly supported profession that has been designated by society to deal with what it defines as its major social problems. Societal definitions, therefore, will clearly affect where social work practice is located. During the period immediately following World War II and throughout the 1950s, there was a major nationwide concern with mental illness, which was defined as the nation's number one health problem.

It is beyond the scope of this article to explore why definitions of problems in one

[19]Lydia Rapoport, Social Casework: An Appraisal and an Affirmation, *Smith College Studies in Social Work*, 39:225 (June 1969).

decade will differ from those in another,[20] but it is clear that such definitions will affect the establishment of priorities and the expenditure of funds. Training and research grants that supported students and practitioners in mental health studies and research as well as the burgeoning community mental health movement all strengthened the preoccupation with psychological variables, psychotherapy, and mental and emotional illness. Scott Briar, describing the casework predicament in 1968, wrote that "the image of the modern caseworker . . . is above all that of a therapist, which is to say that for the most part he performs only a therapeutic function."[21]

This image is conveyed in Emerson's announcement about the Community Service Society. It is an image that is conveyed and reinforced by caseworkers themselves. We have not been explicit in our objectives, nor have we sorted out the areas of our concerns or the locations of our interventions. Could it be that our efforts, over the years, to arrive at some unifying definition have added to the confusion?[22] While reaching for unity, such efforts may have tended to submerge significant differences and to obscure the multiplicity of modes of practice that continue to appear and reappear in various guises. In our effort to be generic, to say that casework is casework, we have perhaps lost what should have been specific. Particularly, the failure to distinguish between the objectives of changing people and meeting those of concrete

needs may have created our most serious confusions.

Hollis's book, *Casework: A Psychosocial Therapy*, has been widely used as a basic text in casework classes in many schools of social work, and for some people it has come to stand as a definition of casework practice. The therapeutic model of casework defined in this book is not "all of casework," as Hollis states in the first paragraph of her introduction. "The concern of this book, is the analysis of a particular segment of casework practice—the treatment of people experiencing problems in their interpersonal relationships."[23] Because of the nature of the problems addressed by the practice studied in this volume, the intervention that is discussed is primarily psychological. People, however, are not likely to read or remember an introduction. One infers from the title that casework is being defined.

The endless discussion concerning the book, *Girls at Vocational High: An Experiment in Social Work Intervention*,[24] presents an example of the kinds of difficulties that emerge when we fail to develop operational definitions of social casework. "Casework" as "done" at Vocational High did not "work." In a sobering review of the book, Alvin Schorr writes, "The service given was of good quality and, in usual practice terms, substantial."[25] What, however, was the nature of the intervention? What was the model of casework practice?

In a later discussion of the project, Mary E. MacDonald raises the issue of evaluating the model of practice.[26] The question becomes not whether the practice was of "good quality"

[20]For an interesting view of this question, see Thomas S. Szasz, *The Manufacture of Madness: A Comparative Study of the Inquisition and the Mental Health Movement* (New York: Harper & Row, 1970).

[21]Scott Briar, The Casework Predicament, *Social Work*, 13:7 (January 1968).

[22]For example, Swithun Bowers's exhaustive and scholarly analysis of casework practice and definitions exposed many differences but then ended with a broad enough definition to reconcile these differences. See Swithun Bowers, The Nature and Definition of Social Casework: Part I, *Journal of Social Casework*, 30:311–17 (October 1949); and Part II, *Journal of Social Casework*, 30:369–75 (November 1949).

[23]Florence Hollis, *Casework: A Psychosocial Therapy* (New York: Random House, 1965), p. 3.

[24]Henry J. Meyer, Edgar F. Borgatta, and Wyatt C. Jones, *Girls at Vocational High: An Experiment in Social Work Intervention* (New York: Russell Sage Foundation, 1965).

[25]Alvin Schorr, Mirror, Mirror on the Wall . . . , *Social Work*, 10:112 (July 1965).

[26]Mary E. MacDonald, Reunion at Vocational High, An Analysis of *Girls at Vocational High: An Experiment in Social Work Intervention*, *Social Service Review*, 40:188 (June 1966).

but rather how it was being defined. We are again confronted with the question, What is social casework? Is it a people-changing activity? Is it a concrete service delivery method? Is it a situation-changing intervention? When the Community Service Society drops casework, what is it dropping?

Casework can be and still is defined by many as primarily a psychotherapeutic method consisting of an extended, open-ended (or, in the briefer version, time-limited) period of interviews, occurring generally in the worker's office, and dealing with the client's problems in living by means of his self-reports in the context of the worker-client relationship. The target of change is the person, and the social is put back into social work as a part of diagnostic thinking but rarely as a focus of direct intervention. In this view, casework is defined as a "thing," a therapeutic service in and of itself that can operate independently from the delivery of any other service. It can even, according to some, be offered in the context of a private practice. It is interesting to note, however, that most caseworkers in private practice change their self-definitions to "psychotherapists," as the headings on their professional stationery will demonstrate. Casework practice, defined as such, may be difficult—if not impossible—to distinguish from other forms of therapy. In fact, the attempt to make or dissolve these distinctions has been a regular definitional exercise practiced by many with varying success in both directions!

There are many variations of psychotherapeutic social work practice, ranging from emphasis on "insight development"—the exploration of genetic material and the alteration of the defensive structure—to a focus that is primarily on executive and adaptive ego-functions in relation to task and role performance. The fundamental objective is growth and change in the individual; the unit of attention or point of intervention is the psychological system; and the interventive measures consist primarily of communications between client and worker and the conscious use of the relationship.

Many caseworkers and casework agencies would conceptualize casework practice in these terms—terms that may or may not be appropriate, depending on the nature of the problem and the objectives of both the client and the agency. The psychotherapeutic model has been criticized, particularly because it is sometimes utilized exclusively or in inappropriate situations. For example, at a children's treatment institution the worker's role may be described as offering to the child one or two weekly therapeutic interviews in the worker's office. The worker does not become involved in the life space of the child because his doing so may "complicate the therapeutic relationship." It is not unheard of for school social workers and even workers in foster care agencies to define practice in a similar way. For example, a caseworker in a foster care agency may define service as "play therapy" with the child and even "treatment" of the foster parents.

It is also important to distinguish between the setting and the method of intervention because an innovative setting does not guarantee an alteration in the style of practice. It is possible to move caseworkers creatively and imaginatively into a single room occupancy hotel, and then, having established a foothold, conceptualize the service offered as psychotherapy. It is clear that Rapoport and Briar are accurate when they say that for many practitioners, casework has become synonymous with psychotherapy.

The person in situation

Moving outward and enlarging the unit of attention and the scope of interventive measures, we come to the newer and more sophisticated versions of Lowry's second form of treatment, which emphasizes the transaction between the person and the situation and approaches the individual by means of the situation. Some would say that this kind of practice is truly casework. Rapoport has written that it is that "blending of psychological understanding and management with social provision, thus giving us a wide and rich range of choice in the instrumentation of the change process," which distinguishes casework from other therapies.[27] The objectives of this mid-

---

[27] Rapoport, Social Casework, p. 226.

dle-range practice are still primarily people changing, but use is made of developmental, educational, or experiential interventions. Life experience is captured and utilized as an instrument of change or as an opportunity for growth.

Crisis intervention is an example of this type of practice. The client, with the help of the worker and the utilization of personal and environmental resources, is enabled to turn a threatening and possibly debilitating life experience into an opportunity to grow, to develop new coping mechanisms, and even to work through old, unresolved losses or conflicts that emerge as a result of the current crisis. Such services are ideally provided at times and in places where populations are likely to be "at risk." Another example of this middle-range change effort is the socialization or social competence model, which has as its objective the development of the client's competence to function in a variety of roles while utilizing the milieu. The milieu must "provide opportunities to improve role performance," and the worker must take the role of a socializing agent who actively "teaches, models, and invites participation."[28]

These and other developmental models of practice rest on a view of the personality as an open system that is in constant and meaningful transaction with environment. Throughout life the personality is available to change at times of crisis, in the exercise of new roles, or in the mastery of new tasks.[29]

Practice is based on the conviction that life experience itself can be the most important and effective instrument of change. Some would say that it is these experiential, developmental models that are truly casework.

Finally we come to that "new-old" activity of caseworkers, that of delivering concrete services. In a transactional view, environmental change and introduction of services will clearly bring about individual and family change, but our concern in this article is with objectives. In considering whether service delivery is really a casework role, it is necessary to determine whether objectives for personal growth or change are an essential part of a definition of casework practice. Hollis, in a recent discussion of the psychosocial model of casework, writes, "The objective of treatment may be to enable change to occur in the individual(s) or in the situation or in both."[30] From this statement it would seem that casework may be practiced with no objectives for client change. Later in the discussion, however, Hollis describes the process of engagement, and her focus changes.

The process of engaging a client in treatment may be simple or quite complicated. It *always* has two primary aspects . . . motivation and resistance. . . . Motivation has to do with how much the client wants to change and how much he is willing to contribute to bringing about change [italics added].[31]

In fact, Hollis's emphasis on motivation and resistance is predicated on objectives of individual growth or change.

In a scholarly appraisal and eloquent affirmation of social casework, Rapoport makes it clear that she defines social casework as "an instrument for individual and family change."[32] She includes advocacy and social

[28]Elizabeth McBroom, Socialization and Social Casework, in *Theories of Social Casework*, ed. Robert W. Roberts and Robert H. Nee (Chicago: University of Chicago Press, 1970), p. 320.

[29]See Louise Bandler, Casework: A Process of Socialization, in *The Drifters*, ed. Eleanor Panenshedt (Boston: Little, Brown, & Co., 1968); and Thomas Gladwin, Social Competence and Clinical Practice, *Psychiatry*, 30:33–37 (February 1967).
The Family Service Association of Nassau County has structured much of its program around a variety of developmental interventions, some of which have been reported in professional journals. See Robert Sunley, New Dimensions in Reaching-out Casework, *Social Work*, 13:64–74 (April 1968); Phyllis Levenstein, Cognitive Growth in Preschoolers Through Verbal Interaction with Mothers, *American Journal of Orthopsychiatry*, 40:426–32

(April 1970); and Salvatore Ambrosino, A Family Agency Reaches Out to a Slum Ghetto, *Social Work*, 11:17–23 (October 1966).

[30]Florence Hollis, The Psychosocial Approach to the Practice of Casework, in Roberts and Nee, *Theories of Social Casework*, p. 37.

[31]Ibid., p. 2.

[32]Rapoport, Social Casework, p. 226.

brokerage as appropriate casework functions or roles but writes, "They are at best a part of the total process. If well and sensitively done, they require the use of judgments as to differential diagnosis and overall treatment planning and thus become part of the total process."[33] She further explicates the essence of casework practice as follows:

Here we have ever-broadening range of modalities to choose from as to dimensions of time, place, frequency, intensity, focus, level of intervention, unit of intervention, use of interpersonal processes exclusively or in conjunction with social provision, and so forth. In all of this, there is the centrality of the helping relationship, a purposeful and consciously directed process involving the use of professional self through which *growth and change in the individual can take place* [italics added].[34]

Defining casework as a problem-solving process, Perlman emphasizes "help" rather than "treatment" and does not describe her objectives in relation to "change." She seems, however, to locate the "problem" with the "person."

The person or family considered to be a prospective user of help via the casework process is one who is experiencing some problem in his relationship with one or more other persons, or in his satisfactory performance of one or more role tasks.[35]

Can one consider the appropriate provision of an individualized service "real" casework when it is simply needed and wanted and there is no implicit or explicit agenda for change or growth in the recipient of service? It would seem that many caseworkers—Hollis, Rapoport, and perhaps Perlman among them—would answer no to this question and would say that objectives in relation to change or growth in the individual or family are an

essential part of a definition of casework practice.

I am not sure we have ever settled this vital issue, although the determination of the objectives of practice in turn determines organizational arrangements and methodology. If objectives for growth or change are an essential part of a definition of casework, then we define and select our clients as those in need of change or growth, and our emphasis is either rehabilitative, therapeutic, or both. Both Reynolds and Lowry included as part of social casework the meeting of social needs and the provision of social services without the objective of what Richmond calls "the development of personality."[36] In our ambivalence about this function or in our concern that we were doing "real casework," we have experienced the need to dignify or professionalize the delivery of service—the meeting of a concrete need—by calling it, and using it, as "a tool in treatment."

Individualized service provision

Some caseworkers would say that casework can be an individualizing method of service provision and can stand alone on this objective. Meyer, in her recently published *Social Work Practice: A Response to the Urban Crisis*, develops such a model from the institutional stance proposed by Reynolds.[37] Her context, however, is the modern urban environment and a systemic view of the person-situation complex.

Although interventions directed at individual growth or change are not ruled out, the existence of individual or personal problems is not the point of entry for the practitioner nor the raison d'être for the practice. The aim of social work practice, in Meyer's view, is to individualize and humanize the urban environment with its complex of service systems to which all citizens must turn in order to meet their social, physical, and economic needs. This individualizing service should not be confined to social agencies that were

---

[33]Ibid.

[34]Ibid., p. 233.

[35]Helen Harris Perlman, Casework: The Problem Solving Model in Social Casework, in Roberts and Nee, *Theories of Social Casework*, p. 134.

[36]Richmond, *What is Social Case Work?*, p. 98.

[37]Carol H. Meyer, *Social Work Practice: A Response to the Urban Crisis* (New York: Free Press, 1970).

established to help people solve their problems. It should exist within all service delivery systems, "at the highways and byways, wherever people go in the natural course of their lives."[38] In this institutional view, "client" becomes "citizen" and "consumer of service." The "problem" is shifted to the dysfunctional aspects of need-meeting systems because there is no assumption that a citizen-client is necessarily in need of growth or change. He is simply in need of and has the right to an appropriately responsive environment. There is an assumption that the urban bureaucratic systems that have been developed to meet needs must be humanized and that their services must be individualized.

A different definition of practice methods and of the worker-client relationship follows when the aims of practice are defined in this way. If needed services are available, practice methods include individualizing and coordinating the services and enabling the client to utilize them. When the services are not available, are being withheld, or are delivered in a dehumanizing way, casework practice, according to some theorists, includes the locating or developing of resources, mediating, negotiating the service systems, advocating for the client, and participating with the client and others to bring about small-scale social change—if that is what is needed. Some people would say that this is real casework, the casework that is truly responsive to the major

---

[38]Ibid., pp. 172–73.

social problems confronting our nation today: poverty, discrimination, and the dehumanization of the individual in a mass society. Certainly the provision of social services is the activity practiced by the largest numbers of caseworkers in this country.

Conclusion

What is social casework? The answer to this question would seem to depend on whom one asks. If casework is to be defined by those who define themselves as caseworkers, objectives including either people changing or situation changing or a combination of both must be considered appropriate. Following from this breadth of objectives comes a broad array of interventive measures that may be included as a part of casework method. Along this wide range of practice—from intensive psychotherapy to picketing—different caseworkers draw different boundaries. Because people who define themselves as caseworkers define the practice so differently and because no one has been elected to determine the definition, I assume that we can all carve out our area and practice it, teach it, and write articles about it as long as the community, clients, universities, and editors will support us.

Because there is such variety and such divergence, let us recognize these differences, examine them, and talk about them. And, when we announce that we are dropping casework or picking it up, diagnosing it as dead or alive, evaluating it as effective or ineffective, let us define it.

A SYSTEMS ORIENTATION

Sister Mary Paul Janchill, R.G.S.

Systems concepts in casework theory and practice

Sister Mary Paul Janchill, R.G.S., is director
of social service, the Euphrasian Residence,
New York, N.Y. At the time this article
was written she was a student in the doctoral
program, Columbia University
School of Social Work, New York, N.Y.

The person-in-situation concept is easily identified as the critical base from which the social work profession has steadily evolved its theory, its art, and its method of practice. In less than half a century since the publication of Mary Richmond's work, a social work literature expanding and developing the concept has come into being. The concept continues as the central dynamic that organizes the tension of the profession to redefine itself in relation to its values, the process by which it gives service, the basis of the skills it seeks to develop in its practitioners, and the relevance of its methods to the attainment of its goals in today's world.

The history of casework can be traced along the path of two converging motifs. The first of these crystallized social work's understanding of broad social forces in the course of the industrialization of the Western World as these affected man. Attempts were made to discriminate the institutional patterns shaped by new production methods, population shifts and migrations, and cultural change, as well as their immediate impact on individuals and families. Retrospective evaluations of these early efforts to distinguish the individual in the environment often take note of a certain motive and need to define the "worthy poor" in the search to comprehend a social problem. Nevertheless, the emphasis was placed on obtaining a factually detailed social history of the client in order to understand the unique situation of the individual, including his feelings and emotional reactions to his environment. Richmond stressed that "broad generalizations about relief, about family life, about desertion, widowhood, immigrants, and the rest" by "wholesalers" were not meaningful either in understanding or treating individual persons.[1] Rather, diagnosis and treatment plan depended fundamentally on locating an array of specific social factors that come to bear on a person's problem. Understanding of "the personality as it now is, together with the ways in which it came to be what it now is," requires a knowledge of the person's life experience.[2]

Richmond's essential formulation that personality growth occurs through "adjustments consciously effected" between the individual and his environment was virtually eclipsed by the revolutionary impact of psychoanalytic theory, which resulted in the development of the second major motif. Though the Great Depression kept alive the need for direct

[1]Mary E. Richmond, Some Next Steps in Social Treatment, in *Proceedings of the National Conference of Social Work* (University of Chicago Press, Chicago, 1920), 254.

[2]Mary E. Richmond, *What Is Social Case Work?* (Russell Sage Foundation, New York, 1922), 103.

SOCIAL CASEWORK, 1969, Vol. 50, No. 2, pp. 74–82.

environmental intervention, it led to a shift in values. There was a growing conviction among caseworkers that the salient features of need were to be understood in the personality of the client: the forces *within his psyche* that served to establish a given relationship between him and his environment.

Gordon Hamilton, in a succinct historical analysis, rendered for today's caseworker the meaning that Freudian theory brought to casework practice, affecting the whole process of study, diagnosis, and treatment and recasting the very definition of task for the caseworker by shifting the focus from *problem* to *person* and from the socioeconomic frame of reference to the psychosocial.[3]

For the purposes of this article it is sufficient to recapture the perspective psychoanalytic theory gave to the understanding of an individual, who was no longer viewed simply as a type in relation to temperament, occupation, ethnicity, and economic status. Rather than being seen as a static aggregate of attributes, personality came to be seen as a dynamic unit of forces standing in relationship to the outside world and at the same time to the self. Freudian theory greatly illuminated the meaning of human behavior by explicating goal-attainment operations on unconscious levels. It explained how contradictory goals that arise in the mind breed conflict and how this conflict is reflected in social relationships. It led to an awareness that emotional energies are manifested in diverse ways and that those that are not volitionally directed may persist and act as chronic stimuli, affecting the individual's social interaction and causing physical alterations. In regard to the developmental pattern of human life psychoanalytic theory showed that sexuality is an aspect of growth from infancy onward and that because it responds delicately to disturbances of personality it often reflects difficulties in the growth process. These insights led to the adoption of a completely new stance by the worker, who began to listen to the client not only to learn facts but also to discover unconscious distor-

tions reflected in various mechanisms of defense.

Limitations of the knowledge base

In the past decade there has been increasing question concerning the use of the psychoanalytic framework in casework. Caseworkers increasingly tend to view Freudian theory as not entirely sufficient for the explanation of the total range of behavior they observe, and the need for an expanded knowledge base is becoming apparent. There is, in particular, a search for conceptualizations of environment, and person-in-environment, to complement the Freudian formulation of intrapsychic processes. For despite an avowed conviction, stated in most expositions of casework, that all casework is psychosocial, that problems are to be understood in terms of both inner and outer factors, and that the caseworker's focus is on the person-in-situation, a persistent pattern of dichotomizing internal and external dimensions manifests itself in the study of psychodynamics and in the delineation of psychotherapeutic methods and goals. There have been notably few attempts to integrate both dimensions in the formulation of diagnostic and treatment classifications. A review of the treatment classifications made by Mary Richmond (1922), Porter Lee (1923), Fern Lowry (1936), Grete Bibring (1947), Lucille Austin (1948), Florence Hollis (1949 and 1964), Gordon Hamilton (1951), and Eleanor Cockerill (1952) have at least one thing in common: Treatment geared to environmental problems is distinguished from treatment geared to psychological problems. As recently as 1964, however, Frances Scherz questioned whether environmental services can be considered treatment and took the position that they cannot.[4] Indeed, the rationale for methods of treatment classification seems to flow from the point of view described by Isabel Stamm:

Treatment has at times been described as though it were a continuum with measures designed to

[3]Gordon Hamilton, A Theory of Personality: Freud's Contribution to Social Work, in Howard J. Parad, ed., *Ego Psychology and Dynamic Casework* (Family Service Association of America, New York, 1958), 15.

[4]Frances H. Scherz, reviewing Florence Hollis' *Casework—A Psychosocial Therapy*, in *Social Service Review*, 38:207 (June 1964).

reduce environmental stress at one end, measures to support and strengthen adaptive functioning somewhere in the middle, and, finally, at the other end a precious therapeutic segment dedicated to the resolution of instinctual conflicts.[5]

Such thinking is based on the assumption that the true goal of therapy is to achieve client insight into the manner in which unconscious conflicts are implicated in affective and cognitive life. In general caseworkers have not explored psychological theories for different interpretations of insight and have tended to keep its definition within the psychoanalytic model. In 1956 Austin pointed out that insight is "developed in different methods of psychotherapy through the use of several techniques,"[6] that there are different kinds of insight, and that insight varies according to the individual who is the client. Social work's lag in developing Austin's leads nevertheless persists. The writings of Carl Duncan and W. Edgar Vinacke, citing other authors, stress the relationship of thinking to the external world as well as to inner processes and requirements. Vinacke, in particular, views insight in a broader context than the analytic, explicating other forms of insight that are basic to problem-solving and that may be highly relevant to treatment task formulation.[7] Duncan suggests that perhaps subjects "could be trained in reorienting as a method of understanding, and that such a skill would transfer to a wide variety of problems."[8] He discusses J. P. van de Geer's phenomenological theory of problem-solving, which asserts that situations differ in "transparency" and that explanation of some factors results in a reduction of the "nontranspar-

ency" of others. Though this approach is not alien to casework, there is little conscious, planned use of methods that would relieve the tendency to separate the inner and the outer in a therapeutic focus.

The consequences of casework's limited theoretical framework and accepted knowledge base are reflected in the current clamor for a redefinition of the task and role of the practitioner. There is growing awareness that the theory upon which social workers rely for practice addresses itself to the individual's mediation of external reality while that reality situation is relatively unspecified and only grossly understood. Social workers have engaged in extended debate about the ensuing limitations of the casework method and the restricted client groups it reaches. They have taken positions that range from a heated defense of practice as it is currently constituted to radical proposals for a restructuring of practice.[9] It is not difficult to identify, in all the arguments, a commitment to the interpretation of the person-in-situation concept.

This . . . is the struggle between the individual and the social, the one and the many, the psychological and the economic, the inner experience and the external event. The developmental view of social work shows what we have seldom been willing to admit, that no great personality in social work has been able to carry both these opposing tendencies in equal development within the self, but that leadership in social work has flourished through individuals who have carried with passionate devotion either one side or the other of this conflict. . . . Casework is clearly that branch of social work which carries forward, protects, and lives out in thought and activity the single strand of devotion to the separate, single human self: the worth of the one. Other branches of social work, such as community organization, program making, social action, all by their nature belong to the opposite tendency which places upon the broad program, the external adjustment, the economic solution, the higher value in interest and feeling.[10]

[5]Isabel L. Stamm, Ego Psychology in the Emerging Theoretical Base of Casework, in Alfred J. Kahn, ed., *Issues in American Social Work* (Columbia University Press, New York, 1959), 84.

[6]Lucille N. Austin, Social Caseworkers, in Qualifications for Psychotherapists, a symposium, *American Journal of Orthopsychiatry*, 26:51 (January 1956).

[7]W. Edgar Vinacke, *The Psychology of Thinking* (McGraw-Hill Book Co., New York, 1952), 160–94.

[8]Carl P. Duncan, Recent Research on Human Problem Solving, *Psychological Bulletin*, 56:424 (November 1959).

[9]See Helen Harris Perlman, Casework Is Dead, SOCIAL CASEWORK, 48:22–25 (January 1967).

[10]Anita J. Faatz, *The Nature of Choice in Casework Process* (University of North Carolina Press, Chapel Hill, North Carolina, 1953), 10.

In developing her thesis, Faatz identifies casework as a process in which the client is helped to achieve internal choice through the sharing that takes place in the worker-client relationship. Her standpoint is in the tradition of the functional school of social work, which includes the Rankian emphasis on the will and choice. Nevertheless, because of the logical consequences of a dichotomy of person and situation, her point of view is shared by many practitioners of the diagnostic school as well.

There are, of course, a great many others in the social work profession who do not concur, and some have contributed to the development of interactional references. Herman Stein, for example, presents a dynamic interpretation of the person-in-situation concept in his clarification of the concept of environment. He begins by identifying the boundaries of the concept that have been proved outdated: "(1) The social environment seen as restricted to what is accessible to immediate perception, and open to direct modification . . . ; (2) the social environment seen as external to the individual [a view which does not· take account of the personality-transforming potentials of social-cultural forces] . . . ; and (3) the social environment perceived as static."[11] Stein examines certain issues of social class stratification, ethnicity, family structure, and role organization in the social agency itself for their dynamic significance and influence on behavior.

Although such relevant issues have now been delineated, the following difficulties remain:

1. The contributions of the social sciences relating to social class, the structures of role and status, the social organization of the family, and the influences of reference groups and ethnicity are found not in any organized body of theory but as many separate contributions from a variety of disciplines. Because of the lack of a coherent theoretical framework incorporating the various contributions, some

social work educators tend to omit them from systematic consideration; others place them side by side, as it were, with the psychoanalytic theory of personality. Omission, of course, exposes the student to error, while "adding" social science theory to a psychoanalytic frame of reference has limited value, and environment thus becomes a secondary consideration.

2. There are aspects of environment that are relatively concrete, static, and still significant, as Stein recognizes, in casework treatment.[12] The profession is left with some of the original problems and value considerations in placing environmental manipulation in perspective.

3. The unorganized selection of unorganized theory makes it difficult to communicate to students and new practitioners the knowledge base for which they are professionally accountable. Specifically, the identification of the referents for the basic concept of person-in-situation are as yet unclear.

General systems theory

It has been proposed that a bridge is needed between psychoanalytic theory and social science theory. Ego psychology and role theory have been most frequently suggested as supplying that bridge, but these appear to fall short of the need. Although both are vital contributions to the knowledge of personality and behavior, they are not in themselves able to incorporate material from the sciences in a sufficiently systematic way. The need, in my view, is not for a theory or a bridge, but for ways of conceptualizing that bring phenomena and events into dynamic relation to each other, taking time span into account and encompassing the steady inflow of life.

General systems theory may effectively meet the profession's current need for conceptual tools that activate an understanding of the relational determinants of behavior in the person-in-situation configuration. Systems theory is not in itself a body of knowledge; it is a way of thinking and of analysis that accommodates knowledge from many sciences. It offers a framework in which social

[11]Herman D. Stein, The Concept of the Social Environment in Social Work Practice, in Howard J. Parad and Robert R. Miller, eds., *Ego-Oriented Casework: Problems and Perspectives* (Family Service Association of America, New York, 1963), 68.

[12]Stein, The Concept . . . , 68.

interaction can be objectively and comprehensively understood without jeopardy to the work of individualization.

Systems, defined by Ludwig von Bertalanffy as "sets of elements standing in interaction,"[13] apparently have some properties and structural uniformities in common. The study of these has become the interest of biologists, physiologists, physicists, engineers, economists, mathematicians, psychologists, sociologists, social psychologists, and a small but growing number of social workers.[14] All have become involved, for example, in the study of homeostasis or equilibrium and the processes and mechanisms contributing to it. Systems theorists work from the assumption that "the essential problems are the organizing relations that result from dynamic interaction and make the behavior of parts different when studied in isolation or within the whole."[15] Their frame of reference also requires that environment is taken into account in identifying and explaining the character and properties of any system. The functional relationships between a given system and its environment (constituted by other systems) become the indicators for an analyst or observer of needs and fulfilling processes.

A first level of analysis in systems theory consists in the specification of open versus closed systems. The latter are self-contained, isolated from their environment in the sense

that they do not depend on that environment for sustainment, and their constituent unit elements are encompassed within a fairly impermeable boundary. By contrast all living organisms are open systems, which are characterized by an active exchange of energy and matter with the environment. The unit elements of such open systems not only have innate capacities for growth and elaboration but are also capable of increasing differentiation, specialization, and effect through environmental exchanges. The qualitative as well as quantitative potentials for individualization and development are implicit in this concept of open system and its dependence on a supporting environment. The analogy of the open system has the virtue of a metaphor that allows choice in the unit of attention (the personality system of an individual, a family, an organization or agency, a total society, or any subsystem of one of these), as well as requiring the relating of that unit to an environment in the form of other systems.

Daniel Katz and Robert Kahn, in an application of systems theory to the behavior of persons in organizations, present a cogent summary of nine characteristics of open systems, derived from many systems theorists, such as James G. Miller, von Bertalanffy, Floyd H. Allport, and Talcott Parsons.[16] The nine common characteristics are presented below with a few selective indications of knowledge areas that are relevant to their use in conceptualizing the person-in-situation configuration.

Importation of energy

The intrinsic characteristic of life is seen as that of dynamic forces. These forces enable the organism to adjust itself to changing conditions. The importation of energy feature of the open system suggests there is need for knowledge of the sources of energy whereby any organism maintains integrity as it confronts internal and external changes. Psychoanalytic theory has been drawn upon in developing understanding of how the instincts serve as sources of psychic energy. Further search is needed in psychology and the other

---

[13]Ludwig von Bertalanffy, General System Theory, in N. J. Demerath III and Richard A. Peterson, eds., *System, Change, and Conflict* (Free Press, New York, 1967), 115–29.

[14]See Gordon Hearn, *Theory Building in Social Work* (University of Toronto Press, Toronto, 1958); Donald E. Lathrope, Use of Social Science in Social Work Practice: Social Systems, in *Trends in Social Work Practice and Knowledge* (National Association of Social Workers, New York, 1966), 212–26; Alan F. Klein, The Application of Social System Theory to Social Work, paper presented at the annual program meeting of the Council on Social Work Education, New York, N.Y., January 25–27, 1966; Carel B. Germain, Social Study: Past and Future, Social Casework, 49: 403–09 (July 1968); and William E. Gordon, Basic Constructs for an Integrative and Generative Conception of Social Work, paper presented at the annual program meeting of the Council on Social Work Education, Minneapolis, Minnesota, January 26, 1968.

[15]von Bertalanffy, General..., 115.

[16]Daniel Katz and Robert L. Kahn, *The Social Psychology of Organizations* (John Wiley & Sons, New York, 1966), 19–26.

sciences to see how cognitive faculties, open to influence by the instincts, may themselves serve as distinct sources of energy. Social encounter, generally, shapes the affective life from which action itself springs, and energic inputs need to be studied in that context. Sociology, social psychology, and cultural anthropology, for example, are of value in understanding how the expectations of others are inputs for an individual in the process of identification, internalization of values, and adaptive and creative activity. Importation of energy suggests an analytic reference for the ways in which the environment serves the individual and is used by him. Specifically in casework, this orientation permits an assessment of an individual's resources in terms of his inner psychic equipment as well as all the outer sources that make contact with the affective life.

Through-put

Through-put is used to denote the process by which the system acts upon the energy imported—the transformation of energy. Once again, psychoanalytic theory sheds much light on the distribution of psychic energy, accounting for it in genetic terms, psychic economy, and topographic and structural dynamisms and laws. On the one hand it illustrates some total systemic effects of object cathexis and, on the other hand, the withdrawal of cathexis. Mechanisms of defense may also be understood in relation to a through-put process. Indeed, insofar as psychoanalytic theory regards the mediation of stimuli and of conflict, it is very valuable here. Additional knowledge is needed, however, for an understanding of internal changes that take place under the influence of role interaction. For example, the mother-child relationship cannot be understood in isolation; the mother must be seen in hyphenated relation to the father, the grandparents, and all her other role partners in all her statuses if one is to achieve an understanding of the characteristics of her relationship with her child.[17] The social sciences demonstrate that the man-

ner in which an individual negotiates his environment is more than, but inclusive of, his inner psychological mechanisms. Talcott Parsons stresses the fact that human motives and values cannot be understood except in terms of the interaction of the personality system, the cultural system, and the social system.[18] Robert Merton, among other sociologists, has also cautioned about the limitations of psychological explanations of behavior that can be better understood in the light of social science. Hypersensitivity in an individual, for example, can be identified as a personality trait stemming from unconscious guilt and the use of projection as a defense. Or, as Robert Merton points out, the same trait may be interpreted sociologically as the product of activated statuses, as when race is constantly made salient for a Negro, either by negative discrimination or the "suffocation of respect," in a variety of cues that tell him he is different.[19] A spate of organizational studies of mental hospitals and treatment centers illustrate the impact of systems on personality. Exacerbation of pathology has been seen in some instances, while in others ego repair and growth are induced.[20] A systems reference is indispensable to the understanding of role interaction and role performance, whether an individual or a family is the center of focus.[21]

Output

The issue of human action in *behavior* of some kind is suggested by this characteristic

[17]Robert K. Merton, *Social Theory and Social Structure*, rev. ed. (Free Press, New York, 1957), 368–84.

[18]Talcott Parsons, *The Social System* (Free Press, Glencoe, Illinois, 1951).

[19]Unpublished lectures, Columbia University, 1966.

[20]Alfred H. Stanton and Morris S. Schwartz, *The Mental Hospital* (Basic Books, New York, 1954); Erving Goffman, *Asylums* (Doubleday & Co., New York, 1961); David Street, Robert D. Vinter, and Charles Perrow, *Organization for Treatment: A Comparative Study of Institutions for Delinquents* (Free Press, New York, 1966); and John Cumming and Elaine Cumming, *Ego and Milieu* (Atherton Press, New York, 1963), are some examples.

[21]Irma Stein, The Application of System Theory to Social Work Practice and Education, paper presented at the annual program meeting of the Council on Social Work Education, New York, N.Y., January 25–27, 1966.

61

of systems, and an immense literature has developed on the language of behavior in psychological and interpersonal terms. Functional analysis, as a sociological method, shows that behavior can also be understood by its consequences for another system. Social work has yet to exploit these insights in attempting to understand psychodynamics and symptomatology. Depression, for example, may be interpreted in psychoanalytic terms: object loss, the incorporation of the object so that there is no longer any difference between the self and the object, and punishment of the incorporated object that was originally the subject of ambivalent feelings. Another way of interpreting depression is by means of its latent functional consequences: the control it gives the patient in environmental systems, such as the family and employment. Systems analysis, then, may be a reference for a larger view of symptomatology. The notion of an output that activates another input also enriches understanding of role complementarity and role induction. Communications theory and learning theory would undoubtedly have greater applicability when used with a systems reference.

Systems as cycles of events

This concept involves the notion that "the product exported into the environment furnishes the sources of energy for the repetition of the cycle of activities. The energy reinforcing the cycle of activities can derive from some exchange of the product in the external world or from the activity itself."[22] This concept leads to examining an output as it becomes involved in interpersonal exchanges to identify how it is reinforced and becomes reinvested with energy. The phenomenon of the double-bind exemplifies this characteristic as a pathogenic kind of communication sustaining a cycle of interaction. Such phenomena are identifiable only within a systems reference, since effects for another environment are revealing of the dynamisms involved. This point of reference promises a rich yield in the study of worker-client expectations, definitions that come to be given to the motivated client, issues involved in

intergroup and racial conflict, and latent consequences of designated social work programs and policies.[23]

Negative entropy

The concept of negative entropy puts a minus sign to the characteristic of closed systems that causes them to move inexorably to decomposition or disintegration, since their impenetrability precludes any new input from the environment. An open system, by contrast, can achieve negative entropy by importing more energy from its environment than it spends. This is a natural area of concern in casework. The health of the individual is seen to be essentially dependent on his openness to new sources of energy in the environment—including its being an outlet for the spending activity of the individual or other unit in focus. Robert White stresses the inherent drive of the organism to have effect,[24] which clearly requires a mutual presence of the individual and an environing system in which the spending of energy is reciprocated, reinforced, and rewarded. The concept of negative entropy has enormous value for guiding the therapeutic task in social work. It is in this perspective —and based on a larger knowledge of social interaction—that supportive treatment needs to be redefined. The notion of support is currently linked with specific techniques within the casework relationship, as opposed to broader attention to environmental inputs that are system-supporting and life-enriching.

Information input, negative feedback, and the coding process

Not only energy but also information and regulating signals from the environment constitute adaptive inputs for a system. Allowing a client to express negative feelings, locate his complaints or conflicts, and sift his experiences has traditionally been part of casework. A complementary approach might consist in

[22]Katz and Kahn, *The Social Psychology . . . .*, 20.

[23]See Winifred Bell, *Aid to Dependent Children* (Columbia University Press, New York, 1965), which illustrates how the ADC program unwittingly put a premium on fatherless families.

[24]Robert W. White, Motivation Reconsidered: The Concept of Competence, *Psychological Review*, 66:297–333 (September 1959).

identifying and releasing feedback mechanisms from other systems so that they reach the individual or group in focus and become operative. Knowledge of the dynamics of social stratification, role organizations, and the structure of authority is of value.

Steady state and dynamic homeostasis

The concept of homeostasis or dynamic equilibrium is central to any theory of systems. A tremendous intellectual effort has been exerted in all the sciences in elucidating the concept. Psychoanalytic theory uses homeostasis as a powerful referent in the explication of integrative, restorative, and compensatory functions within the human psyche. Recently physiologists and biologists have joined psychiatrists in studying the biopsychosocial contributions to equilibrium in the phenomenon of dreams. Charles Fisher and William Dement report studies that seem to validate Freud's theory that dreams are a kind of safety valve for the partial discharge of instinctual energy and that they serve a conservative, economic function in preserving sleep. Experimental studies show that when dreaming (rather than sleep itself) is prevented or frustrated, the individual builds up a deficit that he tends to compensate by dreaming longer in subsequent periods of sleep. When the deficit is not made up, emotional impairment is likely to result.[25] There is a growing literature on homeostatic mechanisms in family interactions, but such analysis needs to be expanded through understanding of intersystem transactions and the place of conflict in a moving equilibrium. Systems theory is valuable in the general area of accommodation to new inputs of several kinds and the process of reorganization toward a steady state that is never the same as the beginning point in the action cycle. This is an important perspective in crisis intervention.

Differentiation

Systems theory calls attention to the tendency of self-elaboration within an organism, as contrasted with the differentiation and specialization that results from the development of external relations. In the physical sciences there has been much interest in studying the relationship of the molecular environment of the brain to actual cognitive processes. Social workers stand to enrich diagnostic and treatment approaches greatly by drawing on a wider knowledge base in the social and behavioral sciences to learn how environmental systems shape patterns of growth and differentiation.

Equifinality

The principle of equifinality indicates that a certain final state can be reached from differing initial conditions and by a variety of paths. It finds its validation in modern ego psychology—and in various sciences—and it is so harmonious with values in social work that it hardly needs elaboration. It is proposed as a subject for renewed cathectic interest by caseworkers that should lead to creative experimentation in methods by which human growth and happiness may be influenced and achieved.

Conclusion

The above comments on the nine characteristics of systems are brief and suggestive, but they may serve in the selection of a framework that accommodates knowledge from many sciences. General systems theory may be seen to have the following potential values for social work:

1. Whereas the present disease model implicit in the study-diagnosis-treatment formulation requires a normative appraisal and reference to pathology, general systems theory may make possible a more value-free exploration of the relational determinants of behavior through its focus on a synchronic analysis of interacting systems. It seeks first to locate the forces that are reaching the person, emotionally and socially, without supposing pathology at the outset.

2. Replacing a linear approach to causation, general systems theory emphasizes an understanding of cause by the observation and interpretation of functional consequences, both manifest and latent. It directs the prac-

---

[25]Charles Fisher and William C. Dement, Studies on the Psychopathology of Sleep and Dreams, *American Journal of Psychiatry*, 119:1160–68 (June 1963).

titioner to see that the reason for behavior may emerge by tracing the function of such action for *another system,* rather than its expression in the person or system of origin.

3. General systems theory could push the development and systematization of knowledge by relating processes to outcomes, thereby enhancing predictive ability for designated interventions in a system relevant to the person-in-situation configuration.

4. General systems theory presents the challenge of identification and selection of appropriate points for intervention but leaves open the question of strategy and technique. It may therefore permit greater creativity in task and method development. It may help to correct social work's current tendency to dwell on process and technique in such a way as to identify them with goals they are meant to serve.

5. General systems theory may assist in the appraisal of those elements in the person-in-situation configuration that are enduring or rigid, or that are fluid or accessible in a reor-ganization of equilibrium. Such appraisal may be particularly helpful in the study of crisis states.

6. Systems theory could provide a richer understanding of symptomatology by seeing symptom in terms of function for and across systems.

7. General systems theory could be very valuable in substituting an enriched metapsychology for the current leanings toward psychic determinism and a closed energy system and thereby widen the scope of clinical social work practice. It allows for consideration of multiple energic sources for the adult as well as for the child, and this has many implications for the programing of services and social policy determination.

Systems theory has had much to offer many scientific disciplines. It may well serve social work in the resolution of the perennial conflict of the many and the one, with the result that the person-in-situation concept can be grounded in meaning and effective practice.

ASSESSMENT: THEORY AND PRACTICE

A THEORY OF GROUP DEVELOPMENT [1]

Warren G. Bennis and Herbert A. Shepard

I F attention is focused on the organic properties of groups, criteria can be established by which phenomena of development, learning, or movement toward maturity can be identified. From this point of view, maturity for the group means something analogous to maturity for the person: a mature group knows very well what it is doing. The group can resolve its internal con-

[1] This theory is based for the most part on observations made over a 5-year period of teaching graduate students "group dynamics". The main function of the seminar as it was set forth by the instructors was to improve the internal communication system of the group, hence, a self-study group.

flicts, mobilize its resources, and take intelligent action only if it has means for consensually validating its experience. The person can resolve his internal conflicts, mobilize his resources, and take intelligent action only if anxiety does not interfere with his ability to profit from his experience, to analyse, discriminate, and foresee. Anxiety prevents the person's internal communication system from functioning appropriately, and improvements in his ability to profit from experience hinge upon overcoming anxiety as a source of distortion. Similarly, group development involves the overcoming of ob-

From *Warren G. Bennis and Herbert A. Shepard,* "A Theory of Group Development," Human Relations, *Vol. 9, No. 4, 1956, pp. 415–457. Some footnotes omitted. Abridged and used by permission.*

Warren G. Bennis, Kenneth D. Benne, and Robert Chin (eds.), THE PLANNING OF CHANGE, 1961, Holt, Rinehart and Winston, Inc., pp. 321–340.

stacles to valid communication among the members, or the development of methods for achieving and testing consensus. Extrapolating from Sullivan's definition of personal maturity we can say a group has reached a state of valid communication when its members are armed with

". . . referential tools for analyzing interpersonal experience, so that its significant differences from, as well as its resemblances to, past experience, are discriminable, and the foresight of relatively near future events will be adequate and appropriate to maintaining one's security and securing one's satisfactions without useless or ultimately troublesome disturbance of self-esteem" (19, p. 111).

Relatively few investigations of the phenomena of group development have been undertaken. This paper outlines a theory of development in groups that have as their explicit goal improvement of their internal communication systems.

A group of strangers, meeting for the first time, has within it many obstacles to valid communication. The more heterogeneous the membership, the more accurately does the group become, for each member, a microcosm of the rest of his interpersonal experience. The problems of understanding, the relationships, that develop in any given group are from one aspect a unique product of the particular constellation of personalities assembled. But to construct a broadly useful theory of group development, it is necessary to identify major areas of internal uncertainty, or obstacles to valid communication, which are common to and important in all groups meeting under a given set of environmental conditions. These areas must be strategic in the sense that until the group has developed methods for reducing uncer-

tainty in them, it cannot reduce uncertainty in other areas, and in its external relations.

The Two Major Areas of Internal Uncertainty: Dependence (Authority Relations) and Interdependence (Personal Relations)

Two major areas of uncertainty can be identified by induction from common experience, at least within our own culture. The first of these is the area of group members' orientations toward authority, or more generally toward the handling and distribution of power in the group. The second is the area of members' orientations toward one another. These areas are not independent of each other: a particular set of inter-member orientations will be associated with a particular authority structure. But the two sets of orientations are as distinct from each other as are the concepts of power and love. A number of authorities have used them as a starting-point for the analysis of group behavior.

In his *Group Psychology and the Analysis of the Ego*, Freud noted that "each member is bound by libidinal ties on the one hand to the leader . . . and on the other hand to the other members of the group" (6, p. 45). Although he described both ties as libidinal, he was uncertain "how these two ties are related to each other, whether they are of the same kind and the same value, and how they are to be described psychologically." Without resolving this question, he noted that (for the Church and the Army) "one of these, the tie with the leader, seems . . . to be more of a ruling factor than the other, which holds between members of the group" (6, p. 52).

More recently, Schutz (17) has made

these two dimensions central to his theory of group compatibility. For him, the strategic determinant of compatibility is the particular blend of orientations toward authority and orientations toward personal intimacy. Bion (1, 2) conceptualizes the major dimensions of the group somewhat differently. His "dependency" and "pairing" modalities correspond to our "dependence" and "interdependence" areas; to them he adds a "fight-flight" modality. For him these modalities are simply alternative modes of behavior; for us, the fight-flight categorization has been useful for characterizing the means used by the group for maintaining a stereotyped orientation during a given subphase.

The core of the theory of group development is that the principal obstacles to the development of valid communication are to be found in the orientations toward authority and intimacy that members bring to the group. Rebelliousness, submissiveness, or withdrawal as the characteristic response to authority figures; destructive competitiveness, emotional exploitiveness, or withdrawal as the characteristic response to peers prevent consensual validation of experience. The behaviors determined by these orientations are directed toward enslavement of the other in the service of the self, enslavement of the self in the service of the other, or disintegration of the situation. Hence, they prevent the setting, clarification of, and movement toward group-shared goals.

In accord with Freud's observation, the orientations toward authority are regarded as being prior to, or partially determining of, orientations toward other members. In its development, the group moves from preoccupation with authority relations to preoccupation

with personal relations. This movement defines the two major phases of group development. Within each phase are three subphases, determined by the ambivalence of orientations in each area. That is, during the authority ("dependence") phase, the group moves from preoccupation with submission to preoccupation with rebellion, to resolution of the dependence problem. Within the personal (or "interdependence") phase the group moves from a preoccupation with intermember identification to a preoccupation with individual identity to a resolution of the interdependence problem.

The Relevant Aspects of Personality in Group Development

The aspects of member personality most heavily involved in group development are called, following Schutz, the dependence and personal aspects.

The dependence aspect is comprised by the member's characteristic patterns related to a leader or to a structure of rules. Members who find comfort in rules of procedure, an agenda, an expert, etc. are called "dependent." Members who are discomfited by authoritative structures are called "counterdependent."

The personal aspect is comprised by the member's characteristic patterns with respect to interpersonal intimacy. Members who cannot rest until they have stabilized a relatively high degree of intimacy with all the others are called "overpersonal." Members who tend to avoid intimacy with any of the others are called "counterpersonal."

Psychodynamically, members who evidence some compulsiveness in the adoption of highly dependent, highly counterdependent, highly personal, or highly counterpersonal roles are regarded as "conflicted." Thus, the person who persists in being dependent upon any and all authorities thereby provides himself with ample evidence that authorities should not be so trustingly relied upon; yet he cannot profit from this experience in governing his future action. Hence, a deep, but unrecognized, distrust is likely to accompany the manifestly submissive behavior, and the highly dependent or highly counterdependent person is thus a person in conflict. The existence of the conflict accounts for the sometimes dramatic movement from extreme dependence to extreme rebelliousness. In this way counterdependence and dependence, while logically the extremes of a scale, are psychologically very close together.

The "unconflicted" person or "independent," who is better able to profit from his experience and assess the present situation more adequately, may of course act at times in rebellious or submissive ways. Psychodynamically, the difference between him and the conflicted is easy to understand. In terms of observable behavior, he lacks the compulsiveness and, significantly, does not create the communicative confusion so characteristic of, say, the conflicted dependent, who manifests submission in that part of his communication of which he is aware, and distrust or rebellion in that part of his communication of which he is unaware.

Persons who are unconflicted with respect to the dependence or personal aspect are considered to be responsible for the major movements of the group toward valid communication. That is, the actions of members unconflicted with respect to the problems of a given phase of group development move the group to the next phase. Such actions are called barometric events, and the initiators are called catalysts. This part of the theory of group development is based on Redl's thesis concerning the "infectiousness of the unconflicted on the conflicted personality constellation." The catalysts (Redl calls them "central persons") are the persons capable of reducing the uncertainty characterizing a given phase. "Leadership" from the standpoint of group development can be defined in terms of catalysts responsible for group movement from one phase to the next. This consideration provides a basis for determining what membership roles are needed for group development. For example, it is expected that a group will have great difficulty in resolving problems of power and authority if it lacks members who are unconflicted with respect to dependence.

Phase Movements

The foregoing summary has introduced the major propositions in the theory of group development. While it is not possible to reproduce the concrete group experience from which the theory is drawn, we can take a step in this direction by discussing in more detail what seem to us to be the dominant features of each phase. The description given below is highly interpretive, and we emphasize what seem to us to be the major themes of each phase, even though many minor themes are present. In the process of abstracting, stereotyping, and interpreting, certain obvious facts about group process are lost. For example, each group meeting is to some extent a recapitulation of its past and a forecast of its future. This means that behavior that is "regressive" or "advanced" often appears.

PHASE I: DEPENDENCE

Subphase 1: Dependence-flight. The first days of group life are filled with behavior whose remote, as well as immediate, aim is to ward off anxiety. Much of the discussion content consists of fruitless searching for a common goal. Some of the security-seeking behavior is group-shared—for example, members may reassure one another by providing interesting and harmless facts about themselves. Some is idiosyncratic—for example, doodling, yawning, intellectualizing.

The search for a common goal is aimed at reducing the cause of anxiety, thus going beyond the satisfaction of immediate security needs. But just as evidencing boredom in this situation is a method of warding off anxiety by denying its proximity, so group goal-seeking is not quite what it is claimed to be. It can best be understood as a dependence plea. The trainer, not the lack of a goal, is the cause of insecurity. This interpretation is likely to be vigorously contested by the group, but it is probably valid. The characteristic expectations of group members are that the trainer will establish rules of the game and distribute rewards. He is presumed to know what the goals are or ought to be. Hence his behavior is regarded as a "technique"; he is merely playing hard to get. The pretense of a fruitless search for goals is a plea for him to tell the group what to do, by simultaneously demonstrating its helplessness without him, and its willingness to work under his direction for his approval and protection.

We are here talking about the dominant theme in group life. Many minor themes are present, and even in connection with the major theme there are differences among members. For some, testing the power of the trainer to affect their futures is the major concern. In others, anxiety may be aroused through a sense of helplessness in a situation made threatening by the protector's desertion. These alternatives can be seen as the beginnings of the counterdependent and dependent adaptations. Those with a dependent orientation look vainly for cues from the trainer for procedure and direction, sometimes paradoxically they infer that the leader must want it that way. Those with a counterdependent orientation strive to detect in the trainer's action elements that would offer ground for rebellion, and may even paradoxically demand rules and leadership from him because he is failing to provide them.

The ambiguity of the situation at this stage quickly becomes intolerable for some, and a variety of ultimately unserviceable resolutions may be invented, many of them idiosyncratic. Alarm at the prospect of future meetings is likely to be group-shared, and at least a gesture may be made in the direction of formulating an agenda for subsequent meetings.

This phase is characterized by behavior that has gained approval from authorities in the past. Since the meetings are to be concerned with groups or with human relations, members offer information on these topics, to satisfy the presumed expectations of the trainer and to indicate expertise, interest, or achievement in these topics (ex-officers from the armed services, from fraternities, etc. have the floor). Topics such as business or political leadership, discrimination and desegregation, are likely to be discussed. During this phase the contributions made by members are designed to gain approval from the trainer, whose reaction to each comment is surreptitiously watched. If the trainer comments that this seems to be the case, or if he notes that the subject under discussion (say, discrimination) may be related to some concerns about membership in this group, he fails again to satisfy the needs of members. Not that the validity of this interpretation is held in much doubt. No one is misled by the "flight" behavior involved in discussing problems external to the group, least of all the group members. Discussion of these matters is filled with perilous uncertainties, however, and so the trainer's observation is politely ignored, as one would ignore a *faux-pas* at a tea-party. The attempts to gain approval based on implicit hypotheses about the potential power of the trainer for good and evil are continued until the active members have run through the repertoire of behaviors that have gained them favor in the past.

Subphase 2: Counterdependence-flight. As the trainer continues to fail miserably in satisfying the needs of the group, discussion takes on a different tone, and counterdependent expressions begin to replace overt dependency phase. In many ways this subphase is the most stressful and unpleasant in the life of the group. It is marked by a paradoxical development of the trainer's role into one of omnipotence and powerlessness, and by division of the group into two warring subgroups. In subphase 1, feelings of hostility were strongly defended; if a slip were made that suggested hostility, particularly toward the trainer, the group members were embarrassed. Now expressions of hostility are more frequent, and are more likely to be supported by other members, or to be met

with equally hostile responses. Power is much more overtly the concern of group members in this subphase. A topic such as leadership may again be discussed, but the undertones of the discussion are no longer dependence pleas. Discussion of leadership in subphase 2 is in part a vehicle for making explicit the trainer's failure as a leader. In part it is perceived by other members as a bid for leadership on the part of any member who participates in it.

The major themes of this subphase are as follows:

1. Two opposed subgroups emerge, together incorporating most of the group members. Characteristically, the subgroups are in disagreement about the group's need for leadership or "structure." One subgroup attempts to elect a chairman, nominate working committees, establish agenda, or otherwise "structure" the meetings; the other subgroup opposes all such efforts. At first this appears to be merely an intellectual disagreement concerning the future organization of group activity. But soon it becomes the basis for destroying any semblance of group unity. Fragmentation is expressed and brought about in many ways: voting is a favorite way of dramatizing the schism; suggestions that the group is too large and should be divided into subgroups for the meetings are frequent; a chairman may be elected and then ignored as a demonstration of the group's ineffectualness. Although control mechanisms are sorely needed and desired, no one is willing to relinquish the rights of leadership and control to anyone else. The trainer's abdication has created a power gap, but no one is allowed to fill it.

2. Disenthrallment with the trainer proceeds rapidly. Group members see him as at best ineffectual, at worst

damaging, to group progress. He is ignored and bullied almost simultaneously. His interventions are perceived by the counterdependents as an attempt to interrupt group progress; by the dependents, as weak and incorrect statements. His silences are regarded by the dependents as desertion; by the counterdependents as manipulation. Much of the group activity is to be understood as punishment of the trainer, for his failure to meet needs and expectations, for getting the group into an unpleasant situation, for being the worst kind of authority figure—a weak and incompetent one, or a manipulative, insincere one. Misunderstanding or ignoring his comments, implying that his observations are paranoid fantasies, demonstrations that the group is cracking up, references to him in the past tense as though he were no longer present—these are the punishments for his failure.

As, in the first subphase, the trainer's wisdom, power, and competence were overtly unquestioned, but secretly suspected; so, in the second subphase, the conviction that he is incompetent and helpless is clearly dramatized, but secretly doubted. Out of this secret doubt arises the belief in the trainer's omnipotence. None of the punishments meted out to the trainer are recognized as such by the group members; in fact, if the trainer suggests that the members feel a need to punish him, they are most likely to respond in injured tones or in tones of contempt that what is going on has nothing to do with him and that he had best stay out of it. The trainer is still too imposing and threatening to challenge directly. There is a secret hope that the chaos in the group is in fact part of the master plan, that he is really leading them in the direction they should be going. That he may really be helpless as they imply, or that the failure may be theirs rather than his, are frightening possibilities. For this reason subphase 2 differs very little in its fundamental dynamics from subphase 1. There is still the secret wish that the trainer will stop all the bedlam which has replaced polite uncertainty, by taking his proper role (so that dependent members can cooperate with him and counterdependent can rebel in the usual ways).

Subphase 2 thus brings the group to the brink of catastrophe. The trainer has consistently failed to meet the group's needs. Not daring to turn directly on him, the group members engage in mutually destructive behavior: in fact, the group threatens suicide as the most extreme expression of dependence. The need to punish the trainer is so strong, however, that his act of salvation would have to be magical indeed.

Subphase 3: Resolution-catharsis. No such magic is available to the trainer. Resolution of the group's difficulties at this point depends upon the presence in the group of other forces, which have until this time been inoperative, or ineffective. Only the degenerative aspects of the chain of events in subphases 1 and 2 have been presented up to this point and they are in fact the salient ones. But there has been a simultaneous, though less obvious, mobilization of constructive forces. First, within each of the warring subgroups bonds of mutual support have grown. The group member no longer feels helpless and isolated. Second, the trainer's role, seen as weak or manipulative in the dependence orientation, can also be perceived as permissive. Third, his interpretations, though openly ignored, have been secretly attended to. And, as the second and third points imply, some members of the group are less the prisoners of the dependence-counterdependence dilemma than others. These members, called the independents, have been relatively ineffective in the group for two reasons. First, they have not developed firm bonds with other members in either of the warring subgroups, because they have not identified with either cause. Typically, they have devoted their energies to an unsuccessful search for a compromise settlement of the disagreements in the group. Since their attitudes toward authority are less ambivalent than those of other members, they have accepted the alleged reason for disagreement in the group—for example, whether a chairman should be elected—at face value, and tried to mediate. Similarly, they have tended to accept the trainer's role and interpretations more nearly at face value. However, his interpretations have seemed inaccurate to them, since in fact the interpretations have applied much less to them than to the rest of the group.

Subphase 3 is the most crucial and fragile in group life up to this point. What occurs is a sudden shift in the whole basis of group action. It is truly a bridging phase; if it occurs at all, it is so rapid and mercurial that the end of subphase 2 appears to give way directly to the first subphase of Phase II. If it does not occur thus rapidly and dramatically, a halting and arduous process of vacillation between Phases I and II is likely to persist for a long period, the total group movement being very gradual.

To summarize the state of affairs at the beginning of subphase 3: 1. The group is polarized into two competing groups, each unable to gain or relinquish power. 2. Those group members who are uncommitted to either subgroup are ineffective in their attempts to resolve the conflict. 3. The trainer's contributions only serve to deepen the cleavage in the group.

As the group enters subphase 3, it is moving rapidly toward extinction: that is, splintering into two or three subgroups. The independents, who have until now been passive or ineffectual, become the only hope for survival, since they have thus far avoided polarization and stereotypic behavior. The imminence of dissolution forces them to recognize the fruitlessness of their attempts at mediation. For this reason, the trainer's hypothesis that fighting one another is off-target behavior is likely to be acted upon at this point. A group member may openly express the opinion that the trainer's presence and comments are holding the group back, suggest that "as an experiment" the trainer leaves the group "to see how things go without him". When the trainer is thus directly challenged, the whole atmosphere of the meeting changes. There is a sudden increase in alertness and tension. Previously, there had been much acting out of the wish that the trainer were absent, but at the same time a conviction that he was the *raison d'être* of the group's existence —that it would fall apart without him. Previously, absence of the trainer would have constituted desertion, or defeat, fulfilment of the members' worst fears as to their own inadequacy or the trainer's. But now leaving the group can have a different meaning. General agreement that the trainer should leave is rarely achieved. However, after a little further discussion it becomes clear that he is at liberty to leave, with the understanding that he wishes to be a member of the group, and will return if and when the group is willing to accept him.

The principal function of the symbolic removal of the trainer is in its effect of freeing the group to bring into awareness the hitherto carefully ignored feelings toward him as an authority figure, and toward the group activity as an off-target dramatization of the ambivalence toward authority. The leadership provided by the independents (whom the group sees as having no vested interest in power) leads to a new orientation toward membership in the group. In the discussion that follows the exit of the trainer, the dependents' assertion that the trainer deserted and the counterdependents' assertion that he was kicked out are soon replaced by consideration of whether his behavior was "responsible" or "irresponsible." The power problem is resolved by being defined in terms of member responsibilities, and the terms of the trainer's return to the group are settled by the requirement that he behave as "just another member of the group". This phrase is then explained as meaning that he should take neither more nor less responsibility for what happens in the group than any other member.

The above description of the process does not do justice to the excitement and involvement characteristic of this period. How much transferable insight ambivalent members acquire from it is difficult to assess. At least within the life of the group, later activity is rarely perceived in terms of submission and rebellion.

An interesting parallel, which throws light on the order of events in group development, is given in Freud's discussion of the myth of the primal horde. In his version:

"These many individuals eventually banded themselves together, killed [the father], and cut him in pieces. . . . They then formed the totemistic community of brothers all with equal rights and united by the totem prohibitions which were to preserve and to expiate the memory of the murder" (6, p. 112).

The horde's act, according to Freud, was soon distorted into an heroic myth: instead of murder by the group, the myth held that the father had been overthrown single-handed by one person, usually the youngest son. In this attribution of the group act to one individual (the hero) Freud saw the "emergence of the individual from group psychology." His definition of a hero is ". . . a man who stands up manfully against his father and in the end victoriously overthrows him" (8, p. 9). (The heroic myth of Freud thus shares much in common with Sullivan's "delusion of unique individuality.")

In the training group, the member who initiates the events leading to the trainer's exit is sometimes referred to as a "hero" by the other members. Responsibility for the act is felt to be shared by the group, however, and out of their experience comes the first strong sense of group solidarity and involvement—a reversal of the original version, where the individual emerges from the group. This turn of events clarifies Freud's remark concerning the libidinal ties to the leader and to the other group members. Libidinal ties toward the other group members cannot be adequately developed until there is a resolution of the ties with the leader. In our terms, those components of group life having to do with intimacy and interdependence

74

cannot be dealt with until those components having to do with authority and dependence have been resolved.

Other aspects of subphase 3 may be understood by investigating the dramatic significance of the revolt. The event is always marked in group history as "a turning-point", "the time we became a group", "when I first got involved", etc. The mounting tension, followed by sometimes uproarious euphoria, cannot be entirely explained by the surface events. It may be that the revolt represents a realization of important fantasies individuals hold in all organizations, that the emotions involved are undercurrents wherever rebellious and submissive tendencies toward existing authorities must be controlled. These are the themes of some of our great dramas—*Antigone, Billy Budd, Hamlet,* and our most recent folk-tale, *The Caine Mutiny.* But the event is more than the presentation of a drama, or an acting-out of fantasies. For it can be argued that the moments of stress and catharsis, when emotions are labile and intense, are the times in the group life when there is readiness for change. Leighton's analysis of a minor revolution at a Japanese relocation camp is worth quoting in full on this point:

"While this [cathartic] situation is fraught with danger because of trends which may make the stress become worse before it gets better, there is also an opportunity for administrative action that is not likely to be found in more secure times. It is fairly well recognized in psychology that at periods of great emotional stir the individual human being can undergo far-reaching and permanent changes in his personality. It is as if the bone structure of his systems of belief and of his habitual patterns of behavior becomes soft, is fused into new shapes and hardens there when the period of tension is over. . . . Possibly the same can be true of whole groups of people, and there are historical examples of social changes and movements occurring when there was widespread emotional tension, usually some form of anxiety. The Crusades, parts of the Reformation, the French Revolution, the change in Zulu life in the reign of Chaca, the Meiji Restoration, the Mormon movement, the Russian Revolution, the rise of Fascism, and alterations in the social sentiments of the United States going on at present are all to some extent examples" (12, p. 360).

Observers of industrial relations have made similar observations. When strikes result from hostile labor-management relations (as contrasted to straight wage demands), there is a fluidity of relationships and a wide repertoire of structural changes during this period not available before the strike act.[2]

So it is, we believe, with the training group. But what are the new values and behavior patterns that emerge out of the emotional experience of Phase I? Principally, they are acceptance by each member of his full share of responsibility for what happens in the group. The outcome is autonomy for the group. After the events of subphase 3, there is no more attribution of magical powers to the trainer—either the dependent fantasy that he sees farther, knows better, is mysteriously guiding the group and protecting it from evil, or the very similar counterdependent fantasy that he is manipulating the group, exploiting it in his own interests, that the experience is one of "brain-washing." The criterion for evaluating a contribution is no longer who said it, but what is said. Thereafter, such power fantasies as the

[2] See A. Gouldner (10), W. F. Whyte, Jr. (22). Robert E. Park, writing in 1928, had considerable insight on some functions of revolution and change. See (14).

trainer himself may have present no different problem from the power fantasies of any other group member. At the same time, the illusion that there is a struggle for power in the group is suddenly dissipated, and the contributions of other members are evaluated in terms of their relevance to shared group goals.

SUMMARY OF PHASE I

The very word development implies not only movement through time, but also a definite order of progression. The group must traverse subphase 1 to reach subphase 2, and subphase 3 before it can move into Phase II. At the same time, lower levels of development coexist with more advanced levels. Blocking and regression occur frequently, and the group may be "stuck" at a certain phase of development. It would, of course, be difficult to imagine a group remaining long in subphase 3—the situation is too tense to be permanent. But the group may founder for some time in subphase 2 with little movement. In short, groups do not inevitably develop through the resolution of the dependence phase to Phase II. This movement may be retarded indefinitely. Obviously much depends upon the trainer's role. In fact, the whole dependence modality may be submerged by certain styles of trainer behavior. The trainer has a certain range of choice as to whether dependency as a source of communication distortion is to be highlighted and made the subject of special experiential and conceptual consideration. The personality and training philosophy of the trainer determine his interest in introducing or avoiding explicit consideration of dependency.

There are other important forces in the group besides the trainer, and these may serve to facilitate or block the development that has been described as typical of Phase I. Occasionally there may be no strong independents capable of bringing about the barometric events that precipitate movement. Or the leaders of opposing subgroups may be the most assertive members of the group. In such cases the group may founder permanently in subphase 2. If a group has the misfortune to experience a "traumatic" event early in its existence—exceedingly schizoid behavior by some member during the first few meetings, for example—anxieties of other members may be aroused to such an extent that all culturally suspect behavior, particularly open expression of feelings, is strongly inhibited in subsequent meetings.

Table I summarizes the major events of Phase I, as it typically proceeds. This phase has dealt primarily with the resolution of dependence needs. It ends with acceptance of mutual responsibility for the fate of the group and a sense of solidarity, but the implications of shared responsibility have yet to be explored. This exploration is reserved for Phase II, which we have chosen to call the Interdependence Phase.

PHASE II: INTERDEPENDENCE

The resolution of dependence problems marks the transfer of group attention (and inattention) to the problems of shared responsibility.

Sullivan's description of the change from childhood to the juvenile era seems pertinent here:

"The juvenile era is marked off from childhood by the appearance of an urgent need for compeers with whom to have one's existence. By 'compeers' I mean peo-

TABLE I   PHASE I.   DEPENDENCE—POWER RELATIONS *

	SUBPHASE 1 DEPENDENCE-SUBMISSION	SUBPHASE 2 COUNTERDEPENDENCE	SUBPHASE 3 RESOLUTION
1. Emotional Modality	Dependence—Flight	Counterdependence—Fight. Off-target fighting among members. Distrust of staff member. Ambivalence.	Pairing. Intense involvement in group task.
2. Content Themes	Discussion of interpersonal problems external to training groups.	Discussion of group organization; i.e. what degree of structuring devices is needed for "effective" group behavior?	Discussion and definition of trainer role.
3. Dominant Roles (Central Persons)	Assertive, aggressive members with rich previous organizational or social science experience.	Most assertive counterdependent and dependent members. Withdrawal of *less* assertive independents and dependents.	Assertive independents.
4. Group Structure	Organized mainly into multisubgroups based on members' past experiences.	Two tight subcliques consisting of leaders and members, of counterdependents and dependents.	Group unifies in pursuit of goal and develops internal authority system.
5. Group Activity	Self-oriented behavior reminiscent of most new social gatherings.	Search for consensus mechanism: Voting, setting up chairmen, search for "valid" content subjects.	Group members take over leadership roles formerly perceived as held by trainer.
6. Group movement facilitated by:	Staff member abnegation of traditional role of structuring situation, setting up rules of fair play, regulation of participation.	Disenthrallment with staff member coupled with absorption of uncertainty by most assertive counterdependent and dependent individuals. Subgroups form to ward off anxiety.	Revolt by assertive independents (catalysts) who fuse subgroups into unity by initiating and engineering trainer exit (barometric event).
7. Main Defenses	Projection Denigration of authority		Group moves into Phase II

* Course terminates at the end of 17 weeks. It is not uncommon for groups to remain through-out the course in this phase.

77

ple who are on our level, and have generically similar attitudes toward authoritative figures, activities and the like. This marks the beginning of the juvenile era, the great developments in which are the talents for cooperation, competition and compromise" (20, pp. 17–18. Emphasis ours).

The remaining barriers to valid communication are those associated with orientations toward interdependence: i.e. intimacy, friendship, identification. While the distribution of power was the cardinal issue during Phase I, the distribution of affection occupies the group during Phase II.

Subphase 4: Enchantment-flight. At the outset of subphase 4, the group is happy, cohesive, relaxed. The atmosphere is one of "sweetness and light". Any slight increase in tension is instantly dissipated by joking and laughter. The fighting of Phase I is still fresh in the memory of the group, and the group's efforts are devoted to patching up differences, healing wounds, and maintaining a harmonious atmosphere. Typically, this is a time of merrymaking and group minstrelsy. Coffee and cake may be served at the meetings. Hours may be passed in organizing a group party. Poetry or songs commemorating the important events and persons in the group's history may be composed by individuals or, more commonly, as a group project. All decisions must be unanimous during this period, since everyone must be happy, but the issues on which decisions are made are mostly ones about which group members have no strong feelings. At first the cathartic, healing function of these activities is clear; there is much spontaneity, playfulness, and pleasure. Soon the pleasures begin to wear thin.

The myth of mutual acceptance and universal harmony must eventually be recognized for what it is. From the beginning of this phase there are frequent evidences of underlying hostilities, unresolved issues in the group. But they are quickly, nervously smoothed over by laughter or misinterpretation. Subphase 4 begins with catharsis, but that is followed by the development of a rigid norm to which all members are forced to conform: "Nothing must be allowed to disturb our harmony in the future; we must avoid the mistakes of the painful past." Not that members have forgotten that the painful past was a necessary preliminary to the autonomous and (it is said) delightful present, though that fact is carefully overlooked. Rather, there is a dim realization that all members must have an experience somewhat analogous to the trainer's in subphase 3, before a mutually understood, accepted, and realistic definition of their own roles in the group can be arrived at.

Resistance of members to the requirement that harmony be maintained at all costs appears in subtle ways. In open group discussion the requirement is imperative: either the member does not dare to endanger harmony with the group or to disturb the *status quo* by denying that all problems have been solved. Much as members may dislike the tedious work of maintaining the appearance of harmony, the alternative is worse. The house of cards would come tumbling down, and the painful and exacting work of building something more substantial would have to begin. The flight from these problems takes a number of forms. Group members may say, "We've had our fighting and are now a group. Thus, further self-study is unnecessary." Very commonly, the possibility of any change may be prevented by not coming together as a total group at all. Thus the members may subgroup through an entire meeting. Those who would disturb the friendly subgroups are accused of "rocking the boat."

The solidarity and harmony become more and more illusory, but the group still clings to the illusion. This perseveration is in a way a consequence of the deprivation that members have experienced in maintaining the atmosphere of harmony. Maintaining it forces members to behave in ways alien to their own feelings; to go still further in group involvement would mean a complete loss of self. The group is therefore torn by a new ambivalence, which might be verbalized as follows: 1. "We all love one another and therefore we must maintain the solidarity of the group and give up whatever is necessary of our selfish desires." 2. "The group demands that I sacrifice my identity as a person; but the group is an evil mechanism which satisfies no dominant needs." As this subphase comes to a close, the happiness that marked its beginning is maintained only as a mask. The "innocent" splitting of the group into subgroups has gone so far that members will even walk around the meeting table to join in the conversation of a subgroup rather than speak across the table at the risk of bringing the whole group together. There is a certain uneasiness about the group; there is a feeling that "we should work together but cannot". There may be a tendency to regress to the orientation of subphase 1: group members would like the trainer to take over.

To recapitulate: subphase 4 begins with a happy sense of group belongingness. Individual identity is eclipsed by a "the group is bigger than all of us" sentiment. But this integration is short

lived: it soon becomes perceived as a fake attempt to resolve interpersonal problems by denying their reality. In the later stages of this subphase, enchantment with the total group is replaced by enchantment with one's subgroup, and out of this breakdown of the group emerges a new organization based on the anxieties aroused out of this first, suffocating, involvement.

Subphase 5: Disenchantment-fight. This subphase is marked by a division into two subgroups—paralleling the experience of subphase 2—but this time based upon orientations toward the degree of intimacy required by group membership. Membership in the two subgroups is not necessarily the same as in subphase 2: for now the fragmentation occurs as a result of opposite and extreme attitudes toward the degree of intimacy desired in interpersonal relations. The counterpersonal members band together to resist further involvement. The overpersonal members band together in a demand for unconditional love. While these subgroups appear as divergent as possible, a common theme underlies them. For the one group, the only means seen for maintaining self-esteem is to avoid any real commitment to others; for the other group, the only way to maintain self-esteem is to obtain a commitment from others to forgive everything. The subgroups share in common the fear that intimacy breeds contempt.

This anxiety is reflected in many ways during subphase 6. For the first time openly disparaging remarks are made about the group. Invidious comparisons are made between it and other groups. Similarly, psychology and social science may be attacked. The inadequacy of the group as a basis for self-esteem is dramatized in many ways—from stating "I don't care what you think", to boredom, to absenteeism. The overpersonals insist that they are happy and comfortable, while the counterpersonals complain about the lack of group morale. Intellectualization by the overpersonals frequently takes on religious overtones concerning Christian love, consideration for others, etc. In explanations of member behavior, the counterpersonal members account for all in terms of motives having nothing to do with the present group; the overpersonals explain all in terms of acceptance and rejection in the present group.

Subphase 5 belongs to the counterpersonals as subphase 4 belonged to the overpersonals. Subphase 4 might be caricatured as hiding in the womb of the group; subphase 5 as hiding out of sight of the group. It seems probable that both of these modalities serve to ward off anxieties associated with intimate interpersonal relations. A theme that links them together can be verbalized as follows: "If others really knew me, they would reject me." The overpersonal's formula for avoiding this rejection seems to be accepting all others so as to be protected by the others' guilt; the counterpersonal's way is by rejecting all others before they have a chance to reject him. Another way of characterizing the counterpersonal orientation is in the phrase, "I would lose my identity as a member of the group." The corresponding overpersonal orientation reads, "I have nothing to lose by identifying with the group." We can now look back on the past two subphases as countermeasures against loss of self-esteem; what Sullivan once referred to as the greatest inhibition to the understanding of what is distinctly human, "the overwhelming conviction of self-hood—

this amounts to a delusion of unique individuality". The sharp swings and fluctuations that occurred between the enchantment and euphoria of subphase 4 and the disenchantment of subphase 5 can be seen as a struggle between the "institutionalization of complacency" on the one hand and anxiety associated with fantasy speculations about intimacy and involvement on the other. This dissociative behavior serves a purpose of its own: a generalized denial of the group and its meaning for individuals. For if the group is important and valid then it has to be taken seriously. If it can wallow in the enchantment of subphase 4, it is safe; if it can continually vilify the goals and objectives of the group, it is also safe. The disenchantment theme in subphase 5 is perhaps a less skilful and more desperate security provision with its elaborate wall of defenses than the "group mind" theme of subphase 4. What should be stressed is that both subphase defenses were created almost entirely on fantastic expectations about the consequences of group involvement. These defenses are homologous to anxiety as it is experienced by the individual; i.e. the state of "anxiety arises as a response to a situation of danger and which will be reproduced thenceforward whenever such a situation recurs" (7, p. 72). In sum, the past two subphases were marked by a conviction that further group involvement would be injurious to members' self-esteem.

Subphase 6: Consensual validation. In the groups of which we write, two forces combine to press the group toward a resolution of the interdependency problem. These are the approaching end of the training course, and the need to establish a method of evaluation (including course grades).

There are, of course, ways of denying or avoiding these realities. The group can agree to continue to meet after the course ends. It can extricate itself from evaluation activities by asking the trainer to perform the task, or by awarding a blanket grade. But turning this job over to the trainer is a regression to dependence; and refusal to discriminate and reward is a failure to resolve the problems of interdependence. If the group has developed in general as we have described, the reality of termination and evaluation cannot be denied, and these regressive modes of adaptation cannot be tolerated.

The characteristic defenses of the two subgroups at first fuse to prevent any movement toward the accomplishment of the evaluation and grading task. The counterpersonals resist evaluation as an invasion of privacy: they foresee catastrophe if members begin to say what they think of one another. The overpersonals resist grading since it involves discriminating among the group members. At the same time, all members have a stake in the outcome of evaluation and grading. In avoiding the task, members of each subgroup are perceived by members of the other as "rationalizing", and the group becomes involved in a vicious circle of mutual disparagement. In this process, the fear of loss of self-esteem through group involvement is near to being realized. As in subphase 3, it is the independents —in this case those whose self-esteem is not threatened by the prospect of intimacy—who restore members' confidence in the group. Sometimes all that is required to reverse the vicious circle quite dramatically is a request by an independent for assessment of his own role. Or it may be an expression of confidence in the group's ability to accomplish the task.

The activity that follows group commitment to the evaluation task does not conform to the expectations of the overpersonal or counterpersonal members. Its chief characteristic is the willingness and ability of group members to validate their self-concepts with other members. The fear of rejection fades when tested against reality. The tensions that developed as a result of these fears diminish in the light of actual discussion of member roles. At the same time, there is revulsion against "capsule evaluations" and "curbstone psychoanalysis." Instead, what ensues is a serious attempt by each group member to verbalize his private conceptual scheme for understanding human behavior—his own and that of others. Bringing these assumptions into explicit communication is the main work of subphase 6. This activity demands a high level of work and of communicative skill. Some of the values that appear to underlie the group's work during this subphase are as follows: 1. Members can accept one another's differences without associating "good" and "bad" with the differences. 2. Conflict exists but is over substantive issues rather than emotional issues. 3. Consensus is reached as a result of rational discussion rather than through a compulsive attempt at unanimity. 4. Members are aware of their own involvement, and of other aspects of group process, without being overwhelmed or alarmed. 5. Through the evaluation process, members take on greater personal meaning to each other. This facilitates communication and creates a deeper understanding of how the other person thinks, feels, behaves; it creates a series of personal expectations, as distinguished from the previous, more stereotyped, role expectations.

81

The above values, and some concomitant values, are of course very close to the authors' conception of a "good group". In actuality they are not always achieved by the end of the group life. The prospect of the death of the group, after much procrastination in the secret hope that it will be over before anything can be done, is likely to force the group into strenuous last-minute efforts to overcome the obstacles that have blocked its progress. As a result, the sixth subphase is too often hurried and incomplete. If the hurdles are not overcome in time, grading is likely to be an exercise that confirms members' worst suspicions about the group. And if role evaluation is attempted, either the initial evaluations contain so much hostile material as to block further efforts, or evaluations are so flowery and vacuous that no one, least of all the recipient, believes them.

In the resolution of interdependence problems, member-personalities count for even more than they do in the resolution of dependence problems. The trainer's behavior is crucial in determining the group's ability to resolve the dependence issue, but in the interdependence issue the group is, so to speak, only as strong as its weakest link. The exceedingly dependent group member can ride through Phase I with a fixed belief in the existence of a private relationship between himself and the trainer; but the person whose anxieties are intense under the threats associated with intimacy can immobilize the group. (*Table II* summarizes the major events of Phase II.)

Conclusions

Dependence and interdependence—power and love, authority and intimacy —are regarded as the central problems of group life. In most organizations and societies, the rules governing the distribution of authority and the degree of intimacy among members are prescribed. In the human relations training group, they are major areas of uncertainty. While the choice of these matters as the focus of group attention and experience rests to some extent with the trainer, his choice is predicated on the belief that they are the core of interpersonal experience. As such, the principal obstacles to valid interpersonal communication lie in rigidities of interpretation and response carried over from the anxious experiences with particular love or power figures into new situations in which they are inappropriate. The existence of such autisms complicates all discussion unduly and in some instances makes an exchange of meanings impossible.

Stating the training goal as the establishment of valid communication means that the relevance of the autistic response to authority and intimacy on the part of any member can be explicitly examined, and at least a provisional alternative formulated by him. Whether this makes a lasting change in the member's flexibility, or whether he will return to his more restricted formula when confronted with a new situation, we do not know, but we expect that it varies with the success of his group experience—particularly his success in understanding it.

We have attempted to portray what we believe to be the typical pattern of group development, and to show the relationship of member orientations and changes in member orientations to the major movements of the group. In this connection, we have emphasized the catalytic role of persons uncon-

TABLE II   PHASE II. INTERDEPENDENCE—PERSONAL RELATIONS

	SUBPHASE 4—ENCHANTMENT	SUBPHASE 5—DISENCHANTMENT	SUBPHASE 6—CONSENSUAL VALIDATION
Emotional Modality	Pairing-Flight. Group becomes a respected icon beyond further analysis.	Fight-Flight. Anxiety reactions. Distrust and suspicion of various group members.	Pairing, understanding, acceptance.
Content Themes	Discussion of "group history", and generally salutary aspects of course, group, and membership.	Revival of content themes used in Subphase 1: What is a group? What are we doing here? What are the goals of the group? What do I have to give up—personally—to belong to this group? (How much intimacy and affection is required?) Invasion of privacy vs. "group giving". Setting up proper codes of social behavior.	Course grading system. Discussion and assessment of member roles.
Dominant Roles (Central Persons)	General distribution of participation for first time. Overpersonals have salience.	Most assertive counterpersonal and overpersonal individuals, with counterpersonals especially salient.	Assertive independents.
Group Structure	Solidarity, fusion. High degree of camaraderie and suggestibility. Le Bon's description of "group mind" would apply here.	Restructuring of membership into two competing predominant subgroups made up of individuals who share similar attitudes concerning degree of intimacy required in social interaction, i.e. the counterpersonal and overpersonal groups. The personal individuals remain uncommitted but act according to needs of situation.	Diminishing of ties based on personal orientation. Group structure now presumably appropriate to needs of situation based on predominantly substantive rather than emotional orientations. Consensus significantly easier on important issues.
Group Activity	Laughter, joking, humor. Planning out-of-class activities such as parties. The institutionalization of happiness to be accomplished by "fun" activities. High rate of interaction and participation.	Disparagement of group in a variety of ways: high rate of absenteeism, tardiness, balkiness in initiating total group interaction, frequent statements concerning worthlessness of group, denial of importance of group. Occasional member asking for individual help finally rejected by the group.	Communication to others of self-system of interpersonal relations; i.e. making conscious to self, and others aware of, conceptual system one uses to predict consequences of personal behavior. Acceptance of group on reality terms.
Group movement facilitated by:	Independence and achievement attained by trainer-rejection and its concomitant, deriving consensually some effective means for authority and control. (Subphase 3 rebellion bridges gap between Subphases 2 and 4.)	Disenchantment of group as a result of *fantasied expectations of group life.* The perceived threat to self-esteem that further group involvement signifies creates schism of group according to amount of affection and intimacy desired. The counterpersonal and overpersonal assertive individuals alleviate source of anxiety by disparaging or abnegating further group involvement. Subgroups form to ward off anxiety.	The external realities, group termination and the prescribed need for a course grading system, comprise the barometric event. Led by the personal individuals, the group tests reality and reduces autistic convictions concerning group involvement.
Main Defences	Denial, isolation, intellectualization, and alienation.		

83

flicted with respect to one or the other of the dependence and interdependence areas. This power to move the group lies mainly in his freedom from anxiety-based reactions to problems of authority (or intimacy): he has the freedom to be creative in searching for a way to reduce tension.

We have also emphasized the "barometric event" or event capable of moving the group from one phase to the next. The major events of this kind are the removal of the trainer as part of the resolution of the dependence problem; and the evaluation-grading requirements at the termination of the course. Both these barometric events require a catalytic agent in the group to bring them about. That is to say, the trainer-exit can take place only at the moment when it is capable of symbolizing the attainment of group autonomy, and it requires a catalytic agent in the group to give it this meaning. And the grading assignment can move the group forward only if the catalytic agent can reverse the vicious circle of disparagement that precedes it.

Whether the incorporation of these barometric events into the training design merely makes our picture of group development a self-fulfilling prophecy, or whether, as we wish to believe, these elements make dramatically clear the major forward movements of the group, and open the gate for a flood of new understanding and communication, can only be decided on the basis of more, and more varied, experience.

The evolution from Phase I to Phase II represents not only a change in emphasis from power to affection, but also from role to personality. Phase I activity generally centers on broad role distinctions such as class, ethnic background, professional interests, etc.; Phase II activity involves a deeper concern with personality modalities, such as reaction to failure, warmth, retaliation, anxiety, etc. This development presents an interesting paradox. For the group in Phase I emerged out of a heterogeneous collectivity of individuals; the individual in Phase II emerged out of the group. This suggests that group therapy, where attention is focused on individual movement, begins at the least enabling time. It is possible that, before group members are able to help each other, the barriers to communication must be partially understood.

References

1. BION, W. R. "Experiences in Groups: I." *Hum. Relat.*, Vol. I, No. 3, pp. 314–320, 1948.
2. BION, W. R. "Experiences in Groups: II." *Hum. Relat.*, Vol. I, No. 4, pp. 487–496, 1948.
5. FRENKEL-BRUNSWIK, E. "Intolerance of Ambiguity as an Emotional and Perceptual Personality Variable." In Bruner, J. S., and Krech, D. (eds.), *Perception and Personality*. Durham, N. C.: Duke Univ. Press, 1949 and 1950, p. 115.
6. FREUD, SIGMUND. *Group Psychology and the Analysis of the Ego.* Translated by J. Strachey. London: International ˙ Psycho-Analytical Press, 1922; New York: Liveright, 1949.
7. FREUD, SIGMUND. *The Problem of Anxiety.* Translated by H. A. Bunker. New York: Psychoanalytic Quarterly Press and W. W. Norton, 1936.
8. FREUD, SIGMUND. *Moses and Monotheism.* London: Hogarth Press, 1939; New York: Vintage Books, 1955.
10. GOULDNER, ALVIN. *Wildcat Strike.*

Yellow Springs, Ohio: Antioch Press, 1954; London: Routledge & Kegan Paul, 1955.

12. LEIGHTON, A. H. *The Governing of Men.* Princeton: Princeton Univ. Press, 1946.

14. PARK, ROBERT E. "The Strike." *Society.* New York: Free Press of Glencoe, 1955.

16. SCHUTZ, W. C. "Group Behavior Studies, I–III." Cambridge, Mass.: Harvard Univ., 1954 (mimeo).

17. SCHUTZ, W. C. "What Makes Groups Productive?" *Hum. Relat.,* Vol. VIII, No. 4, p. 429, 1955.

19. SULLIVAN, H. S. "Tensions, Inter-personal and International." In Cantril, Hadley (ed.), *Tensions that Cause Wars.* Urbana, Ill.: Univ. of Illinois Press, 1950.

20. SULLIVAN, H. S. *Conceptions of Modern Psychiatry.* Washington, D.C.: William Alanson White Psychiatric Foundation, 1940, 1945; London: Tavistock Publications, 1955.

22. WHYTE, W. F., Jr. *Patterns for Industrial Peace.* New York: Harper, 1951.

Carel B. Germain is a doctoral candidate, Columbia University School of Social Work, New York, N.Y. During the academic year 1967–1968, she was a career teacher at Columbia University School of Social Work.

Social Study: Past and Future

CAREL B. GERMAIN

NEW APPROACHES to the practice of social casework are now being considered, implemented, and evaluated in all sectors of the profession. The impetus for innovation derives from a number of sources, including the application of crisis concepts in various areas of practice, the growing use of family treatment, the efforts to develop more effective modes of intervention in work with the poor, the concern about treatment dropout and treatment failure, and the need to use the limited supply of trained personnel more productively. Innovation is an appropriate professional response to new knowledge, to the emergence of new problems and needs, and to the impact of social change on old problems and needs. Nevertheless, the implications of innovation must be recognized. And certain implications in current new approaches seem to cast doubt on long-accepted notions of the psychosocial study as a formalized process essential to the diagnostic understanding on which treatment intervention is based.

The crisis approach assumes a time-limited period of upset, when the usual coping capacity is weakened, anxiety is high, and the individual or family is most accessible to help. Immediacy of preventive or restorative intervention is seen as paramount; a period of study and exploration as a basis for action appears inconsistent with the concept of crisis.

Similarly, family treatment appears to emphasize the here-and-now interaction of family members as the arena for the caseworker's intervention, and longitudinal study-diagnosis of the individual family members is eliminated or at least subordinated to a horizontal focus on current trans-actions, communication patterns, and role relationships. The successes and economies of this approach give weight to prevalent doubts about the usefulness of social study as it has been conceptualized.

Experiences in the use of reaching-out techniques over the past decade and in contemporary efforts to understand and apply social and cultural differentials in casework practice have led to the realization that social study pursued in traditional terms is often experienced by the poor or lower-class client as a frustration and rejection.

Recent research findings have suggested that the dropout problem in the early phase of contact may be referred, in part, to difference in the objectives of caseworker and client, in that the caseworker's goals in the early interviews have been traditionally related to the gathering of information, albeit in a therapeutically oriented way, whereas the client's goal has been to secure immediate help with the presenting problem. Too often the caseworker is left with facts, we are told, but no client. Moreover, concerns about the manpower shortage carry the implication that the days of long-term treatment are over and with them the interview hours spent on study and exploration in order to uncover the "real" problem underlying the request for help.

Perhaps these emphases on speeding up the helping process mean that study, as it has been conceived and taught, is no longer appropriate or even possible. They may represent a growing polarity between theory and practice, and it seems urgent that social casework re-examine its tenets and assumptions concerning social study. Are we so in the grip of yesterday that we are clinging in

SOCIAL CASEWORK, July 1968, Vol. 49, pp. 403–409.

theory to a time-honored principle no longer valid for the requirements of current and future practice? Or, at the other extreme, are we in danger of discarding, through expedience and disuse, what is actually a necessary component in all casework?

It is my conviction that study continues to be an essential element in a scientifically based practice. Indeed, the spirit of scientific inquiry on which study rests is more than ever necessary in the face of the constant change in social needs and conditions that now confronts the caseworker. Yet it must be study that serves today's demands, not yesterday's ideologies.

In order to reshape the study process, the first task is to identify the fundamental concepts in the traditional model of study. They will be identified in this article as relevance, salience, and individualization. It will be suggested that the resolution of practice dilemmas that emerge as these concepts are modified may depend on broadening conceptions of casework practice.[1] The study process will be recast within the framework of systems theory. Attention will be drawn to ways in which such a recast study process can match up with new treatment modalities to deliver services that make more productive use of time and resources for the client, the agency, and the worker.

Relevance, Salience, and Individualization

Mary Richmond set forth the principles of social investigation that gave to social study its initial shape and direction.[2] According to her model, the caseworker's first responsibility in planning treatment was to secure any and all facts that, taken together, would reveal the client's personality and his situation. Thus, the beginning thread of a scientific orientation appeared in the insistence on a factual base that, through logical and inferential reasoning, would lead to a plan of action. It was as if knowledge of all the evidence would reveal the cause of the problem

and hence its remedy; consequently, every source of information was to be utilized.

In the light of increased experience and accretions of knowledge, particularly from psychoanalysis, the routine gathering of massive amounts of data gradually gave way to a more discriminating approach. Social history was obtained with more understanding of its relation to personality dynamics. Concepts clarifying the ego's functions in relation to social reality and to inner forces led away from the earlier preoccupation with repressed content to what is still the unit of attention, the person-in-situation. The impact of these developments on study culminated in Gordon Hamilton's conceptual model.[3]

Whereas Richmond had urged the exhaustive collection of facts followed by separation of the significant from the insignificant, Hamilton introduced the concept of relevance. Sources of data were respecified as the client's own account, the reports of collaterals, documentary evidence, findings of experts, and the worker's observations. Viewed in terms of newly defined psychological and environmental dimensions, they were to be tapped selectively according to the nature of the problem, the wish of the client, the purpose of the agency, and the availability and preventive value of the information itself. Study, guided by professional knowledge, was to be related quantitatively to the degree of intervention indicated and the difficulty of establishing the diagnosis. An important distinction was made between history-taking for diagnosis in the early contacts and the use of history for abreaction in the treatment phase.

Hamilton described two types of social study, the *patterned* type and the *clue* type. The most clearly conceptualized examples of the patterned type are the eligibility study made in public assistance work and the psychogenetic study made in cases focused on behavior disorders or emotional disturbances. In such studies priorities are assigned to certain areas considered relevant, and

[1] See Morris S. Schwartz and Charlotte G. Schwartz, *Social Approaches to Mental Patient Care*, Columbia University Press, New York, 1964.
[2] Mary E. Richmond, *Social Diagnosis*, Russell Sage Foundation, New York, 1917, and Mary E. Richmond, *What Is Social Case Work?*, Russell Sage Foundation, New York, 1922.
[3] Gordon Hamilton, *Theory and Practice of Social Case Work* (2nd ed., rev.), Columbia University Press, New York, 1951. See especially Chapter VII, pp. 181–212.

these areas are held in the foreground of attention. In making the clue type of social study, the worker feels his way on the basis of the request and clues, consciously and unconsciously furnished, in order to collect facts relevant to the problem. It has been recently pointed out, however, that, "as Miss Hamilton suggests, clue and pattern are really interrelated and are perhaps more indicative of ways of envisaging the process of securing data than they are clear-cut types of study. The patterned study may involve a matter of priorities, but it is best developed on a basis of explaining the relevance of the inquiry to the request, and with the client's participation, than on a questionnaire basis. Similarly, the clue approach involves a concept of pattern since criteria for relevance give significance to the clue. Further, the worker controls this approach by injecting attention to priority of subjects for exploration at appropriate points." [4]

The scientific orientation that began in Richmond's approach to social study is firm and clear in the Hamilton model. Since the model requires systematic inquiry into relevant facts, it is useful in considering the model to note *Webster's* definition of *relevant* as "bearing upon, or properly applying to, the case in hand; of a nature to afford evidence tending to prove or to disprove the matters in issue. . . ." [5] It follows that the way in which the problem is cast determines which data are relevant and where the emphasis and direction of inquiry will lie. How the problem is defined, and to some extent the mode of intervention available or selected, determines what data will be perceived as relevant and consequently observed, collected, and interpreted for professional judgment. An inquiry into a set of circumstances viewed as indicative of a personality disturbance, for example, will result in the collection and interpretation of certain data. These data will be quite different from those collected and interpreted

when the same set of circumstances is viewed as indicative of a disjunction between the individual and his familial, organizational, or cultural system or between the individual and his physical environment.

An observation underscored in Hamilton's work but sometimes lost sight of in practice had been made as long ago as 1936 by Fern Lowry, namely, that "the decision what to treat frequently demands greater skill than the decision how to treat." [6] As Lowry suggests, early dropout and treatment failure is frequently attributed to the client or to external factors when it should be attributed, rather, to the caseworker's tendency to assume responsibility for every discoverable need. Such a tendency may even conflict with the client's wish for immediate help in a specific area. Accordingly, Lowry urges that the impulse to treat every need and the urge to cure be restrained. [7] From such a standpoint, study is not an inquiry into all areas and needs.

The work of Schwartz and Schwartz introduces the concept of salience [8]—and *Webster's* defines *salient* as "prominent; conspicuous; noticeable. . . ." [9] A salient feature, then, is one that has an emphatic quality that thrusts itself into attention.

According to the foregoing concepts of relevance and salience, treatment is not properly focused on the total person. It becomes, in fact, more individualized and differential when it is particularized for particular clients having particular needs or problems in particular situations. [10] Individualization is based on choice among needs, modes of treatment, and possible goals. From this perspective, social study must become more individualized in order to specify the salient need or needs for which social casework has professional accountability. Specifying the salient need, however, is not

[4] Lucille N. Austin, on "clue and pattern," as discussed in a doctoral seminar in social casework, Columbia University School of Social Work, New York, Spring 1966.

[5] *Webster's New International Dictionary of the English Language* (2nd ed.), G. & C. Merriam Co., Springfield, Massachusetts, 1950, p. 2104.

[6] Fern Lowry, "The Client's Needs As the Basis for Differential Approach in Treatment," in *Differential Approach in Case Work Treatment,* Family Welfare Association of America, New York, 1936, p. 8.

[7] *Ibid.,* p. 9.

[8] Schwartz and Schwartz, *op. cit.,* pp. 111-35.

[9] *Webster's New International Dictionary of the English Language* (2nd ed.), *op. cit.,* p. 2204.

[10] Schwartz and Schwartz, *op. cit.,* p. 124.

the same as partializing the problem. What is described here is still an organismic approach in which the caseworker remains constantly aware of the whole, and the changing relationships of the parts to the whole, while singling out salient need for individualized treatment.

Although caseworkers have long known of the importance of the role of norms in the assessment of functioning within specific social and cultural contexts, the concept of salience requires a shift in the concept of normalcy and a shift from setting treatment goals in terms of cure. Some shift has already occurred insofar as goals are conceptualized as restoration of a prior level of social functioning or return to a previous equilibrium. A further shift away from notions of cure is required so that some resolution of the presenting problem, easing of precipitating stress, and even remission of symptoms, for example, can be embraced as goals. These become appropriate additions to the array of possible goals as new models of casework intervention develop in response to new knowledge and new conditions. The individual and social value of such goals, in relation to conservation of the client's resources and to manpower issues, seems clear. Moreover, the resemblance of these goals to the processes of natural life situations is striking.

Broadening the Conceptions of Help

In social casework theory and education, if not always in practice, study-diagnosis-treatment has been conceptualized on a psychotherapeutic model in which the worker—and, it is hoped, the client—"will peer down the long avenue of the client's past life," as John Dollard puts it, "to see how the present event matured." [11] This conceptualization has often led to searching for, and giving primacy to, the problems underlying the presenting request, or even unrelated to it.

The dilemma that presents itself when such an approach is viewed in the light of the foregoing discussion may be resolved through broadening the conceptions of case-

[11] John Dollard, *Criteria for the Life History*, Yale University Press, New Haven, Connecticut, 1935, p. 27.

work help within the framework proposed by Schwartz and Schwartz. They distinguish between *treatment* as conventionally accepted clinical procedures and *help* as a large variety of attempts to influence clients in a therapeutic direction. They suggest that the conceptions of help should—

include considerations such as a wider arena within which help might proceed, a different conception of who and what is to be helped, and a different view of the conditions and processes that affect therapeutic progress. . . . Thus, broadening the conceptions of help involves some reorientation. From looking upon the process exclusively as a clinical activity, directed at a disease entity, and undertaken within the boundaries of the conventionally defined therapist-patient relationship, the change is to seeing it, in addition, as a sociopsychological process that attempts to deal with problems in living that are not necessarily serious or well-defined emotional disorders. [12]

The authors advance four objectives to be achieved in broadening the conceptions of help. They are interrelated, and although each may be discussed separately for heuristic purposes, each can only be understood in relation to the other three. These objectives are "reconceptualizing the unit of help, changing the . . . object of help, expanding the role of helper, and re-orienting . . . [the] approach to help processes." [13]

The Unit of Help

The unit of attention in social casework has been the person-situation, although history reveals a shifting in emphasis at times from one to the other side of the hyphen. The newer ego concepts have made possible the appropriate study of psychosocial factors in social functioning. Newly conceptualized elements of the dynamic environment—such as role, class, ethnic and other reference groups, value orientations, family structure, and the agency as a social system—have permitted more accurate definitions of the situation. [14] In spite of much effort, however,

[12] Morris S. Schwartz and Charlotte G. Schwartz, *Social Approaches to Mental Patient Care*, Columbia University Press, New York, 1964, p. 85.
[13] *Ibid.*
[14] Herman Stein, "The Concept of the Social Environment in Social Work Practice," *Smith College Studies in Social Work*, Vol. XXX, June 1960, pp. 187–210.

there has until recently been no way to integrate psychological and social phenomena without invoking the fallacy of reductionism. In this regard, general systems theory offers a fruitful approach to reconceptualizing the unit of attention in a way that will permit a valid redefinition of social study.

The Object of Help

Caseworkers have tended to modify their traditional stance in relation to the client whenever the family, rather than the individual, has been viewed as client—and have frequently misconstrued family-focused treatment of individuals as family treatment. Much work lies ahead in developing, from the knowledge and experience of casework itself, useful study-diagnostic concepts and derivative treatment principles and techniques for the family as a social system.

Also required is an enlarged definition of the object of help to encompass not merely the personality, but the whole human being within a fluid, real-life situation, in order to utilize the therapeutic potential of life processes, adaptive and coping capacities, and social supports.

Still another possibility lies in viewing the agency itself as the object of change or as an instrument for change rather than as a given in the situation. Such a view has some similarity to conceptions of milieu therapy as applied in hospitals and other institutions; it implies the use of organizational structure and the organizational roles of clients and workers within the agency to effect organizational or individual change. Given such a view, social study would embrace a consideration of the impact on clients of organizational variables, of the potential of those variables for fostering or inhibiting growth, and of sources of organizational resistance to change.

The Helper

The discipline of social casework has moved in several ways toward redefining the role of the worker from that of clinician-therapist to that of helper. Whereas the formal, instrumental, functionally specific role was traditionally the only one available to the caseworker, a more informal, expressive,

functionally diffuse role has been evolving. Its inception was in the development of reaching-out techniques in several fields of practice. And the dimensions of the role have become clearer in the course of current attempts to reduce social distance, which are based on increasingly sophisticated knowledge of socialization experiences and life styles in deprived groups.

In addition, there has been expansion in the leadership role of the caseworker on service teams, which may include homemakers, volunteers, case aides, and indigenous helpers. Such a team approach appears to offer varied experiences and interpersonal relationships for clients with salient needs in those areas. Continued experimentation and research in programs in which one practitioner makes combined use of casework, group work, and community organization methods are also expected to expand the caseworker's repertory of roles.

The Help Processes

Conventional treatment procedures require verbal skills, introspection, and motivation, which are not infrequently lacking among clients of casework services. Now, however, the idea of help is being broadened to include informal processes and activities. New uses of the home visit are being developed; searches are being made for ways to provide experiences in a social context that will promote growth and maturation in the client; and new techniques of concretization and demonstration are being utilized.[15] In such efforts the relationship offered the client is viewed as a training ground for living and for assuming social roles in more rewarding ways. The caseworker supports adaptive responses and progressive forces, rather than uncovering coping failures, since the latter tactic tends to foster transference and the attendant regressive needs.

The concept of casework help has been broadened to include the provision of consultation services, and, increasingly, caseworkers are being enlisted to provide con-

[15] See, for example, Louise S. Bandler, "Casework with Multiproblem Families," in *Social Work Practice, 1964,* Columbia University Press, New York, 1964, pp. 158–71.

sultation to community caretakers with respect to the needs and responses of their clientele, either as specific individuals or total groups. Those being helped are not cast in the role of client and are not subject to its prescriptions and proscriptions. They may be merely present, perhaps in a helping arena, such as a day care center, a school, or a sheltered workshop.

These broadened conceptions of help call for new models of intervention and new ways to provide help more appropriately and effectively to supplement the psychotherapeutic model and increase the caseworker's flexibility and adaptiveness. Some, such as the crisis model [16] and the life model,[17] are now being developed. They furnish new ways of conceptualizing needs and problems and new methods and techniques of intervention. The relevance and salience of data vary with a shift from one model to another. For example, it may be necessary to reconceptualize certain disturbances as life crises, maturational or situational, or as role transitions imposing new statuses and ego tasks or as psychosocial disabilities requiring help in developing social competence. Defining problems in these terms demands that study produce new kinds of environmental data for the understanding and utilization of life processes as treatment media. Implicit is an emphasis on rapidity in the collection of data so that decisions can be reached to take action that is timely in terms of the model.

A Systems Approach

Because systems theory, as a way of viewing biological, psychological, and social phenomena, cuts across disciplines and bodies of knowledge, its constructs may be useful for the identification of the relevant and salient data in individualized study. The unit of attention is reformulated as a field of ac-

tion in which the client—his biological and personality subsystems—is in transaction with a variety of biological, psychological, cultural, and social systems within a specific physical, cultural, and historical environment. Though there are important differences among these types of systems, all, as open systems, have important properties in common.[18] Some of these characteristics have to do with the input, transformation, and output of energy from and to the environment, which highlight the interdependence of systems, exchanges across boundaries, and degrees of openness to the environment. Other features pertain to the maintenance of a steady state or dynamic homeostasis—that is, the preservation of the general character of the system—and these highlight feedback processes, subsystem dynamics, and the relation between growth and survival. These and other characteristics draw attention to the functional and dysfunctional consequences, the reciprocal effects and reverberations that occur in the field of systems as the result of the operations of each. Similar observations can be made concerning the relation of its parts to any single system.

In contrast to the two-dimensional person-situation approach, this conception offers a wide range of system variables and encourages a holistic view. It leads to a focus on the disruptive factors in the usual steady state and on the mechanisms for restitution, coping, adaptation, and innovation in all systems. The systems perspective also places the agency as a social system and the worker and the client in the same transactional field. The helping relationship has a larger purview, which adds the reciprocal influences of the roles, norms, and values of several transacting social systems to the clinical aspects of the relationship. The worker's entrance into the client's field

[16] Developments in the crisis model are found in Howard J. Parad (ed.), *Crisis Intervention: Selected Readings,* Family Service Association of America, New York, 1965.

[17] Bernard Bandler, "The Concept of Ego-Supportive Psychotherapy," in *Ego-Oriented Casework: Problems and Perspectives,* Howard J. Parad and Roger R. Miller (eds.), Family Service Association of America, New York, 1963, pp. 27–44.

[18] For further discussion of the characteristics and operations of open systems, see, for example, Daniel Katz and Robert L. Kahn, *The Social Psychology of Organizations,* John Wiley & Sons, New York, 1966, pp. 14–70, and Roy R. Grinker (ed.), *Toward a Unified Theory of Human Behavior,* Basic Books, New York, 1967. All the material in this work is valuable. See also Gordon Hearn, *Theory Building in Social Work,* University of Toronto Press, Toronto, 1958, pp. 38–51.

changes it *de facto*, not only through his effect as an observer on the observed but also through the reverberations of his entrance through the various other systems in the client's field, particularly secondary role networks. Similarly, the client's organizational roles have an impact on agency role-sets, whether they are designed by client groups as in some current public welfare agencies or by other agencies that have provided for planned participation for citizen-clients. In either instance, Heinz Hartmann's view of adaptation, which takes into account the individual's potential for contributing to the modification of existing environments and the creation of new ones, is more likely to be implemented through the systems approach.

Conclusions

We tend to observe and recognize as relevant what is closest to our conceptual model, and the systems perspective allows more indicators of salient and relevant variables to filter through the worker's perceptual screen. This does not mean that in any one case the entire field is covered.[19] On the contrary, the systems perspective enables the worker to comprehend the salient features of the problem as it is systemically conceived, to recognize relevant data within the relevant system or systems, and to reach professional judgments more rapidly. Paradoxically, it enlarges the unit of attention while it sharpens the focus by suggesting additional possible points of entry to effect change, as well as by illuminating the feasibility of change in specific systems. In a systems approach, a rapid gathering of relevant facts related to the salient features of the presenting need requires, however, greater breadth of knowledge, more skill in diagnosis, and greater capacity for communication, relationship, and self-awareness than are required in a tra-

ditional person-situation approach. Rapidity requires confidence in a knowledge base amplified to include all systems, their characteristics and linkages. Even in the first interview, the caseworker's broad knowledge is available to lead him to an understanding of the psychological and social commonalities revealed empirically through verbal and nonverbal clues. Increased knowledge and skill permit him to rely on these clues and signs as indicators that it is not then necessary to explore many phenomena and large areas of the client's experience. As Joseph Eaton has pointed out, this kind of professional confidence and security calls for tolerance of some degree of uncertainty and error.[20]

No matter what types of casework intervention may arise from broadened conceptions of help, the worker with a scientific orientation will always think diagnostically, using logical procedures with respect to evidence, inferential reasoning, and the relating of empirical data to theory and knowledge. He will make disciplined use of prognosis and evaluation, as formulated by Hamilton, against which predicted probable outcomes are measured. Careful analysis will be made of cases that do not have the expected outcome in order to uncover previously unknown variables, which may themselves add to the refinement of study. The worker will be guided in study, as in the total helping process, by social work values. His effectiveness will be enhanced by diversified patterns of communication, differential roles, and helping relationships that give attention to the emotional, cultural, and cognitive forces in growth and change.

For the new demands of practice, social study remains the scientific inquiry Hamilton conceptualized, but it is becoming accelerated and more sharply relevant in its focus on salient system variables. Its newer form and content must go hand in hand with newer treatment modes, newer levels of intervention, and broader conceptions of the flexible helping process that is social casework.

[19] This view departs from that suggested in a pioneer paper, Werner A. Lutz, *Concepts and Principles Underlying Social Casework Practice,* "Social Work Practice in Medical Care and Rehabilitation Settings, Monograph III," Medical Social Work Section, National Association of Social Workers, Washington, D.C., 1956, pp. 72–75. In contrast, the present article is an attempt to apply systems theory to more models than the clinical.

[20] Joseph W. Eaton, "Science, 'Art,' and Uncertainty in Social Work," *Social Work,* Vol. III, July 1958, p. 10.

FOUNDATIONS OF THE THEORY OF ORGANIZATION

PHILIP SELZNICK

University of California,
Los Angeles

Trades unions, governments, business corporations, political parties, and the like are formal structures in the sense that they represent rationally ordered instruments for the achievement of stated goals. "Organization," we are told, "is the arrangement of personnel for facilitating the accomplishment of some agreed purpose through the allocation of functions and responsibilities."[1] Or, defined more generally, formal organization is "a system of consciously coordinated activities or forces of two or more persons."[2] Viewed in this light, formal organization is the structural expression of rational action. The mobilization of technical and managerial skills requires a pattern of coordination, a systematic ordering of positions and duties which defines a chain of command and makes possible the administrative integration. of specialized functions. In this context *delegation* is the primordial organizational act, a precarious venture which requires the continuous elaboration of formal mechanisms of coordination and control. The security of all participants, and of the system as a whole, generates a persistent pressure for the institutionalization of relationships, which are thus removed from the uncertainties of individual fealty or sentiment. Moreover, it is necessary for the relations within the structure to be determined in such a way that individuals will be interchangeable and the organization will thus be free of dependence upon personal qualities.[3] In this way, the formal structure becomes subject to calculable manipulation, an instrument of rational action.

But as we inspect these formal structures we begin to see that they never succeed in conquering the non-rational dimensions of organizational behavior. The latter remain at once indispensable to the continued existence of the system of coordination and at the same time the source of friction, dilemma, doubt, and ruin. This fundamental paradox arises from the fact that rational action systems are inescapably imbedded in an institutional matrix, in two significant senses: (1) the action system—or the formal structure of delegation and control which is its organizational expression—is itself only an aspect of a concrete social structure made up of individuals who may interact as *wholes,* not simply in terms of their formal roles within the system; (2) the formal system, and the social structure within which it finds concrete existence, are alike subject to the pressure of an institutional environment to which some over-all adjustment must be made. The formal administrative design can never adequately or fully reflect the concrete organization to which it refers, for the obvious reason that no abstract plan or pattern can—or may, if it is to be useful—exhaustively describe an empirical totality. At the same time, that which is not included in the abstract design (as reflected, for example, in a staff-and-line organization chart) is vitally relevant to the maintenance and development of the formal system itself.

Organization may be viewed from two standpoints which are analytically distinct but which are empirically united in a context of reciprocal consequences. On the one hand, any concrete organizational system is an *economy;* at the same time, it is an *adap-*

---

[1] John M. Gaus, "A Theory of Organization in Public Administration," in *The Frontiers of Public Administration* (Chicago: University of Chicago Press, 1936), p. 66.

[2] Chester I. Barnard, *The Functions of the Executive* (Cambridge: Harvard University Press, 1938), p. 73.

[3] Cf. Talcott Parsons' generalization (after Max Weber) of the "law of the increasing rationality of action systems," in *The Structure of Social Action* (New York: McGraw-Hill, 1937), p. 752.

AMERICAN SOCIOLOGICAL REVIEW, 1948, Vol. 13, pp. 25-35.

93

tive social structure. Considered as an econ-omy, organization is a system of relation-ships which define the availability of scarce resources and which may be manipulated in terms of efficiency and effectiveness. It is the economic aspect of organization which commands the attention of management technicians and, for the most part, students of public as well as private administration.[4] Such problems as the span of executive con-trol, the role of staff or auxiliary agencies, the relation of headquarters to field offices, and the relative merits of single or multiple executive boards are typical concerns of the science of administration. The coordinative scalar, and functional principles, as elements of the theory of organization, are products of the attempt to explicate the most general features of organization as a "technical prob-lem" or, in our terms, as an economy.

Organization as an economy is, however, necessarily conditioned by the organic states of the concrete structure, outside of the sys-tematics of delegation and control. This be-comes especially evident as the attention of leadership is directed toward such problems as the legitimacy of authority and the dy-namics of persuasion. It is recognized im-plicitly in action and explicitly in the work of a number of students that the possibility of manipulating the system of coordination depends on the extent to which that system is operating within an environment of effec-tive inducement to individual participants and of conditions in which the stability of authority is assured. This is in a sense the fundamental thesis of Barnard's remarkable study, *The Functions of the Executive.* It is also the underlying hypothesis which makes it possible for Urwick to suggest that "proper" or formal channels in fact function to "confirm and record" decisions arrived at

by more personal means.[5] We meet it again in the concept of administration as a process of education, in which the winning of con-sent and support is conceived to be a basic function of leadership.[6] In short, it is recog-nized that control and consent cannot be di-vorced even within formally authoritarian structures.

The indivisibility of control and consent makes it necessary to view formal organiza-tions as *cooperative* systems, widening the frame of reference of those concerned with the manipulation of organizational resources. At the point of action, of executive decision, the economic aspect of organization pro-vides inadequate tools for control over the concrete structure. This idea may be readily grasped if attention is directed to the role of the individual within the organizational economy. From the standpoint of organiza-tion as a formal system, persons are viewed functionally, in respect to their *roles*, as par-ticipants in assigned segments of the co-operative system. But in fact individuals have a propensity to resist depersonalization, to spill over the boundaries of their segmen-tary roles, to participate as *wholes*. The for-mal systems (at an extreme, the disposition of "rifles" at a military perimeter) cannot take account of the deviations thus intro-duced, and consequently break down as in-struments of control when relied upon alone. The whole individual raises new problems for the organization, partly because of the needs of his own personality, partly because he brings with him a set of established habits as well, perhaps, as commitments to special groups outside of the organization.

Unfortunately for the adequacy of formal systems of coordination, the needs of indi-viduals do not permit a single-minded at-tention to the stated goals of the system within which they have been assigned. The hazard inherent in the act of delegation de-rives essentially from this fact. Delegation is

---

[4] See Luther Gulick and Lydall Urwick (editors), *Papers on the Science of Administration* (New York: Institute of Public Administration, Columbia University, 1937); Lydall Urwick, *The Elements of Administration* (New York, Harper, 1943); James D. Mooney and Alan C. Reiley, *The Prin-ciples of Organization* (New York: Harper, 1939); H. S. Dennison, *Organization Engineering* (New York: McGraw-Hill, 1931).

[5] Urwick, *The Elements of Administration, op. cit.,* p. 47.
[6] See Gaus, *op. cit.* Studies of the problem of morale are instances of the same orientation, having received considerable impetus in recent years from the work of the Harvard Business School group.

an organizational act, having to do with formal assignments of functions and powers. Theoretically, these assignments are made to roles or official positions, not to individuals as such. In fact, however, delegation necessarily involves concrete individuals who have interests and goals which do not always coincide with the goals of the formal system. As a consequence, individual personalities may offer resistance to the demands made upon them by the official conditions of delegation. These resistances are not accounted for within the categories of coordination and delegation, so that when they occur they must be considered as unpredictable and accidental. Observations of this type of situation within formal structures are sufficiently commonplace. A familiar example is that of delegation to a subordinate who is also required to train his own replacement. The subordinate may resist this demand in order to maintain unique access to the "mysteries" of the job, and thus insure his indispensability to the organization.

In large organizations, deviations from the formal system tend to become institutionalized, so that "unwritten laws" and informal associations are established. Institutionalization removes such deviations from the realm of personality differences, transforming them into a persistent structural aspect of formal organizations.[7] These institutionalized rules and modes of informal cooperation are normally attempts by participants in the formal organization to control the group relations which form the environment of organizational decisions. The informal patterns (such as cliques) arise spontaneously, are based on personal relationships, and are usually directed to the control of some specific situation. They may be generated anywhere within a hierarchy, often with deleterious consequences for the formal

goals of the organization, but they may also function to widen the available resources of executive control and thus contribute to rather than hinder the achievement of the stated objectives of the organization. The deviations tend to force a shift away from the purely formal system as the effective determinant of behavior to (1) a condition in which informal patterns buttress the formal, as through the manipulation of sentiment within the organization in favor of established authority; or (2) a condition wherein the informal controls effect a consistent modification of formal goals, as in the case of some bureaucratic patterns.[8] This trend will eventually result in the formalization of erstwhile informal activities, with the cycle of deviation and transformation beginning again on a new level.

The relevance of informal structures to organizational analysis underlines the significance of conceiving of formal organizations as cooperative systems. When the totality of interacting groups and individuals becomes the object of inquiry, the latter is not restricted by formal, legal, or procedural dimensions. The *state of the system* emerges as a significant point of analysis, as when an internal situation charged with conflict qualifies and informs actions ostensibly determined by formal relations and objectives. A proper understanding of the organizational process must make it possible to interpret changes in the formal system—new appointments or rules or reorganizations—in their relation to the informal and unavowed ties of friendship, class loyalty, power cliques, or external commitment. This is what it means "to know the score."

The fact that the involvement of individuals as whole personalities tends to limit the adequacy of formal systems of coordination does not mean that organizational characteristics are those of individuals. The organic, emergent character of the formal organization considered as a cooperative system must be recognized. This means that the

[7] The creation of informal structures within various types of organizations has received explicit recognition in recent years. See F. J. Roethlisberger and W. J. Dickson, *Management and the Worker* (Cambridge: Harvard University Press, 1941), p. 524; also Barnard, *op. cit.*, c. ix; and Wilbert E. Moore, *Industrial Relations and the Social Order* (New York: Macmillan, 1946), chap. xv.

[8] For an analysis of the latter in these terms, see Philip Selznick, "An Approach to a Theory of Bureaucracy," *American Sociological Review*, Vol. VIII, No. 1 (February, 1943).

organization reaches decisions, takes action, and makes adjustments. Such a view raises the question of the relation between organizations and persons. The significance of theoretical emphasis upon the cooperative *system* as such is derived from the insight that certain actions and consequences are enjoined independently of the personality of the individuals involved. Thus, if reference is made to the "organization-paradox"—the tension created by the inhibitory consequences of certain types of informal structures within organizations—this does not mean that individuals themselves are in quandaries. It is the nature of the interacting consequences of divergent interests within the organization which creates the condition, a result which may obtain independently of the consciousness or the qualities of the individual participants. Similarly, it seems useful to insist that there are qualities and needs of leader*ship,* having to do with position and role, which are persistent despite variations in the character or personality of individual leaders themselves.

Rational action systems are characteristic of both individuals and organizations. The conscious attempt to mobilize available internal resources (e.g., self-discipline) for the achievement of a stated goal—referred to here as an economy or a formal system—is one aspect of individual psychology. But the personality considered as a dynamic system of interacting wishes, compulsions, and restraints defines a system which is at once essential and yet potentially deleterious to what may be thought of as the "economy of learning" or to individual rational action. At the same time, the individual personality is an adaptive structure, and this, too, requires a broader frame of reference for analysis than the categories of rationality. On a different level, although analogously, we have pointed to the need to consider organizations as cooperative systems and adaptive structures in order to explain the context of and deviations from the formal systems of delegation and coordination.

To recognize the sociological relevance of formal structures is not, however, to have constructed a theory of organization. It is important to set the framework of analysis, and much is accomplished along this line when, for example, the nature of authority in formal organizations is reinterpreted to emphasize the factors of cohesion and persuasion as against legal or coercive sources.[9] This redefinition is logically the same as that which introduced the conception of the self as social. The latter helps make possible, but does not of itself fulfill, the requirements for a dynamic theory of personality. In the same way, the definition of authority as conditioned by sociological factors of sentiment and cohesion—or more generally the definition of formal organizations as cooperative systems—only sets the stage, as an initial requirement, for the formulation of a theory of organization.

STRUCTURAL-FUNCTIONAL ANALYSIS

Cooperative systems are constituted of individuals interacting as wholes in relation to a formal system of coordination. The concrete structure is therefore a resultant of the reciprocal influences of the formal and informal aspects of organization. Furthermore, this structure is itself a totality, an adaptive "organism" reacting to influences upon it from an external environment. These considerations help to define the objects of inquiry; but to progress to a system of predicates *about* these objects it is necessary to set forth an analytical method which seems to be fruitful and significant. The method must have a relevance to empirical materials, which is to say, it must be more specific in its reference than discussions of the logic or methodology of social science.

The organon which may be suggested as peculiarly helpful in the analysis of adaptive structures has been referred to as "structural-functional analysis."[10] This method

---

[9] Robert Michels, "Authority," *Encyclopedia of the Social Sciences* (New York: Macmillan, 1931), pp. 319ff.; also Barnard, *op. cit.,* c. xii.

[10] For a presentation of this approach having a more general reference than the study of formal organizations, see Talcott Parsons, "The Present Position and Prospects of Systematic Theory in Sociology," in Georges Gurvitch and Wilbert E. Moore (ed.), *Twentieth Century Sociology* (New York: The Philosophical Library, 1945).

may be characterized in a sentence: *Structural-functional analysis relates contemporary and variable behavior to a presumptively stable system of needs and mechanisms*. This means that a given empirical system is deemed to have basic needs, essentially related to self-maintenance; the system develops repetitive means of self-defense; and day-to-day activity is interpreted in terms of the function served by that activity for the maintenance and defense of the system. Put thus generally, the approach is applicable on any level in which the determinate "states" of empirically isolable systems undergo self-impelled and repetitive transformations when impinged upon by external conditions. This self-impulsion suggests the relevance of the term "dynamic," which is often used in referring to physiological, psychological, or social systems to which this type of analysis has been applied.[11]

It is a postulate of the structural-functional approach that the basic need of all empirical systems is the maintenance of the integrity and continuity of the system itself. Of course, such a postulate is primarily useful in directing attention to a set of "derived imperatives" or needs which are sufficiently concrete to characterize the system at hand.[12] It is perhaps rash to attempt a catalogue of these imperatives for formal or-ganizations, but some suggestive formulation is needed in the interests of setting forth the type of analysis under discussion. In formal organizations, the "maintenance of the system" as a generic need may be specified in terms of the following imperatives:

(1) *The security of the organization as a whole in relation to social forces in its environment*. This imperative requires continuous attention to the possibilities of encroachment and to the forestalling of threatened aggressions or deleterious (though perhaps unintended) consequences from the actions of others.

(2) *The stability of the lines of authority and communication*. One of the persistent reference-points of administrative decision is the weighing of consequences for the continued capacity of leadership to control and to have access to the personnel or ranks.

(3) *The stability of informal relations within the organization*. Ties of sentiment and self-interest are evolved as unacknowledged but effective mechanisms of adjustment of individuals and sub-groups to the conditions of life within the organization. These ties represent a cementing of relationships which sustains the formal authority in day-to-day operations and widens opportunities for effective communication.[13] Consequently, attempts to "upset" the informal structure, either frontally or as an indirect consequence of formal reorganization, will normally be met with considerable resistance.

(4) *The continuity of policy and of the sources of its determination*. For each level within the organization, and for the organization as a whole, it is necessary that there be a sense that action taken in the light of a given policy will not be placed in continuous jeopardy. Arbitrary or unpredictable changes in policy undermine the significance of (and therefore the attention to) day-to-day action by injecting a note of capriciousness. At the same time, the organization will seek stable roots (or firm statutory authority or popular mandate) so that a sense of the perma-

---

[11] "Structure" refers to both the relationships within the system (formal plus informal patterns in organization) and the set of needs and modes of satisfaction which characterize the given type of empirical system. As the utilization of this type of analysis proceeds, the concept of "need" will require further clarification. In particular, the imputation of a "stable set of needs" to organizational systems must not function as a new instinct theory. At the same time, we cannot avoid using these inductions as to generic needs, for they help us to stake out our area of inquiry. The author is indebted to Robert K. Merton who has, in correspondence, raised some important objections to the use of the term "need" in this context.

[12] For "derived imperative" see Bronislaw Malinowski, *The Dynamics of Culture Change* (New Haven: Yale University Press, 1945), pp. 44ff. For the use of "need" in place of "motive" see the same author's *A Scientific Theory of Culture* (Chapel Hill: University of North Carolina Press, 1944), pp. 89-90.

[13] They may also *destroy* those relationships, as noted above, but the need remains, generating one of the persistent dilemmas of leadership.

nency and legitimacy of its acts will be achieved.

(5) *A homogeneity of outlook with respect to the meaning and role of the organization.* The minimization of disaffection requires a unity derived from a common understanding of what the character of the organization is meant to be. When this homogeneity breaks down, as in situations of internal conflict over basic issues, the continued existence of the organization is endangered. On the other hand, one of the signs of "healthy" organization is the ability to effectively orient new members and readily slough off those who cannot be adapted to the established outlook.

This catalogue of needs cannot be thought of as final, but it approximates the stable system generally characteristic of formal organizations. These imperatives are derived, in the sense that they represent the conditions for survival or self-maintenance of cooperative systems of organized action. An inspection of these needs suggests that organizational survival is intimately connected with the struggle for relative prestige, both for the organization and for elements and individuals within it. It may therefore be useful to refer to a *prestige-survival motif* in organizational behavior as a short-hand way of relating behavior to needs, especially when the exact nature of the needs remains in doubt. However, it must be emphasized that prestige-survival in organizations does not derive simply from like motives in individuals. Loyalty and self-sacrifice may be individual expressions of organizational or group egotism and self-consciousness.

The concept of organizational need directs analysis to the *internal relevance* of organizational behavior. This is especially pertinent with respect to discretionary action undertaken by agents manifestly in pursuit of formal goals. The question then becomes one of relating the specific act of discretion to some presumptively stable organizational need. In other words, it is not simply action plainly oriented internally (such as in-service training) but also action presumably oriented externally which must be inspected for its relevance to internal conditions. This

is of prime importance for the understanding of bureaucratic behavior, for it is of the essence of the latter that action formally undertaken for substantive goals be weighed and transformed in terms of its consequences for the position of the officialdom.

Formal organizations as cooperative systems on the one hand, and individual personalities on the other, involve structural-functional homologies, a point which may help to clarify the nature of this type of analysis. If we say that the individual has a stable set of needs, most generally the need for maintaining and defending the integrity of his personality or ego; that there are recognizable certain repetitive mechanisms which are utilized by the ego in its defense (rationalization, projection, regression, etc.); and that overt and variable behavior may be interpreted in terms of its relation to these needs and mechanisms—on the basis of this logic we may discern the typical pattern of structural-functional analysis as set forth above. In this sense, it is possible to speak of a "Freudian model" for organizational analysis. This does not mean that the substantive insights of individual psychology may be applied to organizations, as in vulgar extrapolations from the individual ego to whole nations or (by a no less vulgar inversion) from strikes to frustrated workers. It is the *logic*, the *type* of analysis which is pertinent.

This homology is also instructive in relation to the applicability of generalizations to concrete cases. The dynamic theory of personality states a set of possible predicates about the ego and its mechanisms of defense, which inform us concerning the propensities of individual personalities under certain general circumstances. But these predicates provide only tools for the analysis of particular individuals, and each concrete case must be examined to tell which operate and in what degree. They are not primarily organs of prediction. In the same way, the predicates within the theory of organization will provide tools for the analysis of particular cases. Each organization, like each personality, represents a resultant of complex forces, an empirical entity which no single relation or no simple formula can explain. The problem of analysis becomes that of selecting among the possible predicates set forth in the theory of organization those which illuminate our understanding of the materials at hand.

The setting of structural-functional analysis as applied to organizations requires some qualification, however. Let us entertain the suggestion that the interesting problem in social science is not so much why men act the way they do as why men in certain circumstances *must* act the way they do. This emphasis upon constraint, if accepted, releases us from an ubiquitous attention to behavior in general, and especially from any undue fixation upon statistics. On the other hand, it has what would seem to be the salutary consequence of focusing inquiry upon certain necessary relationships of the type "if . . . then," for example: If the cultural level of the rank and file members of a formally democratic organization is below that necessary for participation in the formulation of policy, then there will be pressure upon the leaders to use the tools of demagogy.

Is such a statement universal in its applicability? Surely not in the sense that one can predict without remainder the nature of all or even most political groups in a democracy. Concrete behavior is a resultant, a complex vector, shaped by the operation of a number of such general constraints. But there is a test of general applicability: it is that of noting whether the relation made explicit must be *taken into account* in action. This criterion represents an empirical test of the significance of social science generalizations. If a theory is significant it will state a relation which will either (1) be taken into account as an element of achieving control; or (2) be ignored only at the risk of losing control and will evidence itself in a ramification of objective or unintended consequences.[14] It is a corollary of this principle of significance that investigation must

search out the underlying factors in organizational action, which requires a kind of intensive analysis of the same order as psychoanalytic probing.

A frame of reference which invites attention to the constraints upon behavior will tend to highlight tensions and dilemmas, the characteristic paradoxes generated in the course of action. The dilemma may be said to be the handmaiden of structural-functional analysis, for it introduces the concept of *commitment* or *involvement* as fundamental to organizational analysis. A dilemma in human behavior is represented by an inescapable commitment which cannot be reconciled with the needs of the organism or the social system. There are many spurious dilemmas which have to do with verbal contradictions, but inherent dilemmas to which we refer are of a more profound sort, for they reflect the basic nature of the empirical system in question. An economic order committed to profit as its sustaining incentive may, in Marxist terms, sow the seed of its own destruction. Again, the anguish of man, torn between finitude and pride, is not a matter of arbitrary and replaceable assumptions but is a reflection of the psychological needs of the human organism, and is concretized in his commitment to the institutions which command his life; he is in the world and of it, inescapably involved in its goals and demands; at the same time, the needs of the spirit are compelling, proposing modes of salvation which have continuously disquieting consequences for worldly involvements. In still another context, the need of the human organism for affection and response necessitates a commitment to elements of the culture which can provide them; but the rule of the super-ego is uncertain since it cannot be completely reconciled with the need for libidinal satisfactions.

Applying this principle to organizations we may note that there is a general source

---

[14] See R. M. MacIver's discussion of the "dynamic assessment" which "brings the external world selectively into the subjective realm, conferring on it subjective significance for the ends of action." *Social Causation* (Boston: Ginn, 1942), chaps. 11, 12.

The analysis of this assessment within the context of organized action yields the implicit knowledge which guides the choice among alternatives. See also Robert K. Merton, "The Unanticipated Consequences of Purposive Social Action," *American Sociological Review*, I, 6 (December, 1936).

of tension observable in the split between "the motion and the act." Plans and programs reflect the freedom of technical or ideal choice, but organized action cannot escape involvement, a commitment to personnel or institutions or procedures which effectively qualifies the initial plan. *Der Mensch denkt, Gott lenkt*. In organized action, this ultimate wisdom finds a temporal meaning in the recalcitrance of the tools of action. We are inescapably committed to the mediation of human structures which are at once indispensable to our goals and at the same time stand between them and ourselves. The selection of agents generates immediately a bifurcation of interest, expressed in new centers of need and power, placing effective constraints upon the arena of action, and resulting in tensions which are never completely resolved. This is part of what it means to say that there is a "logic" of action which impels us forward from one undesired position to another. Commitment to dynamic, self-activating tools is of the nature of organized action; at the same time, the need for continuity of authority, policy, and character are pressing, and require an unceasing effort to master the instruments generated in the course of action. This generic tension is specified within the terms of each cooperative system. But for all we find a persistent relationship between *need* and *commitment* in which the latter not only qualifies the former but unites with it to produce a continuous state of tension. In this way, the notion of constraint (as reflected in tension or paradox) at once widens and more closely specifies the frame of reference for organizational analysis.

For Malinowski, the core of functionalism was contained in the view that a cultural fact must be analyzed in its setting. Moreover, he apparently conceived of his method as pertinent to the analysis of all aspects of cultural systems. But there is a more specific problem, one involving a principle of selection which serves to guide inquiry along significant lines. Freud conceived of the human organism as an adaptive structure, but he was not concerned with all human needs, nor with all phases of adaptation. For his system, he selected those needs whose expression is blocked in some way, so that such terms as repression, inhibition, and frustration became crucial. All conduct may be thought of as derived from need, and all adjustment represents the reduction of need. But not all needs are relevant to the systematics of dynamic psychology; and it is not adjustment as such but reaction to frustration which generates the characteristic modes of defensive behavior.

Organizational analysis, too, must find its selective principle; otherwise the indiscriminate attempts to relate activity functionally to needs will produce little in the way of significant theory. Such a principle might read as follows: *Our frame of reference is to select out those needs which cannot be fulfilled within approved avenues of expression and thus must have recourse to such adaptive mechanisms as ideology and to the manipulation of formal processes and structures in terms of informal goals*. This formulation has many difficulties, and is not presented as conclusive, but it suggests the kind of principle which is likely to separate the quick and the dead, the meaningful and the trite, in the study of cooperative systems in organized action.[15]

The frame of reference outlined here for the theory of organization may now be identified as involving the following major ideas: (1) the concept of organizations as cooperative systems, adaptive social structures, made up of interacting individuals, sub-groups, and informal plus formal relationships; (2) structural-functional analysis, which relates variable aspects of organization (such as goals) to stable needs and self-defensive mechanisms; (3) the concept of recalcitrance as a quality of the tools of social action, involving a break in the continuum of adjustment and defining an environment of constraint, commitment, and tension. This frame of reference is suggested as providing a specifiable *area of relations* within which

---

[15] This is not meant to deprecate the study of organizations as *economies* or formal systems. The latter represent an independent level, abstracted from organizational structures as cooperative or adaptive systems ("organisms").

predicates in the theory of organization will be sought, and at the same time setting forth principles of selection and relevance in our approach to the data of organization.

It will be noted that we have set forth this frame of reference within the over-all context of social action. The significance of events may be defined by their place and operational role in a means-end scheme. If functional analysis searches out the elements important for the maintenance of a given structure, and that structure is one of the materials to be manipulated in action, then that which is functional in respect to the structure is also functional in respect to the action system. This provides a ground for the significance of functionally derived theories. At the same time, relevance to control in action is the empirical test of their applicability or truth.

COOPTATION AS A MECHANISM OF ADJUSTMENT

The frame of reference stated above is in fact an amalgam of definition, resolution, and substantive theory. There is an element of *definition* in conceiving of formal organizations as cooperative systems, though of course the interaction of informal and formal patterns is a question of fact; in a sense, we are *resolving* to employ structural-functional analysis on the assumption that it will be fruitful to do so, though here, too, the specification of needs or derived imperatives is a matter for empirical inquiry; and our predication of recalcitrance as a quality of the tools of action is itself a *substantive theory*, perhaps fundamental to a general understanding of the nature of social action.

A theory of organization requires more than a general frame of reference, though the latter is indispensable to inform the approach of inquiry to any given set of materials. What is necessary is the construction of generalizations concerning transformations within and among cooperative systems. These generalizations represent, from the standpoint of particular cases, possible predicates which are relevant to the materials as we know them in general, but which are not necessarily controlling in all

circumstances. A theory of transformations in organization would specify those states of the system which resulted typically in predictable, or at least understandable, changes in such aspects of organization as goals, leadership, doctrine, efficiency, effectiveness, and size. These empirical generalizations would be systematized as they were related to the stable needs of the cooperative system.

Changes in the characteristics of organizations may occur as a result of many different conditions, not always or necessarily related to the processes of organization as such. But the theory of organization must be selective, so that explanations of transformations will be sought within its own assumptions or frame of reference. Consider the question of size. Organizations may expand for many reasons—the availability of markets, legislative delegations, the swing of opinion—which may be accidental from the point of view of the organizational process. To explore changes in size (as of, say, a trades union) as related to changes in nonorganizational conditions may be necessitated by the historical events to be described, but it will not of itself advance the frontiers of the theory of organization. However, if "the innate propensity of all organizations to expand" is asserted as a function of "the inherent instability of incentives"[16] then transformations have been stated within the terms of the theory of organization itself. It is likely that in many cases the generalization in question may represent only a minor aspect of the empirical changes, but these organizational relations must be made explicit if the theory is to receive development.

In a frame of reference which specifies needs and anticipates the formulation of a set of self-defensive responses or mechanisms, the latter appear to constitute one kind of empirical generalization or "possible predicate" within the general theory. The needs of organizations (whatever investigation may determine them to be) are posited as attributes of all organizations, but the responses to disequilibrium will be varied.

---

[16] Barnard, *op. cit.*, pp. 158-9.

The mechanisms used by the system in fulfillment of its needs will be repetitive and thus may be described as a specifiable set of assertions within the theory of organization, but any given organization may or may not have recourse to the characteristic modes of response. Certainly no given organization will employ all of the possible mechanisms which are theoretically available. When Barnard speaks of an "innate propensity of organization to expand" he is in fact formulating one of the general mechanisms, namely, expansion, which is a characteristic mode of response available to an organization under pressure from within. These responses necessarily involve a transformation (in this case, size) of some structural aspect of the organization.

Other examples of the self-defensive mechanisms available to organizations may derive primarily from the response of these organizations to the institutional environments in which they live. The tendency to construct ideologies, reflecting the need to come to terms with major social forces, is one such mechanism. Less well understood as a mechanism of organizational adjustment is what we may term *cooptation*. Some statement of the meaning of this concept may aid in clarifying the foregoing analysis.

Cooptation is the process of absorbing new elements into the leadership or policy-determining structure of an organization as a means of averting threats to its stability or existence. This is a defensive mechanism, formulated as one of a number of possible predicates available for the interpretation of organizational behavior. Cooptation tells us something about the process by which an institutional environment impinges itself upon an organization and effects changes in its leadership and policy. Formal authority may resort to cooptation under the following general conditions:

(1) When there exists a hiatus between consent and control, so that the legitimacy of the formal authority is called into question. The "indivisibility" of consent and control refers, of course, to an optimum situation. Where control lacks an adequate measure of consent, it may revert to coercive measures or attempt somehow to win the consent of the governed. One means of winning consent is to coopt elements into the leadership or organization, usually elements which in some way reflect the sentiment, or possess the confidence of the relevant public or mass. As a result, it is expected that the new elements will lend respectability or legitimacy to the organs of control and thus reestablish the stability of formal authority. This process is widely used, and in many different contexts. It is met in colonial countries, where the organs of alien control reaffirm their legitimacy by coopting native leaders into the colonial administration. We find it in the phenomenon of "crisis-patriotism" wherein normally disfranchised groups are temporarily given representation in the councils of government in order to win their solidarity in a time of national stress. Cooptation is presently being considered by the United States Army in its study of proposals to give enlisted personnel representation in the court-martial machinery—a clearly adaptive response to stresses made explicit during the war, the lack of confidence in the administration of army justice. The "unity" parties of totalitarian states are another form of cooptation; company unions or some employee representation plans in industry are still another. In each of these cases, the response of formal authority (private or public, in a large organization or a small one) is an attempt to correct a state of imbalance by *formal* measures. It will be noted, moreover, that what is shared is the *responsibility* for power rather than power itself. These conditions define what we shall refer to as *formal cooptation.*

(2) Cooptation may be a response to the pressure of specific centers of power. This is not necessarily a matter of legitimacy or of a general and diffuse lack of confidence. These may be well established; and yet organized forces which are able to threaten the formal authority may effectively shape its structure and policy. The organization in respect to its institutional environment—or the leadership in respect to its ranks—must take these forces into account. As a consequence, the outside elements may be brought into

the leadership or policy-determining structure, may be given a place as a recognition of and concession to the resources they can independently command. The representation of interests through administrative constituencies is a typical example of this process. Or, within an organization, individuals upon whom the group is dependent for funds or other resources may insist upon and receive a share in the determination of policy. This form of cooptation is typically expressed in informal terms, for the problem is not one of responding to a state of imbalance with respect to the "people as a whole" but rather one of meeting the pressure of specific individuals or interest-groups which are in a position to enforce demands. The latter are interested in the substance of power and not its forms. Moreover, an open acknowledgement of capitulation to specific interests may itself undermine the sense of legitmacy of the formal authority within the community. Consequently, there is a positive pressure to refrain from explicit recognition of the relationship established. This form of the cooptative mechanism, having to do with the sharing of power as a response to specific pressures, may be termed *informal cooptation.*

Cooptation reflects a state of tension between formal authority and social power. The former is embodied in a particular structure and leadership, but the latter has to do with subjective and objective factors which control the loyalties and potential manipulability of the community. Where the formal authority is an expression of social power, its stability is assured. On the other hand, when it becomes divorced from the sources of social power its continued existence is threatened. This threat may arise from the sheer alienation of sentiment or from the fact that other leaderships have control over the sources of social power. Where a formal authority has been accustomed to the assumption that its constitu-

ents respond to it as individuals, there may be a rude awakening when organization of those constituents on a non-governmental basis creates nuclei of power which are able effectively to demand a sharing of power.[17]

The significance of cooptation for organizational analysis is not simply that there is a change in or a broadening of leadership, and that this is an adaptive response, but also that *this change is consequential for the character and role of the organization.* Cooptation involves commitment, so that the groups to which adaptation has been made constrain the field of choice available to the organization or leadership in question. The character of the coopted elements will necessarily shape (inhibit or broaden) the modes of action available to the leadership which has won adaptation and security at the price of commitment. The concept of cooptation thus implicity sets forth the major points of the frame of reference outlined above: it is an adaptive response of a co-operative system to a stable need, generating transformations which reflect constraints enforced by the recalcitrant tools of action.

----

[17] It is perhaps useful to restrict the concept of cooptation to formal organizations, but in fact it probably reflects a process characteristic of all group leaderships. This has received some recognition in the analysis of class structure, wherein the ruling class is interpreted as protecting its own stability by absorbing new elements. Thus Michels made the point that "an aristocracy cannot maintain an enduring stability by sealing itself off hermetically." See Robert Michels, *Umschichtungen in den herrschenden Klassen nach dem Kriege* (Stuttgart: Kohlhammer, 1934), p. 39; also Gaetano Mosca, *The Ruling Class* (New York: McGraw-Hill, 1939), p. 413ff. The alliance or amalgamation of classes in the face of a common threat may be reflected in formal and informal cooptative responses among formal organizations sensitive to class pressures. In a forthcoming volume, *TVA and the Grass Roots,* the author has made extensive use of the concept of cooptation in analyzing some aspects of the organizational behavior of a government agency.

BY FRANCIS P. PURCELL AND HARRY SPECHT

The House on Sixth Street

THE EXTENT TO WHICH social work can affect the course of social problems has not received the full consideration it deserves.[1] For some time the social work profession has taken account of social problems only as they have become manifest in behavioral pathology. Yet it is becoming increasingly apparent that, even allowing for this limitation, it is often necessary for the same agency or worker to intervene by various methods at various points.

In this paper, the case history of a tenement house in New York City is used to illustrate some of the factors that should be considered in selecting intervention methods. Like all first attempts, the approach described can be found wanting in conceptual clarity and systematization. Yet the vital quality of the effort and its implications for social work practice seem clear.

The case of "The House on Sixth Street" is taken from the files of Mobilization For

Youth (MFY), an action-research project that has been in operation since 1962 on New York's Lower East Side.[2] MFY's programs are financed by grants from several public and private sources. The central theoretical contention of MFY is that a major proportion of juvenile delinquency occurs when adolescents from low-income families do not have access to legitimate opportunities by which they can fulfill the aspirations for success they share with all American youth. The action programs of MFY are designed to offer these youths concrete opportunities to offset the debilitating effects of poverty. For example, the employment program helps youngsters ob-

FRANCIS P. PURCELL, MSW, is now Professor of Social Work, Rutgers University, Graduate School of Social Work, New Brunswick, New Jersey. He was formerly Chief, Training and Personnel, Mobilization For Youth, New York, New York. HARRY SPECHT, Ph.D., now Assistant Executive Director, Research Projects, Contra Costa Council of Community Services, Walnut Creek, California, was formerly Assistant Chief, Community Development, Mobilization For Youth.

[1] Social work practitioners sometimes use the term "social problem" to mean "environmental problem." The sense in which it is used here corresponds to the definition developed by the social sciences. That is, a social problem is a disturbance, deviation, or breakdown in social behavior that (1) involves a considerable number of people and (2) is of serious concern to many in the society. It is social in origin and effect, and is a social responsibility. It represents a discrepancy between social standards and social reality. Also, such socially perceived variations must be viewed as corrigible. See Robert K. Merton and Robert A. Nisbet, eds., Contemporary Social Problems (New York: Harcourt, Brace, and World, 1961), pp. 6, 701.

[2] A complete case record of the Sixth Street house will be included in a forthcoming publication of Mobilization For Youth.

Reprinted with permission of the National Association of Social Workers, from SOCIAL WORK, Vol. 10, No. 4, (October 1965), pp. 69-76.

tain jobs; other programs attempt to increase opportunities in public schools. In addition, there are group work and recreation programs. A wide variety of services to individuals and families is offered through Neighborhood Service Centers: a homemaking program, a program for released offenders, and a narcotics information center. Legal services, a housing services unit, a special referral unit, and a community development program are among other services that have been developed or made available. Thus, MFY has an unusually wide range of resources for dealing with social problems.

THE PROBLEM

"The House on Sixth Street" became a case when Mrs. Smith came to an MFY Neighborhood Service Center to complain that there had been no gas, electricity, heat, or hot water in her apartment house for more than four weeks. She asked the agency for help. Mrs. Smith was 23 years old, Negro, and the mother of four children, three of whom had been born out of wedlock. At the time she was unmarried and receiving Aid to Families with Dependent Children. She came to the center in desperation because she was unable to run her household without utilities. Her financial resources were exhausted—but not her courage. The Neighborhood Service Center worker decided that in this case the building—the tenants, the landlord, and circumstances affecting their relationships—was of central concern.

A social worker then visited the Sixth Street building with Mrs. Smith and a community worker. Community workers are members of the community organization staff in a program that attempts to encourage residents to take independent social action. Like many members in other MFY programs, community workers are residents of the particular neighborhood. Most of them have little formal education, their special contribution being their ability to

relate to and communicate with other residents. Because some of the tenants were Puerto Rican, a Spanish-speaking community worker was chosen to accompany the social worker. His easy manner and knowledge of the neighborhood enabled him and the worker to become involved quickly with the tenants.

Their first visits confirmed Mrs. Smith's charge that the house had been without utilities for more than four weeks. Several months before, the city Rent and Rehabilitation Administration had reduced the rent for each apartment to one dollar a month because the landlord was not providing services. However, this agency was slow to take further action. Eleven families were still living in the building, which had twenty-eight apartments. The landlord owed the electric company several thousand dollars. Therefore, the meters had been removed from the house. Because most of the tenants were welfare clients, the Department of Welfare had "reimbursed" the landlord directly for much of the unpaid electric bill and refused to pay any more money to the electric company. The Department of Welfare was slow in meeting the emergency needs of the tenants. Most of the children (forty-eight from the eleven families in the building) had not been to school for a month because they were ill or lacked proper clothing.

The mothers were tired and demoralized. Dirt and disorganization were increasing daily. The tenants were afraid to sleep at night because the building was infested with rats. There was danger of fire because the tenants had to use candles for light. The seventeen abandoned apartments had been invaded by homeless men and drug addicts. Petty thievery is common in such situations. However, the mothers did not want to seek protection from the police for fear that they would chase away all men who were not part of the families in the building (some of the unmarried mothers had men living with them—one of the few means of protection from physical danger available to these women—even though mothers on public assistance are threatened with loss of income if they are not legally married). The anxiety created by these conditions was intense and disabling.

The workers noted that the mothers were not only anxious but "fighting mad"; not only did they seek immediate relief from their physical dangers and discomforts but they were eager to express their fury at the landlord and the public agencies, which they felt had let them down.

The circumstances described are by no means uncommon, at least not in New York City. Twenty percent of all housing in the city is still unfit, despite all the public and private residential building completed since World War II. At least 277,500 dwellings in New York City need major repairs if they are to become safe and adequate shelters. This means that approximately 500,000 people in the city live in inferior dwelling units and as many as 825,000 people in buildings that are considered unsafe.[3] In 1962 the New York City Bureau of Sanitary Inspections reported that 530 children were bitten by rats in their homes and 198 children were poisoned (nine of them fatally) by nibbling at peeling lead paint, even though the use of lead paint has been illegal in the city for more than ten years. Given the difficulties involved in lodging formal complaints with city agencies, it is safe to assume that unreported incidents of rat bites and lead poisoning far exceed these figures.

The effect of such hardships on children is obvious. Of even greater significance is the sense of powerlessness generated when families go into these struggles barehanded. It is this sense of helplessness in the face of adversity that induces pathological anxiety, intergenerational alienation, and social retreatism. Actual physical impoverishment alone is not nearly so debilitating as poverty attended by a sense of unrelieved

impotence that becomes generalized and internalized. The poor then regard much social learning as irrelevant, since they do not believe it can effect any environmental change.[4]

INTERVENTION AND THE SOCIAL SYSTEMS

Selecting a point of intervention in dealing with this problem would have been simpler if the target of change were Mrs. Smith alone, or Mrs. Smith and her co-tenants, the clients in whose behalf intervention was planned. Too often, the client system presenting the problem becomes the major target for intervention, and the intervention method is limited to the one most suitable for that client system. However, Mrs. Smith and the other tenants had a multitude of problems emanating from many sources, any one of which would have warranted the attention of a social agency. The circumstantial fact that in individual contacts an agency that offers services to individuals and families should not be a major factor in determining the method of intervention. Identification of the client merely helps the agency to define goals; other variables are involved in the selection of method. As Burns and Glasser have suggested:

> It may be helpful to consider the primary target of change as distinct from the persons who may be the primary clients. . . . The primary target of change then becomes the human or physical environment toward which professional efforts via direct intervention are aimed in order to facilitate change.[5]

The three major factors that determined

[3] *Facts About Low Income Housing* (New York: Emergency Committee For More Low Income Housing, 1963).

[4] Francis P. Purcell, "The Helping Professions and Problems of the Brief Contact," in Frank Riessman, Jerome Cohen, and Arthur Pearl, eds., *Mental Health of the Poor* (New York: Free Press of Glencoe, 1964), p. 432.

[5] Mary E. Burns and Paul H. Glasser, "Similarities and Differences in Casework and Group Work Practice," *Social Service Review*, Vol. 37, No. 4 (December 1963), p. 423.

MFY's approach to the problem were (1) knowledge of the various social systems within which the social problem was located (i.e., social systems assessment), (2) knowledge of the various methods (including non-social work methods) appropriate for intervention in these different social systems, and (3) the resources available to the agency.[6]

The difficulties of the families in the building were intricately connected with other elements of the social system related to the housing problem. For example, seven different public agencies were involved in maintenance of building services. Later other agencies were involved in relocating the tenants. There is no one agency in New York City that handles all housing problems. Therefore, tenants have little hope of getting help on their own. In order to redress a grievance relating to water supply (which was only one of the building's many problems) it is necessary to know precisely which city department to contact. The following is only a partial listing:

No water—Health Department
Not enough water—Department of Water Supply
No hot water—Buildings Department
Water leaks—Buildings Department
Large water leaks—Department of Water Supply
Water overflowing from apartment above—Police Department
Water sewage in the cellar—Sanitation Department

The task of determining which agencies are responsible for code enforcement in various areas is not simple, and in addition one must know that the benefits and services available for tenants and for the community vary with the course of action chosen. For example, if the building were taken over by the Rent and Rehabilitation Administra-

[6] Harry Specht and Frank Riessman, "Some Notes on a Model for an Integrated Social Work Approach to Social Problems" (New York: Mobilization For Youth, June 1963). (Mimeographed.)

tion under the receivership law, it would be several weeks before services would be re-established, and the tenants would have to remain in the building during its rehabilitation. There would be, however, some compensations: tenants could remain in the neighborhood—indeed, in the same building—and their children would not have to change schools. If, on the other hand, the house were condemned by the Buildings Department, the tenants would have to move, but they would be moved quickly and would receive top relocation priorities and maximum relocation benefits. But once the tenants had been relocated—at city expense—the building could be renovated by the landlord as middle-income housing. In the Sixth Street house, it was suspected that this was the motivation behind the landlord's actions. If the building were condemned and renovated, there would be twenty-eight fewer low-income housing units in the neighborhood.

This is the fate of scores of tenements on the Lower East Side because much new middle-income housing is being built there. Basic services are withheld and tenants are forced to move so that buildings may be renovated for middle-income tenants. Still other buildings are allowed to deteriorate with the expectation that they will be bought by urban renewal agencies.

It is obvious, even limiting analysis to the social systems of one tenement, that the problem is enormous. Although the tenants were the clients in this case, Mrs. Smith, the tenant group, and other community groups were all served at one point or another. It is even conceivable that the landlord might have been selected as the most appropriate recipient of service. Rehabilitation of many slum tenements is at present nearly impossible. Many landlords regard such property purely as an investment. With profit the prime motive, needs of low-income tenants are often overlooked. Under present conditions it is financially impossible for many landlords to correct all the violations in their buildings even if they wanted to. If the social worker chose to intervene at this level of the problem, he might apply to the Municipal Loan Fund, make arrangements with unions for the use of non-union labor in limited rehabilitation projects, or provide expert consultants on reconstruction. These tasks would require social workers to have knowledge similar to that of city planners. If the problems of landlords were not selected as a major point of intervention, they would still have to be considered at some time since they are an integral part of the social context within which this problem exists.

A correct definition of interacting social systems or of the social worker's choice of methods and points of intervention is not the prime concern here. What is to be emphasized is what this case so clearly demonstrates: that although the needs of the client system enable the agency to define its goals, the points and methods of intervention cannot be selected properly without an awareness and substantial knowledge of the social systems within which the problem is rooted.

DEALING WITH THE PROBLEM

The social worker remained with the building throughout a four-month period. In order to deal effectively with the problem, he had to make use of all the social work methods as well as the special talents of a community worker, lawyer, city planner, and various civil rights organizations. The social worker and the community worker functioned as generalists with both individuals and families calling on caseworkers as needed for specialized services or at especially trying times, such as during the first week and when the families were relocated. Because of the division of labor in the agency, much of the social work with individuals was done with the help of a caseworker. Group work, administration, and community organization were handled by the social worker, who had been trained in community organization. In many instances he also dealt with the mothers as individuals, as they encountered one stressful situation after another. Agency caseworkers also provided immediate and concrete assistance to individual families, such as small financial grants, medical care, homemaking services, baby-sitting services, and transportation. This reduced the intensity of pressures on these families. Caseworkers were especially helpful in dealing with some of the knotty and highly technical problems connected with public agencies.

With a caseworker and a lawyer experienced in handling tenement cases, the social worker began to help the families organize their demands for the services and utilities to which they were legally entitled but which the public agencies had consistently failed to provide for them.

The ability of the mothers to take concerted group action was evident from the beginning, and Mrs. Smith proved to be a natural and competent leader. With support, encouragement, and assistance from the staff, the mothers became articulate and effective in negotiating with the various agencies involved. In turn, the interest and concern of the agencies increased markedly when the mothers began to visit them, make frequent telephone calls, and send letters and telegrams to them and to politicians demanding action.

With the lawyer and a city planner (an agency consultant), the mothers and staff members explored various possible solutions to the housing problem. For example, the Department of Welfare had offered to move the families to shelters or hotels. Neither alternative was acceptable to the mothers. Shelters were ruled out because they would not consider splitting up their families, and they rejected hotels because they had discovered from previous experience that many of the "hotels" selected were flop-houses or were inhabited by prostitutes.

The following is taken from the social worker's record during the first week:

Met with the remaining tenants, several

Negro men from the block, and [the city planner]. . . . Three of the mothers said that they would sooner sleep out on the street than go to the Welfare shelter. If nothing else, they felt that this would be a way of protesting their plight . . . One of the mothers said that they couldn't very well do this with most of the children having colds. Mrs. Brown thought that they might do better to ask Reverend Jones if they could move into the cellar of his church temporarily. . . . The other mothers got quite excited about this idea because they thought that the church basement would make excellent living quarters.

After a discussion as to whether the mothers would benefit from embarrassing the public agencies by dramatically exposing their inadequacies, the mothers decided to move into the nearby church. They asked the worker to attempt to have their building condemned. At another meeting, attended by tenants from neighboring buildings and representatives of other local groups, it was concluded that what had happened to the Sixth Street building was a result of discrimination against the tenants as Puerto Ricans and Negroes. The group—which had now become an organization—sent the following telegram to city, state, and federal officials:

We are voters and Puerto Rican and Negro mothers asking for equal rights, for decent housing and enough room. Building has broken windows, no gas or electricity for four weeks, no heat or hot water, holes in floors, loose wiring. Twelve of forty-eight children in building sick. Welfare doctors refuse to walk up dark stairs. Are we human or what? Should innocent children suffer for landlords' brutality and city and state neglect? We are tired of being told to wait with children ill and unable to attend school. Negro and Puerto Rican tenants are forced out while buildings next door are renovated at high rents. We are not being treated as human beings.

For the most part, the lawyer and city planner stayed in the background, acting only as consultants. But as the tenants and worker became more involved with the courts and as other organizations entered the fight, the lawyer and city planner played a more active and direct role.

RESULTANT SIDE-EFFECTS

During this process, tenants in other buildings on the block became more alert to similar problems in their buildings. With the help of the community development staff and the housing consultant, local groups and organizations such as tenants' councils and the local chapter of the Congress of Racial Equality were enlisted to support and work with the mothers.

Some of the city agencies behaved as though MFY had engineered the entire scheme to embarrass them—steadfastly disregarding the fact that the building had been unlivable for many months. Needless to say, the public agencies are overloaded and have inadequate resources. As has been documented, many such bureaucracies develop an amazing insensitivity to the needs of their clients.[7] In this case, the MFY social worker believed that the tenants—and other people in their plight—should make their needs known to the agencies and to the public at large. He knew that when these expressions of need are backed by power—either in numbers or in political knowledge—they are far more likely to have some effect.

Other movements in the city at this time gave encouragement and direction to the people in the community. The March on Washington and the Harlem rent strike are two such actions.

By the time the families had been relocated, several things had been accomplished. Some of the public agencies had

7 See, for example, Reinhard Bendix, "Bureaucracy and the Problem of Power," in Robert K. Merton, Alisa Gray, Barbara Hockey, and Horan C. Sebrin, eds., Reader in Bureaucracy (Glencoe, Ill.: Free Press, 1952), pp. 114–134.

been sufficiently moved by the actions of the families and the local organizations to provide better services for them. When the families refused to relocate in a shelter and moved into a neighborhood church instead, one of the television networks picked up their story. Officials in the housing agencies came to investigate and several local politicians lent the tenants their support. Most important, several weeks after the tenants moved into the church, a bill was passed by the city council designed to prevent some of the abuses that the landlord had practiced with impunity. The councilman who sponsored the new law referred to the house on Sixth Street to support his argument.

Nevertheless, the problems that remain far outweigh the accomplishments. A disappointing epilogue to the story is that in court, two months later, the tenants' case against the landlord was dismissed by the judge on a legal technicality. The judge ruled that because the electric company had removed the meters from the building it was impossible for the landlord to provide services.

Some of the tenants were relocated out of the neighborhood and some in housing almost as poor as that they had left. The organization that began to develop in the neighborhood has continued to grow, but it is a painstaking job. The fact that the poor have the strength to continue to struggle for better living conditions is something to wonder at and admire.

IMPLICATIONS FOR PRACTICE

Social work helping methods as currently classified are so inextricably interwoven in practice that it no longer seems valid to think of a generic practice as consisting of the application of casework, group work, or community organization skills as the nature of the problem demands. Nor does it seem feasible to adapt group methods for traditional casework problems or to use group work skills in community organiza-

tion or community organization method in casework. Such suggestions—when they appear in the literature—either reflect confusion or, what is worse, suggest that no clearcut method exists apart from the auspices that support it.

In this case it is a manifestation of a social problem—housing—that was the major point around which social services were organized. The social worker's major intellectual task was to select the points at which the agency could intervene in the problem and the appropriate methods to use. It seems abundantly clear that in order to select appropriate points of intervention the social worker need not only understand individual patterns of response, but the nature of the social conditions that are the context in which behavior occurs. As this case makes evident, the social system that might be called the "poverty system" is enduring and persistent. Its parts intermesh with precision and disturbing complementarity. Intentionally or not, a function is thereby maintained that produces severe social and economic deprivation. Certain groups profit enormously from the maintenance of this system, but larger groups suffer. Social welfare—and, in particular, its central profession, social work—must examine the part it plays in either maintaining or undermining this socially pernicious poverty system. It is important that the social work profession no longer regard social conditions as immutable and a social reality to be accommodated as service is provided to deprived persons with an ever increasing refinement of technique. Means should be developed whereby agencies can affect social problems more directly, especially through institutional (organizational) change.

The idea advanced by MFY is that the social worker should fulfill his professional function and agency responsibility by seeking a solution to social problems through institutional change rather than by focusing on individual problems in social functioning. This is not to say that individual expressions of a given social problem should be left unattended. On the contrary, this approach is predicated on the belief that individual problems in social functioning are to varying degrees both cause and effect. It rejects the notion that individuals are afflicted with social pathologies, holding, rather, that the same social environment that generates conformity makes payment by the deviance that emerges. As Nisbet points out ". . . socially prized arrangements and values in society can produce socially condemned results." [8] This should direct social work's attention to institutional arrangements and their consequences. This approach does not lose sight of the individual or group, since the social system is composed of various statuses, roles, and classes. It takes cognizance of the systemic relationship of the various parts of the social system, including the client. It recognizes that efforts to deal with one social problem frequently generate others with debilitating results.

Thus it is that such institutional arrangements as public assistance, state prisons, and state mental hospitals, or slum schools are regarded by many as social problems in their own right. The social problems of poverty, criminality, mental illness, and failure to learn that were to be solved or relieved remain, and the proposed solutions pose almost equally egregious problems.

This paper has presented a new approach to social work practice. The knowledge, values, attitudes, and skills were derived from a generalist approach to social work. Agencies that direct their energies to social problems by effecting institutional change will need professional workers whose skills cut across the broad spectrum of social work knowledge.

---

[8] Merton and Nisbet, *op. cit.*, p. 7.

BY SALVATORE AMBROSINO

A Family Agency Reaches Out to a Slum Ghetto

CAN A FAMILY AGENCY help Negro youths and families who live in a ghetto of three thousand population, where more than 50 percent of the children come from broken homes, where 50 percent of the homes have been categorized as "deteriorating" or "dilapidated," where the median family income is $3,200, and where 80 percent of the youths are school dropouts?[1] Can family casework deal adequately with such a widespread and staggering array of problems? If not, is it the function of a family agency to undertake a broader job in order to help families—to branch out into new methods and work with a neighborhood and a total community?

The Family Service Association of Nassau County faced these questions in 1961 as it surveyed conditions in a section of Freeport, New York, an incorporated village with a population of 41,000. A slum ghetto in the village—one of eight seriously depressed areas in Nassau County—was in desperate need of rehabilitation. Meetings with officials of the area's federal low-income housing project confirmed the urgent need to reduce vandalism, delinquency, and family breakdown.

The agency, established in 1958, already

had the task of serving a county whose population was over one million. In addition, it had a long waiting list and received only 25 percent of its support from United Funds. The board of directors and staff, however, decided to accept the challenge and embark on broad-scale intervention.

This paper reviews the development and results of the Youth Service Project—a multiservice program to combat social problems—and points to an expanded role for family agencies in the planning and development of community institutions that affect family life. The Youth Service Project is designed to intervene strategically at different stages in the lives of youths and their families: before they are in difficulty, at the earliest point serious problems appear, and in the midst of crises. The project also intervenes through a variety of services: casework, social group work, a day camp, an interracial nursery school, tutoring, family life education, vocational guidance, and community planning through consultation with a neighborhood action group and a village community development organization. The current staff includes two full-time caseworkers, three full-time group workers, thirty part-time group work specialists and assistants, and approximately one hundred volunteers.

SALVATORE AMBROSINO, Ed.D., is Executive Director, Family Service Association of Nassau County, Mineola, New York. This paper was presented at the Biennial Meeting of Family Service Association of America, Detroit, Michigan, November 12, 1965.

[1] U. S. Bureau of the Census, 1960 Census of Population: General Social and Economic Characteristics (Washington, D. C.: U. S. Government Printing Office, 1961).

PROBLEMS OF THE COMMUNITY

As was anticipated, the problems were found to be so extreme, pervasive, and inextricably related to the social problems and institutions of the community that it was difficult to know where to pinpoint services in order to attain the most needed results. Throughout there has been a constant effort to refine a conceptual framework that establishes the priority of problems and guides the organization of services in the most effective manner. It was clear that only programs of sustained and maximum impact could break the strong patterns of despair that engulfed the community. The current framework places emphasis on three major areas:

1. Primary emphasis is on motivation of youths and families to utilize opportunities for education, employment, and social advancement. This phase of the project has been developed on the basis of a formulation that outlines these as the three major problems resulting from the youths' basic deficits.

2. Secondary emphasis is on social action —the participation of the ghetto community in the vital decisions of village life.

3. Finally, the third emphasis—in time perhaps the most significant—is the development of the village through comprehensive planning that considers human and physical needs and changing institutional functions at one and the same time. The community development concept, used in a number of urban centers such as New Haven and Boston, brings together key institutions of government, education, business, and social agencies in a combined effort to create a viable community to meet a population's broad and changing needs.

Helping youths and families to make use of their opportunities has required an intensive effort to understand the central problems that stand in the way. It is difficult to generalize about the quality of the children's home life, which ranges from extreme neglect to fairly adequate provision of supportive relationships. It is safer to generalize about the deficiencies that result from cultural, social, and economic deprivation. The basic fact is that the children are not vitally connected to life; they have not been encouraged to see, hear, or participate. A sense of nothingness, detachment, and profound frustration and fear of new experiences come from this limited encounter with life. They dip their toes in the water but cannot swim. This is true literally and figuratively and winds up in a progressive helplessness—an inability to give coherence and meaning to life's experiences.

As relationships between staff and children have grown, it has been seen that the children's difficulties have resulted not so much from neurotic conflicts—although these are in evidence—as from deficits in emotional development, support, and guidance; social development and identification; and ability to conceptualize and solve problems. This underdevelopment is expressed by a compelling need for immediate satisfaction and physical action, poor attention span, weak controls, and the lack of motivation and capacity to assimilate life's experiences rewardingly.

The plight of these children and youths was dramatically exposed in 1963 by the decision of the Freeport School Board to close the de facto segregated elementary school in the area served by the project. According to the results of school tests, each child was approximately two to three years behind in academic achievement. Therefore, the project was in the right spot at the right time to help them with this critical change, for which they were distressingly unprepared.

COMMUNITY CENTER PROGRAMS

In 1961 the Family Service Association requested the Freeport Housing Authority to construct a rent-free facility in a basement area of the housing project to be used as a Family Community Center. The center was completed in the fall of 1962.

This paper describes only briefly some of the programs of the Family Community Center, which serves about 325 children. Of this number, 275 children come from the target area, where it is estimated that there are 350 children between the ages of 5 and 18.

Fun and Learn Clubs. This was the first experimental program established to combat the dropout rate. The fourth-graders in the de facto segregated school—which was still in operation at that time—were chosen to strengthen them for junior high school—a critical adjustment period for the potential dropout and predelinquent. Thirty-four of the thirty-five fourth-graders were recruited for four Fun and Learn Clubs, which met twice a week with selected group leaders. A varied program of sports, trips, selected educational activities, homework help, and discussions of vital problems were attempted to motivate the children to extend their social, emotional, and intellectual skills. When they entered junior high school in the fall of 1965, after three years of participation in this special project, most of them had made notable progress in their social and emotional growth, including a number who were considered severe behavior problems at the beginning of the program. Although the staff was pleased with the results, it was troubled by the shortcomings that still remained, especially in the area of intellectual functioning.

Thinking Skills Project. This project is currently receiving the major attention. It is a truly experimental group work program designed for culturally deprived children. The project hypothesizes that the emotional, social, and intellectual components of development are closely related and mutually reinforcing. Therefore, a gain in overcoming thinking deficiencies will also bring relatively greater progress in social and emotional growth. The focus is on the specific cognitive deficiencies of the children—their inability to label and name things, to classify and compare, to form and articulate concepts—as well as

their social and emotional adjustment. The method is to identify specific cognitive deficits or deficiency in thinking skills and then to select and redesign certain group work activities to provide members with progressive opportunities to enhance skills in these areas.

The program, which has drawn on the experiments of Dr. Martin Deutsch with culturally deprived preschool children, began in October 1964 with two groups of first-graders and one group of second-graders, of twelve children each.[2] The groups met twice a week after school with a trained leader and an assistant through June 1965. The children were tested by a procedure devised at the Institute for Developmental Studies.[3] Findings showed them to be seriously behind a control group of white middle-class children in visual and auditory discrimination and language usage.

An evaluation of the Thinking Skills Project indicates it has been successful.[4] Evaluation of the progress of the groups and individual children by group leaders and schoolteachers also indicates that significant changes did occur. An outstanding change was the obvious increase in attention span of all the children. In addition to an improvement in thinking skills, the children showed significant advances in their ability to participate in group activities, control their behavior, and accept

[2] Martin Deutsch, "The Disadvantaged Child and the Learning Process," in A. H. Passow, ed., *Education in Depressed Areas* (New York: Teachers College, 1963), pp. 163–179; Deutsch, "Minority Group and Class Status as Related to Social and Personality Factors in Scholastic Achievement," Monograph 2 (Ithaca, New York: Society for Applied Anthropology, 1960).

[3] Shirley Feldmann and Ida May Mahler, "Reading Prognosis Test" (New York: New York Medical College Institute for Developmental Studies, 1963). (Mimeographed.)

[4] On the basis of tests administered in October 1965 and June 1966 to one experimental group and one control group, improvement shown by the experimental group proved to be statistically significant at the .05 level. Family Service Association of Nassau County, "Social Group Work Thinking Skills Project," unpublished report, Mineola, New York, June 1966.

adult leadership—all areas of importance in school and life adjustment.

Verbal Interaction Project. From the knowledge and experience gained in the Thinking Skills Project, the Youth Service Project developed a plan to help prevent or minimize the cognitive deficits of the disadvantaged children. The pilot phase of this project focuses on the mothers of 2-year-old children, who are at the stage of beginning language and thought development. The disadvantaged mother generally talks infrequently to her young child and does not know how to play with him. The approach chosen was to help the mother and child interact in a verbally meaningful way around basic concepts (visual and auditory discrimination, simple labeling and classification, perceptual-motor co-ordination, and the like). Caseworkers visit the home and demonstrate the use of selected toys, games, and books to the mother and child and review materials on subsequent visits. A preliminary analysis of the test data indicates that the experiment has been favorable. The children in the experimental group showed a gain of 15 percent in IQ, while the control group showed virtually no change.[5] Although the number of children involved is too small (six children) to warrant definitive conclusions, the results point strongly to the impact of this program on disadvantaged families.

Casework. A most distinctive feature of the project is that casework is not an adjunctive service as in most settlement houses and community centers. Instead, it is meshed completely with all the services offered. The caseworkers' assignments include consultation to the nursery school, group work projects, the social action group, and shared responsibility with group work-

5 Phyllis Levenstein, "Project Verbal Interaction— The Fostering of Verbal Intelligence in Culturally Deprived Two-Year-Old Children Through Stimulation of Verbal Interaction in Mother-Child Dyads: A Final Report" (Mineola, N. Y.: Family Service Association of Nassau County, July 1966). (Mimeographed.)

ers to plan and conduct a variety of parent education meetings. Interestingly, a caseworker formulated much of the theoretical framework for the Thinking Skills Project and served as co-ordinator of staff seminars. Primary attention is focused on families of children and youths who attend the center. Teachers' and group workers' reports are used to classify children and youths in one of three categories: adjusting satisfactorily; some problems in school, at home, or at the center; or serious academic and/or behavior problems. Caseworkers and group workers, on a priority basis, plan jointly for reaching out to youths and families to establish treatment objectives and to determine the appropriate functions of the caseworker, group worker, case aide, and other personnel. Other agencies are often involved as well.

Nursery school. The predominantly white, middle-class co-operative nursery school is another integral part of the project. The Family Community Center provides space to the nursery in exchange for scholarships to Negro children in the area. The arrangement has created an enlightening and rewarding experiment in intergroup relations. Of further significance is that the neighborhood children who have attended the nursery school in the past four years have made excellent progress in kindergarten, as contrasted with those who have not attended.

Tutoring. The development of a tutoring program, which could not be undertaken by the school system following desegregation of the neighborhood school in 1963, has received much attention and has had to overcome a number of complications. The project, although hesitant to take on a responsibility that more properly belonged to the school, created a homework help center to fill the vacuum. While a number of children and youths benefited from the initial program, there were many limitations: attendance was uneven, the children played the understandable game of asking for help with subjects they knew best in order to impress the tutors, the tutors were often unsure whether to focus assistance on the immediate homework assignment or on more basic deficiencies. Furthermore, although some children and tutors formed close ties, there was no provision for a "big brother" or continuous relationship between child and volunteer.

In 1964 the project co-sponsored an improved program with the Freeport schools. It was responsible for recruitment and orientation of volunteers and the school was responsible for supervision of the tutors and seminar training. In the present design teachers select third- to fifth-year pupils to meet with volunteer tutors twice a week during or after school to work on a remedial program outlined by the teachers. Most of the children who are participating come from the slum ghetto and from a racially changing area that may become a ghetto—the second area designated by the project for priority service.

In June 1965 the teachers' evaluation of the tutoring program showed that most of the seventy-five children receiving help had advanced in their social and/or academic adjustment. One child who was tutored during the summer made sufficient progress to be returned to a regular class from a class for disturbed children.

Volunteers. It is appropriate here to point to the importance of volunteer manpower and to what can be accomplished with proper professional supervision. Interestingly, teachers and school officials showed a high degree of resistance to the use of volunteers, despite the enthusiasm and encouragement of the school superintendent. The program, however, has overcome this resistance and has won the overall acceptance of the school system. The value of the volunteer tutor has been most apparent in the improved classroom behavior of a number of the children. The moral of this tale for social workers is obvious. Volunteers are a "heart and soul" part of the project and contribute to all aspects of the program. An advisory committee of dedicated volunteers, for exam-

ple, has served as a vital link in gaining wide community support.

Other programs. Other programs that can be mentioned only briefly include the following:

1. Vocational guidance for every youth from the seventh through the twelfth grade by individual conferences scheduled regularly with the group work staff.

2. Family life education with youths and parents to discuss the vital problems and issues of life in the ghetto.

3. A summer day camp which has an enrollment of approximately two hundred children and youths. Its facilities include the use of a county park and state beachfront area as camp sites, and it plans a wide variety of trips to places of interest.

4. A teen-age group that gives service to the community, including a Saturday enrichment program for preschool children and intercultural weekend work camps developed jointly with youth groups in other Nassau County communities.

NEIGHBORHOOD ACTION AND COMMUNITY DEVELOPMENT

The second emphasis of the project has been the organization of a neighborhood action group of parents and teen-agers to spotlight social problems and obtain remedial action with the assistance of appropriate resources. The Community Action Group of Bennington Park—the ghetto area—meets regularly with the mayor, school superintendent, and director of urban renewal. These exchanges have produced increased mutual understanding and have effected important changes. For example, the police have enforced the "play street" regulation on a street that borders the housing project, trucks are forbidden to use another street that fronts the housing project playground, and a crossing guard has been assigned to the street corner that has had one of the highest accident rates in the village.

The action group's complaints to the school superintendent have been specific and carefully documented by periodic interviews with parents in the community. The school superintendent values this important channel of communication, is sympathetic to the demands of the area, and welcomes the group's support in the continuing effort to make necessary changes in the school system. As a result of meetings with the urban renewal office, the ghetto area is now ably represented on the Citizens' Planning Committee. The Community Action Group has learned the basics of how to present issues, the procedures for negotiation, and—most important—the power it has to influence village officials.

In 1964 the Family Service Association was encouraged by the Ford Foundation to stimulate the creation of a community development organization in Freeport, as a model for other suburban areas. This objective has been the third major emphasis of the Youth Service Project. It was accomplished in 1965 with the establishment of the Freeport Community Progress Association, Inc., a broad-based committee of sixty influential Freeport citizens. Its board of directors is composed of important persons including the mayor, school superintendent, and president of the Chamber of Commerce. The association has focused attention on one of Freeport's most critical problems—a racially changing section that threatens to become another ghetto, the project's second priority area for service. The association has sparked an imaginative program to stabilize the community and has become a vital force in the village's efforts to solve its crucial social problems. In a unique arrangement, the village and the school system are co-sponsoring the program and underwriting the cost of hiring a trained social worker, experienced in community organization, to work in the area. The organization has also sponsored a Head Start program with the active participation of the Youth Service Project staff, and is currently designing a poverty program.

ACCOMPLISHMENTS

What are the over-all accomplishments,

measured against four years of work and the expenditure of over one-quarter million dollars? The agency is convinced that the investment is bringing economic return in the form of reduced dependency and greater citizen productivity as well as greater fulfillment to the youths and families served. In general, the atmosphere of apathy and despair is lifting and is giving way to a more realistic appraisal of present-day opportunities and the efforts required to exploit them. The Housing Authority reports a decrease in vandalism and rent delinquency and an improved spirit of co-operation, although these problems still remain and require the teamwork of staff and the housing manager. The behavior of many of the children and youths has changed dramatically. It seems a long time since the early days of the Family Community Center when youths announced in gangland fashion that they were "going to take over the place." They have the same high spirits, but have less volatility, more control, increased confidence and personality intactness, and an improved ability to use the center program and other resources. An important example is the current high attendance of project youth at the Village Recreation Program (outside the ghetto), which they rarely attended in the past. The picture is not all rosy by any means; a number of severely damaged youths have not been reached successfully and another group who have made great strides are now expressing similar conflicts and tensions with which second-generation Americans have struggled. Another concern is that while almost all the older youths are employed, only a few have jobs that offer opportunities for training and advancement.

The most telling index of the project's impact is the sharp reduction in the school dropout rate. The dropout rate began to decline from a high of 80 percent in 1960–61 and by 1964–65 it had been reduced to 15 percent—the same as for the white population—and the number of high school graduates from the target community has more than doubled. Of the thirty-four high school graduates from the area in the past three years, twenty-five (70 percent) have been active in the community center.

Another indicator of progress is the sharp decline in delinquency. Moreover, probation statistics for other communities in Nassau County in this time period have shown alarming increases. The Nassau County Probation Department reported that approximately forty youths from the target area were on probation in 1963. In 1965 five youths were on probation for offenses committed in 1964. More specifically, the director of the probation department gives credit to staff co-operation in an experimental probation service for preventing six youths from being sent to training schools in 1965.

FUTURE EFFECTS

It is difficult to measure objectively the possible effects of the project on the community. One indication, however, is the following excerpt from a study sponsored by the Adelphi University Graduate School of Social Work:

> In addition, since all but three of the families interviewed had used one or more of the services of the Family Service Association, it is very likely that these services in the Bennington Park community over the past three years had a significant influence with regard to the ease with which the initial phase of the school integration was effected.[6]

What does the Freeport community think of the Youth Service Project? The project has evoked a range of reactions, both supportive and critical. Some think that too much attention is being given to the Negro community. Others claim the project has aroused the conscience of the community to solve its social problems. A critical test was passed this year when the

[6] "School Desegregation in a Suburban Community: A Study of Some Effects of School Desegregation as Seen by Negro Families" (Garden City, N. Y.: Adelphi University Graduate School of Social Work, June 1964), p. 82.

project faced a serious fund-raising problem and the community responded to an emergency drive co-sponsored by the mayor and a state assemblyman, a village resident.

A final word about the implications of the project for Nassau County. First, its establishment necessitated supervisory machinery that led to the creation of a County Youth Board that has since undertaken the support of three more programs in other depressed areas. The project also led the way for poverty programs by conceiving and testing out various methods of working with the poor. On the basis of its experience in Freeport, Family Service Association was asked to assist in the development of a poverty program in Glen Cove, New York, and also undertook the responsibility of preparing the over-all poverty program proposal there. On September 1, 1965, the association began operation of its component of the poverty program—a multi-service center in the ghetto area in Glen Cove. The center will provide further opportunities for experimentation. For example, staff includes professionals, untrained caseworkers, paid indigenous aides, and volunteers from the neighborhood and other sections of Glen Cove.

The extensive reaching-out implications of the Youth Service Project can be seen from this report. The internal effects on the agency have also been profound. The experimental nature of the project and its requirements for imagination, flexibility, optimism, and the willingness to take chances have stimulated agency morale and have had a vital influence on the development of the total agency program. The board of directors and staff alike have been caught up in far-ranging discussions of the project and the philosophy of the family agency. The result has been a constant process of evolving new ideas and of questioning and challenging current methods—all directed toward developing more and more effective ways of helping families under stress.

BY ROBERT D. VINTER AND ROSEMARY C. SARRI

Malperformance in the Public School: A Group Work Approach

A VARIETY OF approaches are being undertaken to resolve certain problems within the public school and to enhance educational attainments. These problems include the tendency of some youth to drop out before graduation from high school, underachievement and academic failure among pupils believed to be intellectually capable, and misconduct that disrupts classroom procedures and school discipline. This paper will describe the development of group services as one approach to such problems and will report preliminary findings from a systematic assessment of this approach.

The work reported here has involved innovations in group work practice, in conceptions of pupil problems, and in adapt-

ROBERT D. VINTER, Ph.D., *is Professor of Social Work, and* ROSEMARY C. SARRI, Ph.D., *is Associate Professor, University of Michigan School of Social Work, Ann Arbor. Principal support for this research has been provided by a curriculum development grant from the Office of Juvenile Delinquency and Youth Development, U. S. Department of Health, Education, and Welfare in co-operation with the President's Committee on Juvenile Delinquency and Youth Crime, and by a research grant from the National Institute of Mental Health, United States Public Health Service.*

ing research designs to a comparative framework. Because of these complexities it is necessary to review study formulations and procedures before presenting the findings now available. The study is in its third and final year; although much data analysis remains to be done, the general direction of outcomes is already clear.

Let us begin by outlining the conception of pupil malperformance—and of its sources—used in this study. First, it is known that standards for academic achievement and for desirable conduct vary among schools, and even within the same school. These variations mean that such types of malperformance as "underachievement," "classroom misconduct," and "failure to adjust" are not identically defined, since different standards and judgments are used from one school to the next, and to some extent among teachers in the same school. The aspects of pupil personality, performance, or ability presumably at issue in one situation are not the same, therefore, as those relevant in another.

Second, there are many differences among schools in terms of their curricula, resources, teacher competencies, student bodies, and school organization. These variations produce wide differences in pupil learning environments, in opportunities for achievement or adjustment, and in conditions that shape the meaning of the school experience.

Third, there are significant differences among schools with regard to their procedures for identifying and coping with pupil malperformance. Thus, in one school youngsters manifesting difficulty may become the targets for a full complement of facilitating services. In another school, however, youngsters exhibiting similar difficulty may encounter relative indifference; when attention is given, it may result in loss of status and privileges for such pupils, perhaps leading eventually to their exclusion from classes and even suspension from the school.

It is proposed here that malperformance patterns should be viewed as *resultants of the interaction of both pupil characteristics and school conditions.* Specific conditions of the school may interact with attributes of the student population to enhance or impede educational achievement. Indeed, certain aspects of school organization and practice may contribute, inadvertently and unwittingly, to the very problems they are designed to alleviate. Certain aspects of this issue will be discussed subsequently, but here it is sufficient to assert that, because of variations among schools, pupils at the same level of ability and performance have quite different experiences, depending on which schools they attend. The import of these variations is that any type of malperformance must be considered not as a unitary phenomenon, or as inhering primarily in the attributes of the pupils, but rather as a resultant of the interaction between school and pupil.

This general conception of malperformance leads us to view pupil difficulties as *social* in several important respects. They are manifested within the social context of the school through interaction with other pupils, with teachers, and with the academic tasks of the curriculum. These patterns assume major relevance as they are judged in terms of the social values and objectives of school personnel. Such problems have their origins in and are currently influenced by pupils' social relations and experiences in the school and elsewhere. Thus, once a pupil has been identified as an underachiever or as disruptive, this social recognition may significantly affect his public identity, his self-image, and his motivation to achieve. Such identification, furthermore, has important implications for how the pupil is subsequently dealt with by the school, for how his school career is shaped, and, ultimately, for his life chances.

In a sense there is nothing especially novel about these conceptions. School social workers have long recognized—certainly at the level of direct experience—that schools are dissimilar, and that some of Johnny's lack of success may be due to certain classroom teaching practices. Nevertheless, there has not been an explicit analysis of the essential ways in which schools and pupils interact. This study has attempted to assess both the characteristics of the pupils and the patterns of the schools that are associated with malperformance problems. There has been an attempt, furthermore, to develop means for modifying the latter as well as the former through school social work services.

RESEARCH DESIGN AND PROCEDURE

Five public school systems have been included in all phases of this research.[1] Group work practitioners were assigned in each, as an integral component of school social work services, to assist malperforming pupils at the junior and senior high school grade levels, with elementary grade pupils also served in two systems. Pupils

[1] Five contrasting southeastern Michigan school systems are included in this work: a rural community, a middle-class academic community, two industrial and one nonindustrial urban communities. The implications of differences in type of community will not be reported here but are an important feature of the study.

were identified and referred in all these schools for underachievement or disruptive behavior; the introduction of group services did not alter schools' criteria for referral. Detailed information was collected about each pupil, providing a basis both for study of pupil change and for comparisons between schools. An attempt was made to systematize the selection of pupils receiving group service by use of standardized referral procedures for teachers, examination of school records, and observation of pupil behavior within the school setting. Youngsters were screened out whom school staff judged as retarded, needing intensive psychiatric treatment, or so handicapped they could not participate with their peers.

A control group design was utilized in the five school systems to assess the effectiveness of the group service strategy. Referred pupils were carefully matched in pairs with respect to several characteristics; one of each pair was randomly assigned to the service groups, and the other became a "control" who received whatever attention was customary within each school *except* the group service. Another sample was randomly selected from the rest of the student population at the same grade levels. The design of this study called for the use of a series of "before-and-after" measures, and comparisons between treatment groups and both matched and random control groups. The use of two control samples permits the study of outcomes that can be directly attributed to the group work service rather than to pupil maturation or factors of chance. Also, the design allows for attitudinal and behavioral comparisons at single points in time between malperforming pupils and a sample of the rest of the student population. During 1963–64 approximately four hundred pupils in the service, matched control, and random groups were thus closely observed in the five school systems. A smaller number of pupils from fewer schools were included in the research during the 1962–63 academic year.

Several sets of before-and-after measures were used. (1) School grades, attendance records, and similar official school information provided one important basis for assessment of pupil change. (2) Teachers and other school personnel completed a behavioral rating form on pupils in all samples early in the school year and again at the end of the year. This standardized form elicited observational information about classroom performance and behavioral patterns, and was validated for use as a sensitive indicator of change. (3) Pupils completed questionnaires and were interviewed with respect to their attitudes, self-images, commitment to educational objectives, school experiences, peer relations, and so forth. All the above types of information had additional use in providing knowledge of the characteristics of malperforming pupils and of different school modes for identifying and responding to problem behavior.

These before-and-after measures of pupils served as the primary means for evaluating changes effected by group services. Means for assessing the *processes* of change included systematic review of practitioners' reports and service records, independent interviewing of treatment groups, and direct consultation with service personnel. To provide the necessary basis for comparability, services to groups were quasi-controlled through preparation of a practitioner's manual and regular group conferences with the research team.[2]

School patterns and practices were assessed through direct observation, interviewing of school administrators and teaching personnel, review of documents and file materials, and questionnaires administered to all school staff. These procedures permit measurement of operational differences among schools with reference to the

---

[2] Taken together these multiple measures resolve many of the deficiencies of previous evaluative studies. *See* Robert D. Vinter, "Group Work with Children and Youth: Research Problems and Possibilities," *Social Service Review*, Vol. 30, No. 3 (September 1956), pp. 310–321.

ways in which school conditions affect pupil malperformance problems. Of particular interest have been the kinds of pupils and problem behaviors produced by each school's system for identifying malperformers. Through a series of group conferences with practitioners and another with school administrators there has been joint review of study procedures and preliminary findings. These have afforded opportunities to explore the meaning of results and of their implications for policy and service.

GROUP WORK SERVICE

We turn now to a consideration of the group work services provided in the five school systems. In each school pupils were routinely identified and referred for special services. As indicated, certain youngsters were screened out at this point. Each prospective member of a group was interviewed by the worker to review his school difficulties, to explain why he had been selected for this service and what would happen in the group, and to establish an initial "contract" for work together on his specific problems. Groups were typically composed of five to eight members and were homogeneous with respect to sex and grade level. Under the guidance of professional workers group sessions were conducted regularly during school hours and in school buildings. These group sessions were the primary means by which change was attempted, although individual service to the same pupils was provided as necessary and by the same professionals.

Within the groups there was explicit public recognition of each pupil's school difficulties and mutual assistance in resolving these. Group discussions and activities were focused on actual problems manifested in the school. Emphasis was placed on mobilizing pupil desire to change toward improved achievement and appropriate conduct. Pupils were helped to develop new skills and alternative methods for coping more effectively with certain stressful school experiences.

There were several primary targets of change through this group work approach: pupil values and goals, self-images, motivations and expectations, social interaction skills, and specific academic abilities. Pupil *values and goals* may be at odds with those of the school, especially as achievement goals become reduced because of past failure and difficulty. *Self-images* are often more negative than desirable, with loss of confidence in ability to achieve academically or to interact appropriately within the school. *Means and opportunities* for successful performance may be insufficiently perceived or known among such pupils, increasing their pessimism and reducing their chances for success. Indeed, opportunities for these students may actually be more limited than is either equitable or desirable. This problem requires intervention *on behalf of* the pupils with other school personnel, as well as work within the groups. Such students typically lack certain *social skills* essential for achievement and for adequate interaction with fellow pupils, teachers, and other school personnel. Lastly, these pupils are, of course, deficient in certain *academic skills*, some of which can be effectively improved within the group (e.g., study habits, efficient use of time, test preparation).

Groups were involved in a variety of activities, depending on the particular service goals set for them, the interests and characteristics of the members, and the devolvement and movement of each group.

Problem-focused discussion predominated, but all groups also engaged in other activities to enhance pupils' learning and change. Study habits, test preparation, how to request assistance from teachers, how to obtain help from classmates, and how to carry out assignments were among the matters discussed and about which groups provided mutual assistance to each other. Group sessions sometimes included in-school creative or recreational activities, outside trips to use selected community facilities, and so on.

Although pupils tended to perceive the groups as pleasurable and rewarding, they were continuously aware of the serious purposes of this experience and its relevance to school performance. In part this was accomplished by encouraging them to report incidents and difficulties they were currently experiencing in the school—and for most participants there is no want of opportunities for such reports. The worker then involved the group in joint exploration of the situation, in consideration of the actual cause-and-effect sequence, and in discovery of more appropriate responses the pupil might have made. Because all pupils had witnessed or been involved in similar incidents, they were effective in curbing each other's tendencies toward denial or projection, and in proposing alternative ways for coping with situations. Sometimes group members used role-playing to recreate their stressful encounters and to test out different response patterns. At other times workers engaged groups in review of their grades and other indices of academic performance, with discussion of the barriers to achievement, and training in methods these pupils could use to improve their course work. These suggest some of the means by which the group sessions were directly related to school concerns and served as vehicles for problem-solving that benefited all participants.

One of the special advantages of working with such pupils in groups is that the powerful forces of peer pressure and judgment can be harnessed in the service of desired change, rather than covertly supporting deviance. The researchers noted, as have many others, that pupils identified as underachieving or disruptive tended to seek each other out and to form associations that reinforced deviancy. A boy in one of the groups explained it in these words:

It depends on who you hang around with. Some guys' idea of fun is to see who gets the lowest grades, skipping school, classes, smoking in the bathroom. I started hanging around with guys like that. . . .

The only reason me or anyone else did things like skip school was to make an impression on your friends. They'd think you're chicken otherwise. I feel if you can't get good grades, then brag about getting away with it.

These findings make it clear that malperforming pupils have at least as many friends as do other pupils, and that they tend to associate with those experiencing similar difficulties more than other students do. These friends are not the strongest supporters of achievement standards, but such friendships are highly valued—perhaps for compensatory reasons. These peer influences, which may support either achievement or malperformance among pupils, are largely ignored by other types of special services and individualized methods.

The progress of each pupil in the groups was assessed several times during the school year to determine whether service should be continued, modified, or terminated, but most pupils were served for two semesters. School grades, attendance records, disciplinary reports, and conferences with classroom teachers provided the primary bases for practitioners' assessment of pupil change —or lack of change.

Group work supplements but does not exclude use of other, more traditional services to implement educational objectives. This approach is conceived as an integral phase of school social work services, and must be supported by school personnel and closely co-ordinated with their activities. Group workers maintained frequent contact with classroom teachers, advisers and counselors, and administrative personnel. They conferred and consulted regularly about specific pupils, shared views on individuals' behavior and progress, and exchanged information about current developments. Much of the practitioners' efforts through these contacts was to modify perceptions and practices toward malperforming pupils on the part of school personnel.

Although several more months will be required to complete the study, the nature of the conclusions has already clearly emerged. This statement is neither inclusive nor final, and subsequent reports will present detailed empirical materials. Findings of three kinds will be reviewed briefly, having to do with pupil characteristics, school practices and conditions, and practitioner roles.

PRELIMINARY FINDINGS: PUPIL CHARACTERISTICS

Intensive study of the referred pupils provides new understanding of those who are identified as presenting malperformance problems. Although it seems widely believed that underachievement and misconduct are generally alike among schools, study findings indicate that these behavior patterns are, in fact, shaped by the distinctive organization and practices of each school. Thus, each school's particular system "produced" somewhat different kinds of pupils and problem behaviors. There was a congruence between the kinds and proportions of identified problems and the dominant goal orientations of school personnel. When developmental rather than academic goals were emphasized among teachers, for example, pupils were more often referred for reasons of misconduct than for underachievement.

Despite these variations among schools, certain commonalities became apparent and achieved statistical significance. Most malperforming pupils fell within the average range of innate capability. They had the intellectual resources to achieve satisfactorily, but the large majority were performing well below their capabilities. Most were also manifesting serious behavioral problems, including disruptive conduct in the classroom or in other school areas, poor interpersonal relations with adults and peers, violation of school norms, or withdrawn and isolated behaviors. Nevertheless, these students were as highly committed to long-term educational and community goals as were other pupils.

The malperformers were less committed, however, to short-term academic tasks and behavioral norms. They appeared to lack effective work and study habits—although they seemed to spend as much time on their studies as other pupils did, they reported that they were unable to complete assignments or use their study time efficiently. They did not reject the school or the "system," but believed they were rejected by the school. (Parenthetically it should be noted that many school personnel have been surprised at some of these findings. Malperformers are often regarded as lacking in motivation and commitment to the school and to their learning tasks. Evidence derived from this study shows that most of these students do, in fact, possess sufficient motivation but lack the necessary means and skills to succeed.)

They were doubtful about their prospects for the future and pessimistic about their chances to change their reputations and to achieve. This pessimism about themselves and their future seemed especially important. It was accompanied by a frank and realistic recognition of their misconduct or inadequate performance. They knew they were not doing well, they doubted that they could do much better, and they seemed unable to take the steps necessary to succeed or conform. At the same time, these pupils believed they had poor reputations among teachers—as indeed they had—and suspected that teachers therefore tended to minimize some of their actual accomplishments. These pupils' negative but more or less accurate appraisal of their current situations and fateful predictions for the future seemed to account for much of the reduction in their investment in educational tasks and in their efforts to improve.

One tenth-grade student described his pessimism in these terms:

I don't want to drop out of school. I want to get a good job. I dropped out for a time in the fall—just didn't care. I wasn't getting good grades in the ninth grade. I figured since I wasn't getting good grades then, it wouldn't change so I just didn't care.

This is, of course, the classic frustration response, in which continued failure to achieve desired goals results in withdrawal, resignation, alienation, and may eventually lead to relinquishment of the goals themselves. In work with these pupils there was heavy reliance on the persistence of their commitment to conventional values —including achievement and success—and on their keen desire to reduce the adverse consequences of being regarded and handled as malperformers. Stimulating motivation to develop and use the abilities they actually possessed was emphasized. At least as important, however, was the creation or opening of opportunities for successful performance within the school. Only by finding ways to achieve, even in limited areas, could anticipations of continued failure be disrupted. Experiences within the group sessions offered some opportunities for success, together with supportive encouragement from others in the group, and the development of additional skills and tools for classroom accomplishment. The crucial condition, however, was the extent to which these pupils could also find opportunities for achievement in the classrooms and other phases of school activities, and could be appropriately rewarded for improved performance. The ways in which school practices and conditions may limit these opportunities was a focus of attention in this study.

PRELIMINARY FINDINGS: SCHOOL CONDITIONS

The writers have asserted that it is the *interaction* between certain aspects of the school and characteristics of the pupils that probably accounts for the observed difficulties. To clarify this relation, three features of the school will be considered: sanctioning procedures, record systems, and teacher perspectives.

Sanctioning procedures. In addition to offering rewards and recognition to pupils for acceptable conduct or achievement, teaching personnel use a variety of negative sanctions to curb malperformance. Grades are, of course, the chief means for doing both: higher than passing grades reward exemplary performance, while lower than passing grades represent a net loss to the pupil. In the short run poor grades serve as negative judgments, and in the long run they curtail pupils' future opportunities. It was observed that students were frequently exposed to a kind of double—or even triple—penalty. Those who performed below a certain standard received adverse grades and might *also* be denied, as a direct consequence, a wide variety of privileges and opportunities within the school. They lost esteem among their classmates, they were seldom chosen for minor but prestigeful classroom or school assignments, and they were excluded from participation in certain extracurricular activities. This process, in turn, often subjected such pupils to negative parental responses, representing a third penalty.

The linking of secondary rewards and sanctions to grades may result in far more than reinforcement of academic criteria, since it denies the poor performer legitimate *alternative* opportunities for recognition and success. His motivation to continue trying and his commitment to educational objectives is thereby jeopardized at the very time when additional supports may be needed to stimulate effort. In these situations the underachieving pupil receives little support for his efforts to improve, as continued failure subjects him to new deprivations.

Record systems. Schools' extensive files on students were found to be most detailed and reliable with respect to grades and other academic performance information. These files tended to be deficient or highly variable with respect to other kinds of facts, such as family characteristics, agency contacts, and so on. Whatever their differences, however, school record systems ap-

125

peared alike in the retention of information that documented malperformance. Disciplinary actions, contacts with parents about critical situations, notice of probationary status, suspensions, and class absences were among the kinds of facts most often recorded in student files. These files followed students from grade to grade and from school to school. The collection and retention of such information, together with grade records, appears to present a number of difficulties. First, it is much easier for pupils to acquire negative than positive formal reputations since, except for grades and at the upper high school level, "good" events are less often recorded (e.g., special classroom duties). Second, it is hard for the pupil to "live down" his past, especially when he moves upward to another school, since the record follows him and is examined there by teaching personnel. Third, there are few ways to certify in the record—except for an unusual improvement in grades—that particular pupils are no longer malperforming or having difficulties. Serious question must be raised about the emphasis on "early identification" when for so many youngsters it results not in service, but in the assignment of negative reputations that cannot easily be surmounted, even if subsequent behavior is acceptable.

Pupils were very much aware of these peculiarities of school file systems and of informal communication among staff that supplemented and extended the official record. They suspected that they were judged to some extent in terms of their reputations *apart* from the objective facts of their current performance. They felt burdened with their negative histories and overwhelmed with the likelihood that they had to do far better than simply "behave themselves" in order to cancel out the past. They became frustrated, finally, with the ambiguous means for clearly establishing that they were *now* conforming or making modest gains, since the evidence of this was less dramatic than that of being in trouble.

Interviews with pupils who were having difficulty illustrated their belief that past events would shape future chances:

When you get in trouble, they never let up on you. They keep calling you in. Like you get caught for smoking and they suspend you. Then they watch out for you so they can catch you again.

I have a bad reputation here. Last year in junior high I gave teachers a lot of trouble and I guess the record follows everywhere I go. Teachers here (in high school) have the record. They have to find out about all the kids.

Teacher perspectives. Interviews with teachers early in this research suggested two aspects of pupil behavior that were of particular concern and that should become foci in group work service. Subsequent findings from teacher questionnaires and from their ratings of pupils have underscored the importance of these issues. On the one hand, teachers regarded pupil motivation toward academic achievement as crucial to either success or failure. They perceived malperforming students as being uncommitted to educational objectives, as lacking incentive to study, and as not trying to learn. These views provided the rationale for the double penalty system, since secondary rewards and sanctions were believed necessary to mobilize pupil concern. Because of these perceptions it has been difficult for school personnel to accept study findings that reveal relatively high levels of commitment and aspiration among malperformers, and that indicate the problem may be more one of means and skills than of deficient motivation. It is possible that student awareness of teachers' skepticism contributes to the pessimism and frustration evidenced among malperformers.

On the other hand, teachers showed much concern about maintaining desirable conditions within the classroom and effective control over their students. They shared an understandable belief that misconduct and disruptive behavior jeopardized the necessary learning climate and their own management of the classroom sit-

126

uation. Many, but not all, malperforming students were perceived as challenging teachers' authority and in some schools teachers were much more concerned about this problem than in others. Information from pupils manifesting difficulties and intensive work within the service groups indicated that most of these youngsters were deficient in the social skills needed for positive relations within the classroom. They did not know how to ask for help, how to accept constructive criticism, or how to withdraw from spiraling conflict situations. Partly because of their self-doubt and their suspicion that they were being singled out by teachers, they tended to misinterpret situations and could tolerate little stress. The escalation of minor incidents into major crises was to be expected, given these orientations among teachers and students.

Even though all these findings were not available to the practitioners, most of them focused their group sessions on resolving problem situations in the classroom. Had the results of the teacher questionnaire been fully anticipated it is likely that even greater emphasis would have been placed on helping pupils make manifest their positive attitudes, and on development of social skills relevant to the classroom and to pupil-teacher interaction. This would have been especially important in those schools where teacher perceptions and expectations were of most significance to malperformers. Impressive gains were achieved, nevertheless, as indicated by teachers' ratings of pupils before and after group work service. Those in the service groups, as compared to their matched controls, showed significant improvement in most areas of performance. Improvement was generally judged to be greatest in the areas of "classroom conduct" and "academic motivation and performance." [3]

---

[3] The "pupil rating form" developed in this research has proved to be a sensitive but simple instrument for assessing pupil behavior and change. A manual for use of this device will soon be published with full statistical evidence of its reliability and validity.

PRELIMINARY FINDINGS: ROLES OF SOCIAL WORKERS IN SCHOOLS

The conception of malperformance as a resultant of interaction between school conditions and pupil characteristics had certain other implications for this study. It argued for attention to the ways in which special services (including social work) were oriented toward the particular circumstances of each school. It also impelled study of social worker roles as these might be simultaneously addressed to changing features of school operation as well as attributes of malperforming pupils. The group work practitioners were the main but not the only helping persons observed in these terms within the five school systems.

Social workers and certain other special service personnel were found to be engaged in several types of activities. Some tended to concentrate on one area of effort, while others concentrated on different areas. These variations in task patterns appeared related to the skills and preferences of individual professionals, to the specific definitions of the social worker role within schools, and to other features of each school's staff and organization. Although analysis of these variations is still incomplete, the preliminary findings are of interest.

Four major types of activities were undertaken by social workers in the schools. *Direct work* with pupils was obviously an important area of effort, involving service contacts with students singly and in groups. In some schools pupils worked with were primarily those whose behavior was disruptive of classroom management, sometimes they were pupils performing far below known abilities, or in other schools they were pupils manifesting both kinds of malperformance. *Mediation* with teachers and other school personnel was another important phase of activity, when staff contacts were focused on specific pupils in difficulty. Such mediation could take the form of information exchange, joint planning about how to handle individuals, or attempts to modify teacher practices on behalf of certain pupils. Social workers in the schools also served as *consultants* to teaching personnel, when attention was directed not so much at specific individuals as at improvement of classroom patterns, modification of teacher perceptions, or changes in school policy and procedure. Next, effort in some situations was devoted to *negotiating* with families and agencies in the community. The primary aim was usually to resolve a particular situation by helping the family or by obtaining agency resources for a pupil or his family. The intent was occasionally more general, such as participation in community planning for troubled children, attempts to change community practices, and the like. In the latter case, the professional served as a kind of "lobbyist" on behalf of such youngsters and services for them.

Most social workers in the schools engaged in each of these activities at one time or another, but among different schools there seemed to be definite patterns by which certain efforts were emphasized and others were minimized. It is apparent that social workers in schools might concentrate on working directly with pupils, working with teachers and other personnel within the school, or working with families and agencies outside the school. Whether social workers were assigned to more than one school appeared to be a significant determinant of their roles. Those who spent part time in several schools were less likely to be used to handle daily crises, while they also had less time for continuous contact with teaching personnel in each school.

Apart from direct work with the service groups there was no attempt to achieve uniformity in role patterns among the social workers who co-operated in this study. However, these service role differences are being taken into account in tracing out those patterns associated with improvement among pupils. The researchers' initial belief that school practices and conditions are a significant factor in malperformance has been buttressed by study findings. The implications of this view for the design of effective school social work patterns are worthy of note.

It appears essential that social work practitioners must address themselves more fully to the conditions of the school, and not limit their efforts to contacts with pupils. Unless the practitioner has intimate knowledge of teachers and their practices, classroom climates, and general school conditions, he cannot understand the particular circumstances that contribute to each pupil's problem situation. Unless there is close contact with other school personnel, the social worker cannot foster those opportunities for success and achievement here suggested as necessary for positive change. The pupil's motivation to learn and to conform that may not appear in the classroom becomes known to the practitioner and must be communicated to teachers. Lastly, and perhaps most important, when positive change does occur, in one area or another, and even in limited degree, the social worker must certify this improvement to teaching personnel. Because of the unintended negative bias of the official record system, the pupil–social worker–teacher informational channel is of central importance. Attempts to help malperforming pupils by treating them in isolation or as though abstracted from the context of school circumstances must be viewed with extreme skepticism. As has been indicated, group work offers a special opportunity to guide the informal peer influences that appear as another potent aspect of the school environment.

Because of their close acquaintance with malperforming pupils, and their knowledge of the conditions that impinge on these pupils, social workers in schools occupy a strategic location. They have the opportunity to assist teachers and administrators in identifying those school practices and arrangements that inadvertently contribute to malperformance, and that curtail learning and adjustment. As has been discussed, some of these problem conditions are integral to each school's system for identifying and coping with pupil deviance.' If the social worker concentrates his energies mainly on helping *some* pupils accommodate to the school, he can do little to ameliorate the patterns that will continue to generate difficulties for many *other* students. If he addresses himself primarily to attributes of the pupil (or his family situation) which seem to be contributing to malperformance, the effectiveness of his helping efforts will be greatly reduced. It seems important, therefore, that the social worker retain dual perspectives, and attempt to resolve problem *situations* or *processes:* both pupils and school conditions should be targets of his interventive activity. He must find ways of serving specific individuals while simultaneously dealing with the sources of pupil difficulties within the school.

GROUP WORK IN THE SCHOOL

This study is now in the final phase of data analysis but the findings are already clear that group work can be an effective supplement to conventional modes of social work practice within the school. When this research is completed, it is expected there can be more precise understanding of the kinds of improvement possible through group services, and guidelines for the selection of malperforming pupils to receive such service. Group work has already been incorporated within the special service programs of the five school systems on the basis of this experience. A revised practitioner's manual is in preparation and will soon be available for general distribution, together with the manual which presents the behavioral rating device.

Perhaps more important will be the new knowledge of value to both educator and social worker. Additional reports will be forthcoming from this research and from related studies being conducted elsewhere. On the basis of such knowledge it will become possible to identify and deliberately modify those features of the school that shape pupil performance and that may curtail achievement of educational goals.

INSTITUTIONAL RACISM AND

SOCIAL WORK PRACTICE

Lou M. Beasley

A beginning attempt
to eradicate racist attitudes

Lou M. Beasley is assistant professor, University of
Tennessee School of Social Work, Nashville,
Tennessee. Her article is based on a paper she
presented to the Middle Tennessee Chapter of the
National Association of Social Workers, Nashville,
Tennessee, June 24, 1971.

Two events in 1969 caused the staff members of Family and Children's Service of
Nashville, Tennessee, to conduct an in-depth
study of racism and its effects on the agency
and on themselves as individuals. (The
agency, a member of Family Service Association of America [FSAA] and Child Welfare League of America, serves residents of
the Nashville Metropolitan United Givers
Fund area.)

The first event occurred when the agency
published its long-range goals and plans. The
following statement appears in the publication.

Family and Children's Service is dedicated to
preserving the dignity of the individual and
the strength of the family. So it is impelled to
keep closer company with individuals and
groups in our society who are fighting the
causes of social ills. It is called upon to ally itself with an enlarged corps of professions and
disciplines who are laboring to rescue persons
and families from poverty, degradation, and injustice. Our agency must become, then, an informed and competent spokesman on social issues; for it must challenge the community to
create conditions which enhance wholesome

family life. It must place the problems of family
welfare upon the community's conscience. In its
advocacy of constructive measures on behalf of
families, Family and Children's Service must
earn the right to be consulted about proposed
changes in social welfare programs.[1]

The second event was the FSAA Biennial
Meeting in Philadelphia in November, with
its theme of "Meeting Change with Change"
and the formation of a Black Caucus and a
White Caucus. The Black Caucus made clear
its belief that FSAA was a racist institution,
despite the national organization's claims that
it was tryng to eradicate any vestiges of
racism. The demand was made that FSAA
immediately stop studying black people and
appoint a task force, which would include
a greater number of minority members, to
study white racism and the damage it has
done to black and other minority families.
The task force would make its recommendations to FSAA and to the Black Caucus. Both the Black Caucus and the White
Caucus asked for immediate reallocation of
existing resources and for allocation of staff
time to the Family Advocacy Program in
order to study and fight the forces and institutions which undermine and exploit family
life.

In April 1970, a staff member of Family

[1]Family and Children's Service, *Long-Range Goals
for Family and Children's Service* (Nashville,
Tenn.: Family and Children's Service, 1969), p. 5.

SOCIAL CASEWORK, January 1972, pp. 9–13.

and Children's Service, as a result of her own interest, conducted two staff development sessions of one and one-half hours each, with the purpose of examining the problems of staff members in their relationships with black clients. During the spring and summer months, the agency struggled to identify its role in the whole realm of family advocacy through staff discussion and more intensive work by the Staff Development Committee and the Board Committee on Public Issues. The high level of staff interest in becoming advocates for families in jeopardy was apparent when almost every staff member attended a regional meeting in Atlanta on October 5, 1970, to hear Mrs. Frances Brisbane, advocacy specialist for FSAA. With the exception of the two social work assistants, the staff members who attended the Atlanta meeting were required to pay the major part of their own expenses.

In November 1970, the Committee on Black Adoptions was formed. This committee purports (1) to provide leadership in the recruitment of black adoptive parents for numbers of black children in our community social agencies for whom little or no planning was being done, and (2) to alert social agencies to those policies and practices that tend to exclude black prospective adoptive parents. The Committee on Black Adoptions consists of black staff members from Family and Children's Service, a black adoption worker from the Department of Public Welfare, and three lay persons from the black community.

As the committee went about its work, the staff showed considerable interest and requested that seminars be conducted in this area of practice. The discussion of racism in adoptive practice led to the development of additional seminars on individual racism and on racism within the agency structure.

Staff seminars on racism

Seven sessions were devoted to the seminars on racism, which began on April 19 and were concluded on May 21, 1971. The staff then comprised thirteen professionals and two social work assistants, who are not usually involved in seminars with the professional staff. Because there were only two black professionals on the staff, the black social work assistant, the Department of Public Welfare caseworker who is a member of the Committee on Black Adoptions, the agency's receptionist, and the agency secretary were included in this series of seminars. The inclusion of these additional interested persons provided a wider range of the black experience to be represented and served to dispel the notion that all black people are alike and have had exactly the same experiences.

Although the discussions were supplemented by extensive reading, no outside speakers were used. This writer served as discussion leader to keep the participants focused on the issue and to avoid the intrusion of extraneous content.

While serving with the Black Adoptions Committee, the writer had reviewed all available information on black couples who, over a six-year period, had made inquiries of Family and Children's Service about adoption. It was thought that these couples might continue to be resources for children available for adoption. Examination of these records revealed the pervasive anxiety of both the caseworker and the couple. Illustrations of this anxiety were cited during the seminars. For example, there were several instances described in which the worker did not explore the client's feelings about unmarried parenthood simply because the client himself was born out of wedlock. Some workers also tended to overemphasize a well-balanced marriage as though it is expected that black people do not have good marriages. It was early in the seminars that caseworkers became aware of their occasional unconscious tendency to stereotype rather than to react to the individual. A white worker's use of the interview situation with a black client—not only for the stated purpose, but also for an opportunity to have contact with a black person—provided the theme of a discussion of the cross purposes of some interviews. For example, a couple may have come to the agency to discuss adopting a child, or an individual may have come for help, but the worker may first attempt to have the client like her. This contact, therefore, becomes an opportunity for the white liberal to succeed in a relationship with a black person. Rather than being just a client, the black person may become a cause for the white worker whose normal contacts with blacks is limited.

With this kind of early discussion, the next three seminar sessions were more intense, with white workers becoming aware that frequently they are overly solicitous to black clients because of their own need to reach out and be helpful. They had been operating with little awareness of the black experience and were now beginning to question their understanding of the life situation of the black client. They displayed a lack of knowledge about the kinds of experiences a black person may have had with other whites and how these past experiences affect the casework relationship.

The black participants were forceful in informing white workers that blacks are faced with racism daily and that they handle this problem much more aggressively than did their parents. The black participants wanted the white participants to know that hostility is not exclusively characteristic of extremists, but that all blacks are angry.

The group discussed the issue of whether trust between blacks and whites is possible at this time. A black participant proposed that social workers must realize their inability to overcome the bitterness of blacks, although they can still provide agency services to the black person. Family service agencies in other parts of the country have accepted the challenge in their move toward greater use of outposts, which appeared to reflect the importance of the commitment of agencies to learn about the particular needs of a community from the people living there and to develop appropriate services to meet those needs. Some workers expressed fears that this meeting of community needs would be indicative of a trend back toward segregation. This writer, however, considers this process as integral to the rights of individuals and communities to determine their own destinies.

The white participants apparently felt the need to talk about their experiences in the casework relationship with black clients. During these sessions they were able to go one step further, and they began to examine their personal attitudes and experiences with black people on a nonprofessional level. In several instances, white workers appeared to be asking for patience and understanding from the black participants and from other white participants.

A white caseworker expressed the pain she felt during this period as follows:

It seemed that these first sessions were a mixture of trying to intellectualize and rationalize racism with occasional glimmers of our own feelings and inadequacies coming through at a gut level. These were quickly covered by the individual's discomfort, as well as the group's discomfort.

I became angry when several of the blacks in the group seemed to be making light of our attempts to. involve ourselves in the problem, especially when a black participant asked, "Do you have to be liked by a black person in order to help him?" I was also very angry when two other blacks asked repeatedly, "So what are you going to do about your racist attitudes?" It seemed they did not realize how deep down prejudice is.

This same worker continued:

After several sessions I became much more aware of myself. It was not my concern anymore that "we out there" look at the problem; I needed to look at *me* and where I was. I went to my black friend in the agency for more discussion, but I felt her drawing the line, as if she were saying, "I am black; you are white; I can't help you with your racism."

As much as I wanted to let go of the whole thing, I could not. Over the weekend I read about black families, black history, about all the terrible injustices black people suffer in this country, and then I made a list of my contacts with black people and my feelings about black people. I found that I had put on blinders; I am very much a part of the system that supports racism. This is not a good feeling. I hope it will not go away—I do not believe it will.

During this great outpouring of feelings by white workers, a black participant said:

I try to be understanding. I try to believe that the white social workers are honestly trying to bring their prejudices to the surface, but deep down within, I believe they are trying to find the Aunt Jemima in me and appeal to her for comfort.

By the fifth seminar, participants were reading everything that was accessible to them. Clippings from the newspaper, magazine advertisements that were racist, and a large number of books were visible around the table. Several workers also participated in the workshop which was presented by the Concerned Citizens for Integrated Schools (CCIS), and they talked enthusiastically about CCIS's plan for integration.

Some workers had questions about the decision that was made concerning the method of conducting the sixth session. The participants were to be assigned to three groups, which were to meet in different areas of the building. There would be two white groups and one black group. When a white worker asked why all the blacks were meeting together, another white worker answered, "The blacks have told us all along that in the final analysis we have to work it out for ourselves." Provisions were made for each group to report to the larger group its recommendations for further growth as persons, staff, and agency.

One group came back with the following brief summary:

We recognized the value of meeting in racially separate groups because there are aspects of racism with which blacks cannot help whites. We believed that previous meetings had been helpful to us in examining our own racism and its effects, even though this feeling was not necessarily verbalized by all. It was felt that we needed to consider solutions next. White racism was seen as closely tied to white experiences, and these experiences vary widely among whites. This aspect of white racism was illustrated well as we shared with each other early experiences with or in relation to blacks. Some of these experiences, which involved painfully remembered cruelty or injustice to blacks, seemed to tie in closely with present tendencies to be overly solicitous.

The question was raised as to how whites and blacks can move more quickly past the point of playing games or roles with each other and into less superficial relationships. We wondered about the element of fear that is often present in relationships with blacks. Was this fear a fear of failure in the relationship or a fear of how black hostility toward whites might be acted out? Was there a residue of childhood in connecting black with things bad or scary, or was it the element of fear of that which is unknown and unfamiliar? Another element mentioned was the white worker's sense of impotence if the black client withholds information about himself as a protective device. There is also the increased self-consciousness and awkwardness in the white worker as she works with the black client now that blacks are speaking out more.

The black social workers in the group of black participants were equally concerned about the casework relationship with both black and white clients. They were aware that one of the evils of racism is that it has taught the black individual a kind of self-hatred that is transferable to other black individuals. Consequently, the black client will often inquire about the possibility of seeing a white worker because of feeling that white people take more interest, are better qualified, or are in a better position to be helpful. They make statements such as, "Your hands are tied just as mine are." One of the sad lessons that black people learn very early in life is, "If you are white, you are right; if you are brown, stick around; if you are black, stay back."

The white client with a black worker may, early in the relationship, express special admiration for the black therapist and seek a favored position. On the other hand, one black worker expressed her discomfort because several of her clients view her as a "superworker" and believe her to have her superior ability because of her presence on a predominantly white staff. The black worker with a black adoptive couple who refuses to accept a dark-skinned child may have punitive feelings toward the couple because of her identification with the black struggle for liberation.

Outcome of group discussion

From these small group discussions black and white participants, as agency staff members, made recommendations for agency action.

1. To deal with racism among whites whenever and wherever possible.

2. To learn as much as possible about what is going on in the black and white communities and what improvements can be made. An illustration would be the present economic withdrawal, or school integration.

3. To deal more thoroughly with cases in order to assess the worker-client relationship. This process would also include examining experiences of workers who are responsible for parents' discussion groups.

4. To balance the number of black and white participants in seminars on racism. It is recommended that we continue to include black clerical staff to achieve greater black representation.

5. To become more receptive to both black and white nonagency participants who may be considered as resources for staff in relation to the black experience.

6. To encourage white staff to avoid retreating to a level on which they can deny their prejudice. Consequently, it was proposed to hold one staff development session on racism every three months.

7. To have staff members who, as individuals, are continually open, sensitive, and perceptive to black and white experiences and who are knowledgeable through life experiences, as well as through current reading and other available means.

There were also several recommendations concerning the agency's policies and practices which were given to the executive director for action by the Board.

Outcome of seminars

It was suggested that a place be made available in the agency for the accumulation of reading material on racism, as well as the compilation of comments and suggestions from workers for the content of future seminars on racism. The staff also voted to make a presentation to the local chapter of the National Association of Social Workers in order to stress that eliminating racism is everybody's business and that this staff had made a beginning.

One worker's opinion of the seminars on racism was as follows:

I felt the seminars were very helpful in opening up each of us, both to each other and to ourselves. They were helpful not in determining if there is prejudice, but in helping each of us—white and black—become more aware of where our prejudices are and how we can best deal with these feelings and work around them and seek gradually to overcome them.

Clearly, the seminars gave the staff a chance to discover each other and to look more closely at the image of the agency. It appears that in view of the goals of one of our national accrediting agencies, FSAA, and our long-range plans and goals, we have no choice but to examine our personal and professional commitment to people. There can be no real service to people until an organization makes itself capable of serving. With racism inherent in an organization, all its energy goes to preserving this evil and accommodating its own institutionalism, and it cannot move forward with the times.

As a black social work practitioner, this writer is unable to conclude this article. As each social worker and social agency in the country at least makes a beginning, perhaps each agency can add its own chapter.

Esther Fibush and BeAlva Turnquest

A black and white approach to the problem of racism

Esther Fibush and BeAlva Turnquest are
caseworkers, Family Service Bureau,
Oakland, California.

The basic commitment of casework is a dual one—to both the social and the psychological approaches to human problems. Because of this commitment, "a diagnosis of an individual's unhappiness . . . cannot ignore a diagnosis of the sickness of society and what it is doing to the person's life."[1] There can be no doubt that white racism qualifies as major social pathology in the United States. Its significance to the lives of its black victims has been powerfully documented, and there is increasing recognition of its contribution to the problems of other minority groups.[2]

From the environmental standpoint, racism is expressed in political, socioeconomic, and cultural institutions that enable the dominant white group to promote its own material interests at the expense of other groups. From the psychological standpoint, it is expressed in a number of related attitudes whereby white individuals attempt to promote their own psychic security through an assumed su-

periority to members of other groups. Racism is thus not only a means by which white people maintain a very real environmental advantage but also a mechanism for attempting to maintain a psychological advantage.[3]

Racist attitudes in individuals both arise from and contribute to racist institutions. In the treatment situation, the caseworker sees the ways in which the social pathology is interwoven with individual psychopathology. Although psychological racism takes a variety of forms and serves a variety of purposes, depending on both the social and the individual dynamics involved, it always includes the assertion of an assumed superiority on the basis of race. Identification with one's own racial group does not in itself constitute racism. Racism arises when racial identity is seen and used as a mark of superiority or inferiority inherent in a person by reason of his racial group membership. Racism ranges from overt white supremacist attitudes to various covert attitudes, including unconscious fantasies about imagined racial characteristics.

Institutionalized racism is a flagrant wrong

[1] Bertha C. Reynolds, The Social Casework of an Uncharted Journey, Social Work, 9:16 (October 1964).

[2] Documentation exists in great variety, dating back to abolition days. A notable recent addition to the literature is William H. Grier and Price M. Cobbs, Black Rage (New York: Basic Books, 1968).

[3] The concept of racism used here is formulated from several sources. It rests in a general way on Gordon W. Allport, The Nature of Prejudice (Cambridge, Mass.: Addison-Wesley, 1954). It is also influenced by Stokely Carmichael and Charles V. Hamilton, Black Power: The Politics of Liberation in America (New York: Vintage Books, 1967); and by Whitney M. Young, Jr., Beyond Racism (New York: McGraw-Hill, 1969).

SOCIAL CASEWORK, 1970, Vol. 51, No. 8, pp. 459-466.

and must be eliminated through social and political action. Casework treatment is in no way a substitute for such change, nor is the caseworker excused from participating in advocacy or activism when these are indicated. In his daily practice, however, the caseworker remains primarily a therapist and a clinician. In this capacity he conducts with the client, white or black, a search for mental health that rejects the concept of superiority or inferiority on the basis of color.

There have been numerous studies of the social and psychological factors associated with prejudice in white people.[4] There has also been some discussion of the impact of racism on the treatment of white patients by black therapists.[5] The scarcity of literature by white caseworkers on the subject of white racist clients suggests that there has been avoidance, denial, or repression of a painful subject. Caseworkers have concentrated a great deal of attention on the black victims of racism. It seems high time that more attention be given its white carriers.

Clinical study

This article is the outcome of a collaborative exploration into white racism by a black caseworker and a white caseworker. Its purpose was to understand the ways in which racism plays a part in the client's problems or defense against problems, in the interaction between client and caseworker, and in the caseworker's attitude toward the client. It was

[4] See T. W. Adorno et al., *The Authoritarian Personality* (New York: Harper & Brothers, 1950); George Simpson and J. Milton Yinger, *Racial and Cultural Minorities: An Analysis of Prejudice and Discrimination* (New York: Harper & Brothers, 1958); and Bruno Bettelheim and Morris Janowitz, *Social Change and Prejudice* (New York: Free Press of Glencoe, 1964).

[5] See Leonard C. Simmons, "Crow Jim": Implications for Social Work, *Social Work*, 8:24–30 (July 1963); and Andrew E. Curry, The Negro Worker and the White Client: A Commentary on the Treatment Relationship, SOCIAL CASEWORK, 45:131–36 (March 1964). From the standpoint of psychoanalytic psychotherapy, see interview with Dr. William H. Grier, A Negro Therapist Discusses Treating the White Patient, *Roche Report: Frontiers of Clinical Psychiatry*, 4:5, 11 (March 15, 1967).

believed that the black-white relationship is a significant factor in casework treatment and might be used as an important tool in the treatment of white racist clients.[6]

The setting was a family service agency in a west coast urban community that has presently a minority population of 40 percent and a "minority" school population of approximately 70 percent. Although the agency continues to serve a substantial number of white middle-class clients, a survey conducted in February 1969 showed that minority clients constituted 44 percent of all clients seen, and that 22 percent of agency clients had incomes below the $4,000 "poverty" level, with another 32 percent at incomes below $7,000. It is an agency that has no present access to funds for financial assistance nor to any other direct means of altering the environmental reality for economically deprived clients. It must, therefore, count heavily on what can be accomplished by casework alone.

Clients who come to a family agency are not representative of the population at large. They are a highly selected group—in large measure a self-selected one. They see themselves in need of a kind of help that their image of the family agency suggests will be offered them. Within this client population there are few white clients who express extreme racist attitudes, just as there are few black clients who express extreme hostility toward whites—this situation is doubtless a factor of the self-selection involved. Of this client population, a number of cases were examined from the standpoint of racism as a treatment consideration; some of them were chosen as case examples.[7]

Attention was given not only to the case material but also to the caseworkers' reaction to it and to their reaction to each other in the course of their discussion. Discussion

[6] Curry, The Negro Worker and the White Client, p. 135.

[7] For the sake of simplicity, examples presented in this study are all of individual treatment cases. Both workers also carried cases in family group therapy and in joint marital counseling in which racism was a factor. The black worker also was conducting group therapy with two racially mixed groups in which, of course, racist attitudes played some part.

was deliberately free-flowing, to encourage the expression of personal as well as professional reactions. There was a conscious effort to recognize factors related to racism wherever they were found—in client or caseworker, black or white—and to trace them to their psychological and social sources.

It became clear very quickly that there could be no simplistic application of either sociological or psychological concepts, that each case had its unique configuration of factors from both sources, and that the caseworker's interpretation might in itself be a stereotype of psychoanalytic, sociological, or personal derivation. Discussion between caseworkers provided a check on each other's assumptions, with the black worker speaking from the standpoint of a black life experience and the white worker from that of a white life experience.

As a working hypothesis for this study, racism in the white client was defined as a defense mechanism indicative of the individual's failure to achieve a sense of identity as a human being of dignity and worth. It was seen as being used primarily in defense against anxiety-provoking feelings of inferiority or inadequacy, shame or guilt. It was thought also to exist in a latent state, coming to conscious awareness or overt expression when other, more habitual modes of defense were threatened.

This definition of racism was adopted for purposes of casework treatment and may or may not have wider application. It represents primarily an effort to find a more therapeutic approach to racism in white clients than just to deplore it.

Some case examples

There were many white clients with whom the subject of race did not seem to need discussion. Some of these clients were obviously so engrossed in other problems in their lives that it would have been inappropriate to introduce the subject. Others had already begun to come to grips with the problem of racism and were actively combating it in some way, so that discussion would have been superfluous. A few white clients brought up the subject of race with the black worker;

there were others, however, with whom the caseworker felt an undercurrent of feeling that suggested that the matter of color be brought into the open.

The purpose in discussing the subject was primarily to free the treatment situation from unnecessary anger and guilt arising from avoidance or denial of the difference in color. It was found that whenever it was possible to discuss the black-white confrontation with a white client (whenever, that is, the subject was not too threatening to the client), the discussion proved to be ego-strengthening. Not only did it free emotional energy for the pursuit of treatment, but it often enabled the client to grapple with other, more realistically threatening situations in his life. The need for such discussion did not arise with the white caseworker, but it was felt that the coincidental advantage of the opportunity to explore and help the client understand the meaning of a special kind of emotional encounter was thereby lost.

The person-to-person encounter between black worker and white client means different things to different clients. For some it is so highly charged emotionally that the worker's blackness becomes a paramount factor in treatment. Such was the case with Miss G.

Miss G was a young white woman who was described by the white intake worker as attractive and articulate, with a problem involving the excessive use of fantasy but with no apparent difficulty entering into a casework relationship. Miss G was assigned to the black worker, who immediately noticed that Miss G was acting out some fantasied role in the casework setting just as she did in her real life situation. During the first treatment hour, the black worker felt that her blackness was interfering in some way, but she did not feel sure enough of this appraisal to bring it up during the session. Miss G canceled her second appointment.

In the next session, Miss G plunged into a discussion of her feelings about black people, her surprise at the worker's being black, and her fear that she might inadvertently say something offensive to the worker. Exploring these remarks, the worker found that some of Miss G's feelings were attributable to her lack of contact with black people and her considerable contact with white people who spoke of black people in a derogatory way. Surprisingly, in this area Miss

G had not made use of fantasy, and exploration of the subject of black-white relationships proved to be her first venture into a search for authenticity.

In this instance, the black-white encounter precipitated the client into a "real" relationship in which she had to grapple honestly with authentic feelings, thus bypassing the habitual defense system and laying the groundwork for the development of healthy ego-functioning.

There are some white clients who appear to have such deep feelings of empathy with black people that one would expect to find them actively engaged in combating racism. When in fact they are not so engaged, the black caseworker might well suspect an effort at ingratiation. This is not always the case, however, as exemplified by Mrs. T.

Mrs. T's problem was her inability to take action. She suffered from anxiety about her own aggression and was unable to assert herself or even to express her feelings in most situations. This was especially true in her marriage, and it was the marriage that was the focus of casework treatment. As Mrs. T gained insight into her problem, she was delighted to find herself openly and freely expressing disagreement on racial issues with her covertly and sometimes overtly racist acquaintances.

At the other extreme, there are white clients who show evidence of deep feelings of anger and hatred toward black people, yet can accept psychological help from a black caseworker.

Mr. S came to the agency reluctantly at the urging of a relative. He was entertaining ideas of suicide and had, over a period of several months, almost starved himself to death. His depression had been precipitated when his wife of many years had left him for another man. Mr. S told of the many plans he had in mind to kill this man. There was something about the way Mr. S talked that prompted the worker to ask if the "other man" had been black. Mr. S confirmed this and added that he had to admit that it was this fact that prompted such murderous feelings.

Having been helped to bring this emotionally fraught matter into the open, Mr. S was able to continue the interview in a more spontaneous way. Because the black caseworker had reacted to him with positive subjective feelings, a rapport was established that enabled Mr. S to recognize his need for treatment and made it possible for him to follow through on the worker's referral to a clinic. One might speculate that the black worker's ability to accept Mr. S's racist feelings provided relief from his immobilizing anger and guilt, freeing him from his obsessive murderous fantasies sufficiently to seek the psychiatric treatment he needed.

The white client may initially have a greater feeling of safety with a black caseworker than with a white worker. Ironically, this sense of trust arises in part from the inferior position imposed upon the black person in a white-dominated society. Moreover, because the black worker may seem at so great a social distance from the realities of his own life, the white client may experience an additional feeling of safety. As treatment progresses, however, there may be development of regressive transference with all its hostile negative elements.

Mrs. L was divorced from her husband but continued to cling to him through a variety of manipulative maneuvers that indicated a severe dependency problem. She was assigned to a white worker and responded to supportive treatment by making some progress toward more independent functioning. The basic problem went untouched, however, and when the white worker left the agency, Mrs. L felt she needed to continue. She asked to be assigned to the black worker who had seen her at intake. This worker had initially had a negative reaction to Mrs. L although Mrs. L had not at that time expressed any racist attitudes.

When the black worker shifted from a simple supportive role to a focus on the intense dependency needs, the negative transference came to the fore, and with it all the previously concealed racist attitudes. Exploration of these feelings indicated that Mrs. L had fastened onto those stereotypes of black people that most reflected her own character problem: dependency, efforts to win acceptance by ingratiating behavior, and various other aspects of childlike or impulse-indulging action. The black worker had intuitively reacted at intake to a defense mechanism in Mrs. L that touched directly on the problems and adaptive techniques developed by black people in a racist society and on Mrs. L's unconscious racist feelings. It became clear that Mrs. L was attempting to deal with ego-dystonic traits by means of projection onto a scapegoat.

The black worker must find some way of handling his own feelings about racist material for the therapeutic benefit of the client.

As the negative transference emerged, Mrs. L's derogatory remarks about black people became more and more difficult to tolerate. The fact that Mrs. L tried to resolve her guilt by seeing her black caseworker as the one exception to the stereotypes served only to "add insult to injury." Mrs. L was not ready for an interpretation of the stereotypes as a projection of her own problems, and the worker feared that any attempt at such an intepretation would be an acting out of her own anger at Mrs. L and therefore destructive to the client.

Discussing the countertransference problem with her white colleague, the worker realized that her attempt to suppress her own anger at racist remarks was unrealistic, despite her awareness of the underlying psychological problems that prompted them. She therefore decided to talk with Mrs. L about her anger.

Mrs. L's reaction was surprise. Recognizing that the worker did indeed feel anger and that such anger was a natural response by a black person to racist remarks, Mrs. L could see that she tended to be unaware of other people's feelings in all her relationships. This was a problem she was ready to work on. Treatment could then proceed on the basis of Mrs. L's insight into her interaction with people in her real-life situations, and the development of further negative transference and countertransference was avoided.

If treatment can accomplish its purpose without special attention to racist attitudes, there is some possibility that the client's racist attitude may simply drop away as he no longer needs it.

Miss J was illegitimately pregnant. Her problems involved conflict with her mother, anger at rejection by her father, and inability to compete successfully with her more demanding siblings for the limited emotional and material supplies in the family. She was from a white, low-income, working-class family that often had to seek help from "the welfare" and that habitually used racist sentiments to deny their own feelings of inferiority and inadequacy. She was able to function well at work but was in danger of losing her job when her pregnancy became known. Miss J quite freely expressed occasional racist opinions.

The white worker ignored these expressions, concentrating on helping Miss J make a plan for leave of absence from work, adoption placement for the baby, and a program for additional education. The crucial factor was to bypass "welfare" in the process, thus effectively separating Miss J from the family pattern of recourse to a kind of help that she felt degrading and humiliating. As Miss J worked her way up the status scale, her self-esteem grew, she no longer needed to feel superior by means of racist attitudes, and she began associating on equal and friendly terms with black colleagues and acquaintances.

Judging from the limited evidence obtained, Miss J's use of racism may have been superficial, primarily a status factor. She had sufficient ego-strength so that when a few doors were opened for her, she could satisfy her need for upward mobility and was then able to adopt a value system appropriate to her more secure environmental situation. One might speculate that because she had not been using racism as a basic personality support, she might have given up her racist attitudes more quickly with a black worker who symbolized the middle-class values toward which she was striving.

There is an occasional instance of a white client for whom racism is not merely a defense mechanism but the very ground on which he stands.

Mr. R came to the agency because he disapproved of his daughter's association with "hippies," a group of white liberal high school students who were tutoring black children in a ghetto area. Mr. R, at fifty-eight, was essentially a defeated person, separated from his wife and alienated from his children, struggling to maintain upper middle-class status among more successful business and professional men within his own reference group. He not only disapproved of his daughter's being in direct contact with black people, whom he saw in every way as inferior, but also of her having close social contact with "gentiles" for fear she might marry

141

outside her faith. Mr. R's sense of personal failure was so great, both emotionally and socioeconomically, that he had retreated into a fantastically narrow concept of his own "in-group" and viewed all outsiders as dangerous threats to what little security he could feel within his self-imposed ghetto.

Mr. R was himself the victim of one variety of racism and the carrier of another. His "identification with the aggressor" had become for him a necessity of life. The white worker decided not to attempt any confrontation with him; whether or not the confrontation implicit in a black caseworker's presence in a counseling capacity might have been more therapeutic for him is questionable. Fortunately, it was clear from Mr. R's report that his daughter had sufficient ego-strength to pursue her own purposes despite her father's objections.

From the standpoint of casework treatment, the matter of racism seemed to be a peripheral factor with Miss J and a central one with Mr. R. In neither instance did the casework relationship itself provide the opportunity for a direct therapeutic encounter. The significant factor from the standpoint of treatment, however, was that the casework relationship could proceed successfully where racist stereotypes were not an essential defense mechanism, as with Miss J, but was entirely blocked where racism constituted a major character defense, as with Mr. R. This finding suggests that the ways in which racist attitudes are used in the defense system may provide an important diagnostic and prognostic clue for treatment.

The treatment possibilities are ordinarily not so easily evaluated, however, because racism is likely to be but one component of a complicated network of defense mechanisms within the personality structure. When it is difficult to assess the significance of racist attitudes to the total treatment picture, the white worker may be confronted with his own conflicts in regard to racism. He may wish to disassociate himself immediately from the client's attitudes, but if he does so, he risks the possibility that the client will feel rejected or attacked and will drop out of treatment. If he disregards the racism, he must be able to handle his own sense of participation in racist guilt so that his own emotional reactions will not block treatment.

Because racist attitudes often provide a defense against awareness of anxiety, such attitudes may contribute to the resistance that arises during the course of treatment and must be dealt with in some way. Dealing with these attitudes will be doubly difficult when racism is ego-syntonic to the client, not only because it contributes to his psychic comfort but also because it corresponds to his perception of a real-life situation. If the white caseworker attempts to deal with racist stereotypes as an incorrect perception of reality, the client may experience this attempt as an attack on his cognitive functions; the matter could then easily degenerate into an "argument" that encouraged the client in intellectualization and rationalization.

It may be necessary for the caseworker to remind himself that the primary purpose of casework treatment is not to attack the defense mechanisms as such, but to strengthen the client's ego capacity sufficiently so that he no longer has need of destructive or self-destructive defenses. It is the ego that perceives reality and that provides the means for dealing with the life situations so as to maximize the attainment of satisfaction. The ego also, however, erects defenses against the awareness of painful emotions and thus blocks its perception of some very significant inner realities; in the pursuit of psychic comfort, the ego often handicaps itself in performing its own basic task. The caseworker must therefore be prepared to enlist the ego in an exploration of inner emotional factors as well as of outer reality circumstances.

Mrs. M came to the agency about her son, age seven, who was soiling. On exploring the social situation, it became apparent that Mrs. M needed supplemental financial assistance and was probably eligible for Aid to Families with Dependent Children (AFDC). She was unwilling to apply, stating that the welfare department favored "Negroes," and indicated her feelings about black people by a facial expression that suggested she was smelling something unpleasant.

The white worker commented on her statement and was able to help Mrs. M decide to make an AFDC application. She did not comment on the facial expression because her own reaction to it was so intensely negative. It was obvious, however, that the facial expression was a nonverbal clue to the meaning of the child's symptom. It later became apparent that Mrs. M's background of economic and emotional deprivation had produced in her a self-hatred that her son was acting out, and that her feelings about black people were actually her feelings about herself.

The worker focused on the reality problem of financial need without also exploring the psychological implications of the nonverbal communication. Having failed to come to grips in the initial encounter with the racist attitude, the worker's guilt mounted, and when Mrs. M again made a racist statement, the caseworker expressed direct disagreement. By that time, regressive transference elements were operating, and Mrs. M ostensibly accepted the disagreement without objection. She then became involved in a sadomasochistic relationship with a man of minority group identification, acting out her problem instead of trying to understand and deal with it in therapy. Ego-oriented casework provided no direct access to the unconscious factors involved, the opportunity for using the racist material to reach a deeper level of emotion was gone, and the case was eventually closed without any real progress having been made.

The case of Mrs. M exemplifies the dilemma for the white caseworker. Had the racist attitude been picked up immediately, the caseworker would have found it extremely difficult to use it in some constructive way. An immediate response would have had the advantage, however, of eliciting a "real" rather than a "transference" reaction from the client, and thus might have prevented the client's acting out later in treatment. By the time this study was undertaken, the damage had already been done, and it was too late to test the proposition that discussion with a black colleague might be the most useful kind of consultation for such a problem.

In handling his own feelings about racism, the white worker is often a novice. The black worker has the painful advantage of having had to cope with his reactions to racist attitudes all his life. The problem of dealing with racist defense mechanisms therapeutically requires all the understanding and

creativity that black and white workers together can bring to it. Even so, it is possible that the treatment of choice for certain racist clients would be group therapy in a racially mixed group, in which the client could face the irrationality of his racist attitudes without direct confrontation with a caseworker.

Conclusion

Judging from the clients studied, racist attitudes in clients must be viewed as an important casework consideration, both from the standpoint of diagnosis and of treatment. The evidence suggests that the presence of a black caseworker sometimes represents a therapeutic encounter in itself. There is also some indication that confrontation by a black worker taps a deeper emotional level with some white clients than is available in ego-oriented treatment with a white caseworker, indicating that the racial composition of a staff has direct bearing on the effectiveness of its treatment program. This evidence does not, however, excuse the white caseworker from facing his own problems in working with racist clients—and perhaps, in some instances, disqualifying himself.

It would also seem that while black people necessarily suffer from the white assumption of superiority, white people do not necessarily gain a corresponding advantage in psychic security (despite their very real advantage from the exploitation of racist institutions). Racist defense mechanisms do not promote, at least in white applicants for casework help, a viable sense of self-esteem, and may indeed be a diagnostic clue indicative of failure in some important ego task. There seems to be considerable reason for caseworkers to shift some of their attention at this time from the black victims of racism to its white carriers. The carriers of the disease may in fact be sicker than its victims.

Where there is sickness in society, everyone is in need of healing—the carrier as well as the victim, the caseworker as well as the client. The first and basic task is to make whatever changes are necessary to bring the society from sickness to health. The caseworker who deals with the individual client, family, or small group is obviously not contributing much to this larger task. Nevertheless, in his daily practice, he may be doing something to limit the spread of the disease.

During the course of this study, both caseworkers realized that any conclusions they might hope to reach would be less important than their growing sense of security in talking together about a subject that is as emotionally charged for caseworkers as for clients. What had started primarily as an intellectual enterprise became an emotional experience in which they were able to share openly and honestly their feelings about black-white relationships. Both became convinced that without such emotional communication between black and white staff members, casework practice will take on its own sterile and intellectualized stereotypes, with both black and white clients.

Caseworkers may read all the "right" books, say all the "right" things, and participate in all the "right" causes, but if black and white do not share their feeling as well as their thinking, they will remain handicapped in achieving their goals. In view of the experience of one such venture, it would appear that when black and white caseworkers talk together freely, the black-white relationship becomes a source of strength and security that has a direct carry-over to work with all clients, black and white.

Intellectually speaking, this study represents only a tentative and preliminary effort to understand and deal with the problem of racism in the treatment situation. Emotionally speaking, however, the implications could be as vast as was James Baldwin's vision in *The Fire Next Time*:

If we—and now I mean the relatively conscious whites and the relatively conscious blacks, who must, like lovers, insist on, or create, the consciousness of the others—do not falter in our duty now, we may be able, handful that we are, to end the racial nightmare, and achieve our country, and change the history of the world....[8]

---

[8]James Baldwin, *The Fire Next Time* (New York: Dial Press, 1963), p. 119.

VALUE ISSUES AND SOCIAL WORK PRACTICE

BY THE AD HOC COMMITTEE ON ADVOCACY

The Social Worker As Advocate: Champion of Social Victims

THE NEW INTEREST in advocacy among social workers can be traced directly to the growing social and political ferment in our cities in the past decade. Social workers connected with Mobilization For Youth [1] (which took its form in the context of this ferment) first brought the advocacy role to the attention of the profession.[2] But the notion that the social worker needs to become the champion of social victims who cannot defend themselves was voiced long ago by others, and has recently been revived.[3]

Present events are forcing the issue with new urgency. Externally the urban crisis and the social revolution of which it is the most jarring aspect are placing new demands on social work; internally, the profession is re-examining itself with an intensity that has few precedents. The profession's faith in its own essential viability is being severely tested. It is especially timely that social work turn its attention to the role of advocate at this time, both because of its clear relevance to the urban crisis and because it has been an integral part of the philosophy and practice of the profession since its earliest days.

WHAT IS ADVOCACY?

The dictionary defines advocate in two ways. On one hand, he is "one that pleads the cause of another." [4] This is the meaning given to the legal advocate—the lawyer—who zealously guards the interests of his

THE AD HOC COMMITTEE ON ADVOCACY *was established by the NASW Task Force on the Urban Crisis and Public Welfare Problems, which itself had been established by the Board of Directors early in 1968 to co-ordinate and redirect NASW's program to make it more responsive to current national crises. Members of the advocacy committee were Willard C. Richan (chairman), William Denham, Charlotte Dunmore, Norma Levine, Howard McClary, Eva Schindler-Rainman, Sue Spencer, Jacob Zukerman, Alfred Stamm (staff), Sam Negrin (liaison with Division of Practice and Knowledge).*

[1] Mobilization For Youth, Inc., started as an action-research program in juvenile delinquency control on New York City's Lower East Side.

[2] See George A. Brager, "Advocacy and Political Behavior," *Social Work*, Vol. 13, No. 2 (April 1968), pp. 5–15; and Charles F. Grosser, "Community Development Programs Serving the Urban Poor," *Social Work*, Vol. 10, No. 3 (July 1965), pp. 18–19.

[3] See, for example, Nathan E. Cohen, ed., *Social Work and Social Problems* (New York: National Association of Social Workers, 1964), p. 374.

[4] *Webster's Third New International Dictionary* (Springfield, Mass.: G. & C. Merriam Co., 1961), p. 32.

client over all others. Another definition describes the advocate as "one who argues for, defends, maintains, or recommends a cause or a proposal." [5] This definition incorporates the political meaning ascribed to the word in which the interests of a class of people are represented; implicitly, the issues are universalistic rather than particularistic.

Both meanings of advocacy have been espoused in the social work literature. Briar describes the historical concept of the caseworker-advocate who is

> ... his client's supporter, his adviser, his champion, and, if need be, his representative in his dealings with the court, the police, the social agency, and other organizations that [affect] his well-being.[6]

For Briar, the social worker's commitment to the civil rights of *his own client* "takes precedence over all other commitments." [7] This is, in essence, the orientation of the lawyer-advocate.

Brager takes another view. He posits the "advocate-reformer" who

> ... identifies with the plight of the disadvantaged. He sees as his primary responsibility the tough-minded and partisan representation of their interests, and this supersedes his fealty to others. This role inevitably requires that the practitioner function as a political tactician.[8]

Brager does not rule out of his definition the direct-service practitioner who takes on the individual grievances of his client, but his emphasis is on the advocacy of the interests of an aggrieved *class* of people through policy change. The two conceptions do overlap at many points, as for

instance when the worker must engage in action to change basic policies and institutions in order to deal effectively with his client's grievances.

SOCIAL WORK'S COMMITMENT TO ADVOCACY

Advocacy has been an important thread running throughout social work's history. Some individuals have been elevated to heroic status because they have fulfilled this role—Dorothea Dix and Jane Addams come most readily to mind. However, it would be safe to say that most social workers have honored advocacy more in rhetoric than in practice, and for this there are at least two reasons.

To begin with, professional education and practice have tended to legitimate a consensus orientation and oppose an adversary one, and this has been perpetuated in the literature. A combative stance, often an essential ingredient in the kind of partisan alignment implied by the concept of advocacy, is not a natural one for many social workers. As a result, most social workers lack both the orientation and the technical skills necessary to engage in effective advocacy. Finally, the employee status of social workers has often restricted their ability to act as advocates.[9]

At the same time that the current upheaval in society adds a note of urgency to the issue of social work's commitment to advocacy, it also adds complications to the task of fulfilling that commitment because of the emotion surrounding many of the issues. For example, some members of the profession feel strongly that fighting racism and deepening the social conscience are the only means to combat these social evils; others—equally adamant—feel that social workers are not equipped to solve

[5] *Ibid.*,
[6] Scott Briar, "The Current Crisis in Social Casework," *Social Work Practice, 1967* (New York: Columbia University Press, 1967), p. 28. *See also* Briar, "The Casework Predicament," *Social Work,* Vol. 13, No. 1 (January 1968), pp. 5–11.
[7] Scott Briar, "The Social Worker's Responsibility for the Civil Rights of Clients," *New Perspectives,* Vol. 1, No. 1 (Spring 1967), p. 90.
[8] *Op. cit.,* p. 6.

[9] It is not the intent to blame the agencies entirely for lack of advocacy in the discharge of a worker's daily duties. It is recognized that progressive agencies have already inculcated advocacy in their workers, often in the face of adverse community reactions and resistance by staff.

these ills, which are a problem of the whole society. There is still another group of social workers who tend to avoid involvement with controversial issues at any cost. What is needed is a consistent approach on the basis of which each social worker can feel confident in fulfilling his professional commitment, an approach that can be responsive to the current crisis but must also outlive it.

OBLIGATIONS OF THE INDIVIDUAL SOCIAL WORKER

The obligation of social workers to become advocates flows directly from the social worker's Code of Ethics.[10] Therefore, why should it be difficult for a profession that is "based on humanitarian, democratic ideals" and "dedicated to service for the welfare of mankind" to act on behalf of those whose human rights are in jeopardy. According to Wickenden:

In the relationship of individuals to the society in which they live, dignity, freedom and security rest upon a maximum range of objectively defined rights and entitlements.[11]

As a profession that "requires of its practitioners . . . belief in the dignity and worth of human beings"[12] social work must commit itself to defending the rights of those who are treated unjustly, for, as Briar asserts:

The sense of individual dignity and of capacity to be self-determining . . . can exist only if the person sees himself and is regarded as a rights bearing citizen with legitimate, enforceable claims on, as well as obligations to, society.[13]

---

[10] This code was adopted by the Delegate Assembly of the National Association of Social Workers, October 13, 1960, and amended April 11, 1967.
[11] Elizabeth Wickenden, "The Indigent and Welfare Administration," in *The Extension of Legal Services to the Poor* (Washington, D.C.: U.S. Department of Health, Education, and Welfare, 1964).
[12] "Code of Ethics."
[13] Briar, "The Social Worker's Responsibility for the Civil Rights of Clients."

Each member of the professional association, in subscribing to the Code of Ethics, declares, "I regard as my primary obligation the welfare of the individual or group served, which includes action to improve social conditions." It is implicit, but clear, in this prescript that the obligation to the client takes primacy over the obligation to the employer when the two interests compete with one another.

The code singles out for special attention the obligation to "the individual or group served." The meaning seems clearest with respect to the caseworker or group worker who is delivering services to identified individuals and groups. It would appear to be entirely consistent with this interpretation to extend the obligation to the line supervisor or the social agency administrator who then is bound to act as an advocate on behalf of clients under his jurisdiction. A collateral obligation would be the responsibility of the supervisor or administrator to create the climate in which direct-service workers can discharge their advocacy obligations. As one moves to consider other social work roles, such as the consultant, the community planner, and the social work educator, the principle becomes more difficult to apply. But how can an obligation be imposed on one segment of the profession and not on another?

The inherent obligation is with respect to the work role and to those persons on whose lives the practitioner impinges by dint of his work role. It is in this role that the individual social worker is most clearly accountable for behaving in accordance with professional social work norms. Through this role he is implicated in the lives of certain groups of people; thus his actions affect their lives directly, for good or ill. Similarly, his work role gives him authority and influence over the lives of his clients; thus he has special ethical obligations regarding them. Finally, there are expected behaviors inherent in the work role on the basis of which it is possible to judge professional performance.

At this point it is important to remind ourselves of the distinction between the obligation of the social worker to be an advocate within and outside of his work role, both of which constitute an obligation of equal weight. However, the obligation to be an advocate outside the work role is general, not specific, and does not have the same force as the obligation to the client. In a sense, this obligation is gratuitous, or, as some might say, "above and beyond the call of duty." An additional problem is that there are no external criteria for judging whether a person is fulfilling this broad responsibility adequately. To use an extreme example: voting might be considered a way of carrying out the role of the advocate-reformer, yet would one say that failure to vote was failure to fulfill a professional obligation? To lump together the two obligations, i.e., to be an advocate in one's work role and outside of it, might appear to reinforce the latter. In reality, it only weakens the former.

Yet the profession as a whole has consistently treated the broad social responsibilities of social workers as important to fulfillment of their responsibilities. Schools of social work make an effort to provide their students with both the orientation and skills to become involved in social issues well outside their future assigned responsibilities. The difference between the two obligations is a moral, not a formal, one. In other words, enforcement of the obligation to be an advocate outside the work role would have to be self-enforcement.

COMPETING CLAIMS

Until now, most discussions of the advocacy role in social work have limited their consideration of competing claims to those of the employing agency [14] or society as a whole.[15] These have overlooked the possi-

bility that in promoting his clients' interest the social worker may be injuring other aggrieved persons with an equally just claim. Suppose, for instance, that a child welfare worker has as a client a child who is in need of care that can only be provided by a treatment institution with limited intake. Does he then become a complete partisan in order to gain admission of his client at the expense of other children in need? What of the public assistance worker seeking emergency clothing allowances for his clients when the demand is greater than the supply? Quite clearly, in either case the worker should be seeking to increase the total availability of the scarce resource. But while working toward this end, he faces the dilemma of competing individual claims. In such a situation, professional norms would appear to dictate that the relative urgency of the respective claims be weighed.

A second dilemma involves conflict between the two types of advocacy—on behalf of client or class. Such conflicts are quite possible in an era of confrontation politics. To what extent does one risk injury to his client's interests in the short run on behalf of institutional changes in the long run? It seems clear that there can be no hard and fast rules governing such situations. One cannot arbitrarily write off any action that may temporarily cause his clients hardship if he believes the ultimate benefits of his action will outweigh any initial harm. Both ethical commitment and judgment appear to be involved here. (Is it, perhaps, unnecessary to add that institutional change does not always involve confrontation?)

A third dilemma is the choice between direct intercession by the worker and mobilization of clients in their own behalf. This is less an ethical than a technical matter. One can err in two directions: it is possible to emasculate clients by being overly protective or to abdicate one's responsibility and leave them to fend for themselves against powerful adversaries.

---

[14] *See* George A. Brager, *op. cit.*
[15] *See* Scott Briar, "The Current Crisis in Social Casework," p. 91.

TECHNICAL COMPETENCE

Questions of competence can compound these dilemmas, for good intentions are not enough for the fulfillment of the advocacy role. Workers must not only be competent, they must also be sophisticated in understanding the appropriate machinery for redressing grievances and skilled in using it. If social workers are required by the profession to carry the obligation to be advocates, they must be equipped to fulfill the role.

While any responsible profession constantly strives to improve its technology, the dissatisfaction of social workers with their skills at advocacy seems to go beyond this. For a variety of reasons, most social workers seem wholly deficient in this area. On the direct practice level, the traditional techniques of environmental manipulation have tended to become peripheral to the practice of social workers, as they have become more sophisticated in the dynamics of inter- and intrapersonal functioning. Second, knowledge of the law, which is vitally tied up with client entitlements, has had less emphasis in the social work curriculum in recent years. Even though increased attention has been given to the client in deprived circumstances—the one who is most likely to need an advocate—this emphasis in the curriculum must be further strengthened.

Regardless of the type of advocacy in which the practitioner engages, knowledge of service delivery systems, institutional dynamics, and institutional change strategies are crucial. Although great advances in this technology have taken place in certain sectors of practice and education, they must be disseminated to the field.

Among the basic content areas that need development and expansion both in school curricula and in continuing education of social workers are the following:

1. Sensitization to the need for and appropriateness of advocacy.
2. Techniques of environmental manipulation and allied practice components.
3. Knowledge of the law, particularly as it bears on individual rights and entitlements.
4. Knowledge of service delivery systems and other institutions that impinge on people's lives and from which they must obtain resources.
5. Knowledge and skill in effecting institutional change.
6. Knowledge and skill in reaching and using the influence and power systems in a community.

The relative emphasis on these different components would vary, depending on the specific work role, although all are necessary in some degree for all social workers.

PROFESSIONAL AUTONOMY AND THE ROLE OF NASW

But lack of technical skills is not the greatest deterrent to advocacy by social workers; actually, it is their status as employees of organizations—organizations that are frequently the object of clients' grievances. Unless social workers can be protected against retaliation by their agencies or by other special interest groups in the community, few of them will venture into the advocacy role, ethical prescripts notwithstanding. It would seem to be a sine qua non of a profession that it must create the conditions in which its members can act professionally. For the profession to make demands on the individual and then not back them up with tangible support would betray a lack of serious intent.

This does not mean that all risks for the worker can or should be eliminated. A worker's job may be protected—but there is no insurance that he will advance within his organization as far or as fast as he would have if he had not been an advocate. Rather, the object is to increase the social worker's willingness to take risks to his self-interest in behalf of his professional commitment.

This brings us to the role and obligation of the professional association—NASW—and once again back to the context of social unrest, social change, and militancy in which this discussion is taking place. In view of the need for the profession to act quickly and decisively to focus on advocacy as being germane to the effective practice of social work, a program is needed—one that should be undertaken by NASW as soon as possible.[16] This program would do the following:

1. Urge social workers to exercise actively and diligently, in the conduct of their practice, their professional responsibility to give first priority to the rights and needs of their clients.

2. Assist social workers—by providing information and other resources—in their effort to exercise this responsibility.

3. Protect social workers against the reprisals, some of them inevitable, that they will incur in the course of acting as advocates for the rights of their clients.[17]

Certain assumptions are implicit in these three program objectives, namely:

■ That the social worker has an obligation under the Code of Ethics to be an advocate.

■ That this obligation requires more than mere "urging."

■ That under certain circumstances, as discussed later, the obligation is enforceable under the Code of Ethics.

■ That the *moral* obligation to be an advocate is not limited to one's own clients, although this cannot be enforced in the same way.

■ That encouragement of advocacy and provision of certain kinds of assistance to advocates need not be limited to members of the professional association.

To return to the relationship of NASW to the social work advocate who gets into trouble with his agency because of his attempts to fulfill a professional obligation: *NASW has an obligation to the worker that takes priority over its obligation to the agency.* In effect, the worker is acting in behalf of the professional community. While the conditions of such responsibility of NASW must be spelled out precisely (to avoid misleading members or jeopardizing the interests of the profession), there can be no question about the member's prior claim on NASW support. Without this principle, the association's claim on the member is meaningless.

The Committee on Advocacy considered two extensions of NASW's obligation. One was in relation to the social work employee who is not a member of NASW. Should the same aids and protections be offered to nonmembers of NASW as to members? It was recognized that a majority of social work positions are held by nonmembers and that they are concentrated particularly in public agencies, which are often the object of client grievances. Furthermore, many indigenous workers in poverty and other neighborhood programs are especially likely to be performing an advocacy function. Obviously, the profession cannot impose a professional obligation on such persons, yet it is consistent with professional concerns that such efforts be supported even when NASW members are not involved. As is spelled out later, the committee recommends that certain types of help be provided, but states that NASW is not in a position to offer the same range of support to nonmembers as to members.

The other extension of NASW's obligation is the possible assumption by NASW of the role of advocate when a client has no alternative channel for his grievances. The committee agreed that NASW could not become, in effect, a service agency, offering an advocacy service to all who request it, although it was felt that the association should work toward the development of such alternative channels. The association should be encouraged to engage in selected advocacy actions when the outcome has potential implications for policy formulation and implementation in general. An example of this would be partici-

16 As the first step in implementing the program, the Commission on Ethics reviewed these findings of the Ad Hoc Committee on Advocacy and recommended that they be widely disseminated. The commission interprets the Code of Ethics as giving full support to advocacy as a professional obligation.

17 This is the wording of the charge given to the Ad Hoc Committee on Advocacy by the NASW urban crisis task force.

pation in litigation against a state welfare agency for alleged violation of clients' constitutional rights; in this instance NASW would be using the courts to help bring about social policy change instead of interceding in behalf of the specific plaintiffs in the case.

Broadly stated, then, the proposed program for NASW calls for concentrated and aggressive activities co-ordinated at local, regional, and national levels, to achieve the needed involvement by individual social workers, backstopped by members in policy-making and administrative positions and community leaders, through education, demonstration, and consultation in program planning; adaptation of NASW complaint machinery to facilitate the adjudication of complaints against agencies with stringent sanctions when indicated; and assistance to individuals who may experience retaliatory action by agencies or communities, ranging from intervention with employers to aid in obtaining legal counsel or finding suitable new employment.

BY HENRY MILLER

Social Work in the Black Ghetto: The New Colonialism

IT HAS BECOME quite fashionable to use the analogy of colonialism when discussing the black man and his relation to the rest of American society. It is not only Black Nationalists who discourse in the dialectic of Fanon; white intellectuals also invoke the image of Algerian peasants grappling with French paratroopers—a struggle leading to existential and political liberation.[1] The purveyors of the analogue see a people constrained by a network of forces to live within the confines of an American Casbah; a people exploited economically; a people forced to live with laws conceived by aliens, administered by aliens, and, indeed, enforced by aliens.

But colonialism takes many forms and is fed by diverse motivations. The colonial metaphor frequently gets out of hand when applied in the current context. Harlem is not the Casbah, South Chicago is not Lagos, and Mississippi is not Vietnam. The differences have to do with the events of the past 350 years, which serve to make the American racial dilemma quite unique.

HENRY MILLER, DSW, is Associate Professor, School of Social Welfare, University of California, Berkeley, California. This paper was presented at the National Conference on Social Welfare, San Francisco, California, May 1968.

The colonial rhetoric ought to be applied with selectivity and with care.

It is, for example, a serious error to see colonialism—at least in its nineteenth- and twentieth-century versions—as being based primarily on Machiavellian premises or to view it through the lens of a Marxian analysis. It may well be true that the edifice of empire is rooted in a web of markets, cotton, rum, and economic inputs and outputs. Surely if the textile mills of Manchester were to operate, Egyptian cotton was needed, and Ceylon supplied the tea for the four o'clock break. It is conceivable, then, that the gunboats were originally powered by such considerations. And it is

[1] Frantz Fanon, especially in his *The Wretched of the Earth* (New York: Grove Press, 1963), provided the ideological base for the colonial model of race relations. Negro spokesmen quickly took it up. *See*, for example, Kenneth B. Clark, *Dark Ghetto: Dilemmas of Social Power* (New York: Harper & Row, 1965); Stokely Carmichael and Charles Hamilton, *Black Power* (New York: Vintage Books, 1967); and the spate of press interviews, television panel shows, and so on with Carmichael, H. Rap Brown, Eldridge Cleaver, and other Black Nationalists. The white use of the colonial model is best illustrated by Charles Silberman, *Crisis in Black and White* (New York: Random House, 1964). *See also* Robert Blauner, "Whitewash Over Watts," *Transaction*, Vol. 3, No. 3 (March–April 1966), pp. 3–9, 54.

Reprinted with permission of the National Association of Social Workers, from SOCIAL WORK, Vol. 14, No. 3, (July 1969), pp. 65–76.

equally conceivable that the sight of the Union Jack or the Tricolor was in itself sufficient rationale for the spread of empire. But whatever the original impetus of the colonizer, a new motivation emerged to be added to the complexity of the phenomenon—the humanitarian ideology of "uplift." Kipling provided the linguistic flag for this new philanthropy—"the white man's burden." [2] We might refer to it as philanthropic colonialism.

PHILANTHROPIC COLONIALISM

We must be careful not to misconstrue the precise nature of such a colonialism. It was real, powerful, and motivated by that most relentless of all propellants—good intention. If the notion of the white man's burden is seen only as a mask for the atrocity of economic spoilage or political machination, an important point is missed. It is necessary to see the idea for what it was and still is, for it is the ideology of the white man's burden that characterizes the posture of social welfare programs and policies in regard to the black man.

Nor should we be deceived by crass and primitive formulations of the white man's burden. Only stupid theoreticians built the doctrine on a base of race and racism. Surely there were those who argued that it was the heaven-sent duty of the white man to care for the lives and souls of God's colored children because they could not care for themselves. And they could not care for themselves because they were not quite men; left to their own devices they would live as they had lived for ages, with cannibalism, sacrifices, incest, infanticide, and the other abominations made necessary by a savage nature. Such was the heart of the system of thought developed by the racist philanthropist: for the sake of civilization and the souls of brown and black child-men, he would spread his benign umbrella of colonial uplift. The colonized were inferior, and just as the biblical patriarchs

rested their oxen, so did the colonizer—in the tradition of humanity—care for his charges.[3]

But this was a crass and crude position. Although it has always been an important strand in the fabric of the doctrine, it offended the enlightened, those committed to an ideology of equality and steeped in biological theory. The white man's burden was a much more subtle ideology; it was built not on a base of racial inferiority, but rather on the firmer bedrock of cultural inferiority. The colonized needed the colonizer, not because of genetic accident, but because of historical accident; not because of a stunted cerebral cortex, but because of a stunted social structure; not because of intellectual insufficiency, but because of technological insufficiency. The distinction is crucial. To put down a rebellion of Sepoys in the name of white superiority is criminal, to put it down in the name of law and order is just, but to put it down in the name of eventual self-determination is downright charitable.

The stance of the philanthropic colonialist might be paraphrased as follows: The modern world is complex; nation-states, in order to survive in any meaningful way, require a minimum level of economic maturity. This implies much more than bustling steel mills, communications networks, and national airlines. It implies a skilled labor force. Moreover, it requires a constitution, a legislature, an executive, a judiciary, and all the other elements of a society governed by the rule of calculated law. The contemporary nation-state demands a complex administrative machinery to moderate its economy and its polity. It requires stability and the blessing of tranquil transition, for it must live not only with itself but with its neighbor states, which, in this shrunken world, comprise all nation-states.

---

[2] From his poem, "The White Man's Burden."

[3] Indeed, such was the rationale provided by some southern apologists for the institution of slavery. *See*, for example, Ulrich B. Phillips, *American Negro Slavery* (Magnolia, Miss.: Peter Smith, 1918).

The precondition for a viable nation-state, then, is an educated, enlightened, and self-controlled population. Now, the philanthropic colonialist will add, it was only through the caprice of historical fortune that Western man developed the attributes requisite to the task of bearing the white man's burden. He might even continue, modestly, that European man, in and of himself, had little to do with such requisites; rather, it is the fortuitous combination of random variables—climate, topography, Caesars, mercantilism, and an apple falling from a tree—that accounts for the efficiency of Western man. If he is contrite he might even add that Europe initially had no business in Africa, Asia, or America; he will wince at the chronicle of the conquistadores or the pillage of Africans. But it happened, and now, he goes on, we have no choice but to be responsible and take on the burden of bringing wrongly subjugated people into the twentieth century.

Note the sweet reason of the philanthropist. He is much too decent a fellow to allow a racist taint to color his good deeds. He is a realist governed by a soft heart. His analysis is predicated on scholarship and empiricism. It was not superiority but randomness that allowed for the dominance of Western civilization. It is a relentless technology that has created the plight of the colonized. The modern colonialist ministers to the underdeveloped rather than to the primitive—to the deprived rather than to the despised. Most pernicious of all, he looks to the future with hope; through charity and patient instruction his charges will be brought into today with strength and vigor and the real equality that comes from competitive viability.[4]

The writer has not invented this portrait of the philanthropic colonialist. Queen Victoria, in many missives to her ministers, anguished over the sufferings of her Indian subjects. She cared more for hospitals and schools than she did for commerce.[5] Moreover, the doctrine of philanthropic colonialism is explicitly articulated in the collective policies of Western states. The white man's burden was mandated by the League of Nations, in its Covenant, to the philanthropic powers who happened to win the Great War.[6] More recently, the Charter of the United Nations allows for the trusteeship of underdeveloped peoples.[7] The charge to the Trusteeship Council is to work toward the self-determination of peoples, but only when, in the wisdom of the council, the colony is ready—that is, when it has become equal to the task.

The impact of this colonialist stance or the serious generosity with which it was promulgated cannot be overemphasized. And it is not a dead or even dying position. Take, for example, the sad shaking of heads when, in 1956, President Nasser of Egypt expropriated the Suez Canal. Certainly a substantial part of the negative Western reaction to this event was premised on economic and political considerations. But there were some who said that the Egyptians simply would not be able to run the canal. They did not have the pilots whose skill was needed to navigate the ships; they did not have the engineers to keep the ditch from filling with sand.[8]

---

[4] The stance here described has been called by some neo-racism. *See* Robert Blauner, "Internal Colonialism and Ghetto Revolt." Paper presented at the University of California Centennial Program, "Studies in Violence," Los Angeles, June 1968.

[5] In writing to the Earl of Derby in August 1858, she urged that the forthcoming India proclamation ". . . should breathe feelings of generosity, benevolence, and religious feeling, pointing out the privileges which the Indians will receive in being placed on an equality with the subjects of the British Crown, and the prosperity following in the train of civilization." John Raymond, ed., *Queen Victoria's Early Letters* (New York: Macmillan Co., 1907).

[6] *See* Article 22 of the Covenant of the League of Nations, which established the mandate system.

[7] *See* Chaps. XI, XII, and XIII.

[8] *See*, for example, the following: "In addition a steady flow of large scale revenue from the canal must involve the question of technical operation and maintenance. It is extremely doubtful if

When it soon became apparent that the canal was being run quite efficiently, there was a note of puzzlement among the philanthropists; somehow it just did not seem right that a backward nation could operate such a marvel of engineering.

A second example is, however, much more tragic. When the Belgians left the Congo (it is more accurate to say when they were forced to leave), they left with every expectation of coming back. It was as though they said, "Foolish children, do you think you can run this vast country without our help?" And with a smiling indulgence they said, "Well, try it and see what happens." The Western world felt a smug satisfaction as it surveyed the turbulence that followed Independence Day in Leopoldville. It seemed to be as they said it would be—the Congo was not yet ready to govern itself. It still needed a period of instruction and guidance.[9]

SOCIAL WELFARE'S ATTITUDE

Social welfare as an institution and many social workers as individuals adopt a posture toward the black man and the ghetto that is nearly identical to the one just detailed. The ideology that characterizes our perception of Black America can best be described as philanthropic colonialism. Again, it must be emphasized that this is *not* a racist position. Indeed, it is counter-racist. It is motivated by dogmas of equality, opportunity, and true integration. And these dogmas are held sincerely. It is in this respect that the advocates of Black Power—both white and black—make their

---

President Nasser has the required skills at his command. He cannot keep non-Egyptians as virtual prisoners indefinitely and it will take time, pains and skill to train their replacements. This has nothing to do with nationality. It is simply a matter of training and experience." Editorial, *New York Times,* July 30, 1956.

[9] Thomas Hamilton, for example, wrote: "In the Congo, however, the problem arises from the fact that a new government in a primitive backward country—no doubt because of past Belgian policies—is unable to govern itself." *New York Times,* July 17, 1960.

most serious error. They fail to see that there may be an evil more terrible than racism, an enemy more powerful than ignorant prejudice, a doctrine more insidious than exploitation. That iniquitous and pernicious doctrine is, of course, the kind of philanthropy just discussed.

Let us look at it more carefully, this time within the context of the United States. The diagnosis made by white America for the black ghetto is, apart from historical detail, very much like that made for the Congo. It would run as follows: The Negro was brought to this country some 350 years ago, in chains, after having been torn from his African culture. He was dispersed among the plantations, exploited in the most barbarous of fashions; his status was that of private property; his women were not his own, nor were his children; he was, in sum, brutalized, emasculated, looked upon as a nonperson, and robbed of his heritage. The seeds of matriarchy were sown during these two and a half centuries of slavery—unparalleled in its ferocity. Emancipation brought nothing but a fictitious freedom. For one hundred additional years the black man, although nominally free, was exploited and victimized. Without dignity, without integrity, without that essence of identity that goes by the name of manhood, without education, without skills—he has become more and more marginal to the mainstream of American life.

These things have happened, so the colonialist argues, through no fault of the black man. But 350 years have left their mark and it shows itself in a life-style that is essentially maladaptive to the wider society. This culture, if you will, was forced on the black man. In order to survive he had to develop structured mechanisms of an ingenious order. His culture, then, is marvelously adaptive to the realities of his unhappy life situation, but serves to work against him now that the democratic processes are beginning to operate in his favor.

The solution, then, is one of uplift. The

black man must first have opportunity, but in order to avail himself of opportunity he must "get with it." And so social welfare has constructed a network of institutions that have as their aim the uplift of the Negro; services that include job training and retraining, education, housing, and, of course, a wide variety of rehabilitative and therapeutic services.

PATERNALISM

There are two aspects to the kind of colonialism being discussed that need further elaboration. The first is more fundamental: it is *paternalism*, a paternalism predicated on the assumption of cultural underdevelopment. The idea is that the black man living in a ghetto must endure a period of preparation before he can participate effectively in the world of middle-class America. This does not mean that he is to be deprived of his civil rights; he is, of course, equal, but his equality is that of a child to an adult. He can be indulged with all the trappings of adulthood—voting rights, open housing, and the rest—but in those matters that really count—commitment to a system of values, aspiration, competence, political sophistication—he needs instruction. This paternalistic stance is not exclusive to social welfare; it characterizes the point of view of white America generally, and social work has probably been more uncomfortable with the position than most other segments of society. Yet it exists and it is pervasive.

For example, in a paper describing casework techniques with low-income families, a professional social worker wrote:

> With many families I appear weekly with the notebook, see the paycheck stub (if I am lucky) and plan with the wife on how the money is to be spent. In a few instances, at their request, I have served as banker, holding money for rent or other necessities until it is due. In crisis periods, and if there is a good reason, I run innumerable errands, get prescriptions filled, take the family to pick up surplus foods. I have gone with clients to see

creditors and discuss refinancing of debts.[10]

There may be some commendable elements to this kind of activity, but surely an underlying dimension of parenthood can be detected—of doing things warmly and kindly for childlike people.

Hollis, describing a special project in Boston, wrote:

> The workers in this program found that they could visit these clients without an invitation and that if they returned regularly, chatted in a neighborly fashion, and offered help with practical problems when they could, they would be allowed to stay. They might then have the chance to demonstrate that a baby stops crying more quickly if someone feeds him, changes his diaper, turns him over, or picks him up than if he is yelled at or hit. Gradually the workers learned that even these little-girl mothers wanted to do better by their children than they themselves had been done by; that the mother yelled at the baby and hit him partly because she actually did not know why he was crying or what else to do and partly because the crying made her feel so bad—so inadequate in the care she was giving her child.[11]

An extremely influential work that triggered a wave of concern for the multiproblem family—the *Casework Notebook*—articulates the paternalistic nature of the white man's burden as a credo:

> We believe in social work's responsibility for the most deprived families, who are failing their central function of child care. These families are a basic and proper charge upon the community; therefore the citizens who support social work have a right to expect us to give them top priority in service.
>
> . . . . .
>
> You don't wear a uniform or carry a

---

10 Janet E. Weinandy, "Techniques of Service," in Frank Reissman, Jerome Cohen, and Arthur Pearl, eds., *Mental Health of the Poor* (New York: Free Press of Glencoe, 1964), p. 372.

11 Florence Hollis, "Casework and Social Class," *Social Casework*, Vol. 46, No. 8 (October 1965), p. 466.

gun, nor need you, because that isn't your job. . . . Yet in a sense, you too have a badge, but it is a symbol of authority rather than something you wear on your coat. . . . You as a social worker are an instrument of social control. You represent the community's intent to influence people to accept social control, rather than force them to submit.[12]

In answer to the question of what the social worker is to do if his child-man client wants no part of him, this document states:

What will you do if you are ordered out? This is one of the reasons for careful advance preparation to give yourself a stronger initial position. If you have this, you will feel so concerned about this family that you can't back away. You will be able to stand up to hostility by a full statement of your concern. . . . The fact that we have returned in the face of initial rebuff has been one of the strongest points in our favor with the families.[13]

What is interesting about these citations is that their referent is not exclusively the Negro family—rather it is a class of families of which Negroes comprise a substantial segment. It is exquisitely nonracial; paternalism knows no skin color.

CLINICALISM

Social work's unique contribution to the ideology of the white man's burden could be called *clinicalism*. It is founded on a presumption of damage—that is, as a result of the sad and brutal history of the Negro people the individual member of that race is likely to have been psychologically injured. The nature of the damage is seen as multifaceted.

One instance of such damage concerns the vital matter of sexual identity; the villain is the infamous matriarchy. The argument holds that as a result of the domi-

nance of the maternal figure and a lack of consistent and esteemed male objects in the early developmental years, the Negro male reaches adulthood with a confused and deprecated masculine identification. After all, the males he had to emulate were held in contempt not only by the larger society but also by Negro women; they were transitory, drifting, and aloof men who held no status except in the harsh and cruel environment of the "cool world." So, the clinician tells us, the Negro male is damaged in that most decisive of all arenas —that of manhood and sexual identity.[14]

The philanthropic solution to this damage is directed at the very soul of black culture. The family must be molded into a different kind of structure. As the controversial Moynihan report states:

. . . Three centuries of sometimes unimaginable mistreatment have taken their toll on the Negro people. The harsh fact is that as a group, at the present time, in terms of ability to win out in the competition of American life, they are not equal to most of those groups with which they will be competing. Individually, Negro Americans reach the highest peaks of achievement. But collectively, in the spectrum of American ethnic and religious and regional groups, where some get plenty and some get none, where some send eighty percent of their children to college and others pull them out of school at the 8th grade, Negroes are among the weakest. . . .

. . . these events, in combination, confront the nation with a new kind of problem. Measures that have worked in the past or would work for most groups in the present, will not work here. A national effort is required that will give a unity of purpose to the many activities of the Federal Government in this area, directed to a new kind of national goal:

---

[12] Alice Overton, Katherine Tinker, and Associates, *A Casework Notebook* (St. Paul: Greater St. Paul Community Chest and Council, 1959), pp. 160, 137.

[13] *Ibid.*, p. 66.

[14] The impact of slavery and postslavery racism on the Negro male has been described by many observers. As a start, the reader may refer to E. Franklin Frazier, *The Negro Family in the United States* (Chicago: University of Chicago Press, 1939); and Elliot Liebow, *Tally's Corner* (Boston: Little, Brown & Co., 1967).

the establishment of a stable Negro family structure.[15]

Moynihan has been much misunderstood; he was not arguing for a crash program in family therapy (much to the chagrin of many clinicians), and he was not for the abandonment of a push toward a massive program of employment and income redistribution. He was saying, however, that if the Negro is ever to become economically self-sufficient the damage must be repaired; he must acquire both the cultural and individual attributes necessary to make him a competitive member of the labor force. It is because of such considerations that the alleged matriarchal character of the Negro family is seen as most obnoxious. It is essential within the context of the larger American society that manhood be defined in terms of wage-earning, vocational competence, and employment security. The homily of "bringing home the bacon" is the summarization of the American concept of manhood. If there is no home there is no need for the bacon, hence the inextricable matrix of family, manhood, and employment.

But as if such damage were not enough, the clinicians see other wounds in the most important structure of the mind—the ego. It is well known, clinicalism argues, that an important function of the ego is to delay gratification and otherwise control the instinctual impulses. The Negro has suffered serious damage in this instance. Immediacy is the rule: nowness, instant gratification, the essential irrelevance of a future orientation are seen as the hallmarks of Negro character. To further confound the damage, the clinician adds a predilection for aggressive expression rather than the more cultivated verbal expression. Action rather than deliberation, wanting rather than working, today rather than tomorrow—these are seen as signs of ego damage. Indeed, they are signs of the human being in

the process of development—the signs of the child.[16]

Hollis argues along Moynihanian lines:

Both experience and study show that long-time poverty results not only in actual deprivation of food, inadequate and shabby clothing, crowded and run-down housing but also in illness or at least depleted energy, a strong sense of inferiority or lack of self-esteem, and often a great sensitivity to criticism, even though this sensitivity may be overlaid by defensive hostility, denial, and projection. The client who is the victim of persistent poverty is often discouraged to the point of being chronically depressed. He almost surely has underlying resentment, anger, and disbelief that the caseworker—a well-dressed, healthy, well-educated member of the middle class—can respect him or be relied upon to help him. Motivation and aspiration are often not absent; but disappointment after disappointment and frustration after frustration may have forced him to bury his hopes for himself —if not for his children—so that he will no longer be vulnerable to so much pain.[17]

In all fairness it should be noted that Hollis, like Moynihan, is all for the elimination of poverty through the implementation of massive programs of public welfare; she is definitely *not* a proponent of psychotherapy as a means of lifting people out of poverty. But she does note that poverty has left its mark on them.

Such is also the thesis of the authors of *The Mark of Oppression,* who, in a careful analysis could claim:

The result of the continuous frustrations in childhood is to create a personality devoid of confidence in human relations, of an eternal vigilance and distrust of others. This is purely a defensive maneuver which purports to protect the individual against the repeatedly traumatic

---

[15] Daniel P. Moynihan, *The Negro Family: The Case for National Action* (Washington, D.C.: U.S. Department of Labor, March 1967), Preface.

[16] The most persuasive case for this point of view can be found in Abram Kardiner and Lionel Ovesey, *The Mark of Oppression* (Cleveland: Meridian Books, 1962). The counterargument is graphically articulated in Liebow, *op. cit.,* p. 308.

[17] *Op. cit.,* p. 466.

effects of disappointment and frustration. He must operate on the assumption that the world is hostile. The self-referential aspect of this is contained in the formula "I am not a lovable creature." This, together with the same idea drawn from the caste situation, leads to a reinforcement of the basic destruction of self-esteem.[18]

The profound subtlety of clinicalism must be recognized. It is based on high-level and sophisticated theory and it appeals to impartial empiricism. There are case histories. There are articles in learned journals. It is not racism, it is not ideology, it is not bias—it is objective reality. The conclusions of psychological damage are based on disciplined observations and these data can be explained by an elaborate theory of cause and effect. And they are made by men of goodwill, men pained by the findings a relentless objectivity yields, men righteously angry at the evil system that led to such far-reaching damage. But these men are also hopeful and they allow for change; individuals can be healed, the damage can be undone, but more important, the system can be changed to preclude further damage in future generations. Prophylaxis is the clinicians' contribution to the ideology of civil rights.

What is found, then, in the welfare stance toward the black man in this country is the philanthropy of the healing father: a welfare system designed to bring damaged and bewildered children to health and clear vision so that at last the American dream can be fulfilled. Whereas Queen Victoria's burden was that of bringing a culturally retarded people into the adult community of nations, social welfare added an element of clinical uplift and we are now charged with bringing a people both culturally deprived *and* psychologically damaged into the adult community of middle-class America.

WHAT IS WRONG WITH SOCIAL WELFARE?

What is this axe-grinding all about? Where lies the evil in philanthropy and what

is wrong with a social welfare that helps people make it? The point has to do with a scheme of values and is this: Nations cannot be backward, men are not children, and ethnic diversity is necessary to the good life.

First, within the context of nation-states, the issue is not that the Congo lacks a well-trained bureaucracy, not that there is a high infant mortality rate in Guinea, not that there is tribal vengeance in Nigeria. The issue is that of self-determination. It is the only issue. People have the right to determine their own destiny, for good or ill, with or without strife, wisely or foolishly—it is their business. This is not an empirical matter; it is a matter of right. In the face of such a right the white man's burden becomes a moral atrocity. Kindness and benevolence become anathema when they transcend the supreme value of a people's choice of life-style and destiny. It is not for Victoria or Gladstone to pass judgment on a culture. In a hierarchy of values that places self-determination at the top, it does no good to argue mortality rates, economic viability, tribalism, or political chaos.

But how do these considerations apply to the ghetto? In this respect the philanthropy of social work errs on two counts. First, the diagnosis of psychological damage, when applied to a people, is an absurdity.[19] Individuals may be sick, but ethnic or social entities cannot be. They may be Apollonian or Dionysian, sacred or secular, autocratic or democratic, matriarchal or patriarchal, but they can hardly be sick in any absolute sense.[20] They can

---

[18] Kardiner and Ovesey, *op. cit.*, p. 308.

[19] The different conclusions one can arrive at, in this regard, by adopting another perspective can be found in Robert Coles, *Children of Crisis: A Study of Courage and Fear* (Boston: Little, Brown & Co., 1967).

[20] This is the most important lesson of contemporary anthropology: Mankind is exquisitely versatile in the kinds of institutionally sanctioned behaviors he can invent; cultures may be different from each other but, unless one makes the chauvinistic error of claiming a unique vision of right, one culture cannot be seen as superior to another.

be evaluated, but the evaluation must take place along dimensions exterior to the system itself. Herein lies the error of clinicalism. The standard of health is embodied in the ethos of the wider society. When collectivities are characterized as sick, the metric is found in a quantum of disparity from the standard. Clinicalism, when applied to ethnic entities, flounders on the rock of an arbitrary standard.

But even if this were not so, the ethic of philanthropic colonialism in regard to the ghetto would be wrong. And this is a central point: The value of ethnic self-determination in America takes its operational form in an ideology of cultural pluralism. To the extent that social welfare's allegiance to a colonialist model subverts that ideology it becomes an evil enterprise.

A SUCCESSFUL MELTING POT

This country has had a long and tortured history of attempting to accommodate to diverse ethnic groups. The attempt has been governed by a principle that, although it has faltered at times, has been surprisingly successful. This is the principle of the melting pot. Irishmen, Czechs, Poles, Germans, Greeks, Jews, Italians, Slavs, and many more have been admitted to this country (not always warmly), housed in this country (not always comfortably), employed in this country (not always fairly), educated in this country (not always diligently), and melted down into what many thought would be a new breed—an American. Although there is controversy about this, the writer claims that this melting process has been successful.[21] In spite of reluctance, resistance, and recalcitrance, in spite of hostility and downright prejudice, in spite of the conscious attempt by some groups to avoid it, within

---

[21] For a counterargument *see* Nathan Glazer and Daniel P. Moynihan, *Beyond the Melting Pot* (Cambridge, Mass.: MIT Press, 1963). A more thorough discussion of the success or failure of the melting pot can be found in Milton Gordon, *Assimilation in American Life* (New York: Oxford University Press, 1964).

the course of two, three, or at most four generations the melting pot notion has prevailed.

It has prevailed—or more accurately, it is prevailing—because of calculated public policy and the homogenizing nature of our institutional life. The ethnic entities that once made up the patchwork quilt of this country have either died or are in the process of dying. Remnants remain and they will continue to be with us for some time. Certain groups were denied entry into the crucible; the black man is the striking example of that denial. But the ideology of the melting pot—or, speaking pejoratively, America as homogenizer—runs deep in this country and has powerful machinery. Television is only the latest in a series of devices used to propagate a mass culture.

The Sons of Italy, the Franco-Americans, the Pulaskis, even the tongs, are rapidly becoming anachronisms. The Italo-American Club can hardly compete with Kiwanis and Lions; when a Jew can become a Mason and join the Westchester Country Club he hardly has use for the B'nai B'rith. When the melting pot is well fired, the process of homogenization can take place with amazing rapidity. The great wave of Jewish immigration into this country took place during the first quarter of this century. The grandparents of contemporary young Jews were greenhorn immigrants; the old ones died in New York knowing but a handful of English words. Their children made it to Westchester County and the country clubs. And their children, in turn, are now making it in Haight-Ashbury. These semitic hippies have little in common with their grandparents; a spastic nostalgia or the improvisation of Hassidic mandala may be groovy, but it is hardly Jewish. The swinger knowns no ethnicity; the American dream is realized when the Sons of Italy make it with the daughters of Erin.

CULTURAL PLURALISM

The ideology of the melting pot, however, is not the only one that could have governed public policy. A less influential ideology, that of cultural pluralism—equally compatible with the spirit of democracy—could have set the tone for this country.[22] And it is even remotely possible that it could still prevail, which, of course, is the rationale for this paper. The difference in ideologies can best be illustrated by their spokesmen. First, the notion of the melting pot by its great protagonist, Israel Zangwill:

> America is God's crucible, the great Melting Pot where all the races of Europe are melting and re-forming! Here you stand, good folk, think I, when I see them at Ellis Island, here you stand in your fifty groups, with your fifty languages and histories, and your fifty blood hatreds and rivalries. But you won't be long like that, brothers, for these are the fires of God you've come to—these are the fires of God. A fig for your feuds and vendettas! Germans and Frenchmen, Irishmen and Englishmen, Jews and Russians—into the Crucible with you all! God is making the American.[23]

It is a noble idea, it governs our policies, and if it has not worked perfectly, our stance is to make it work more perfectly. But here is an alternative:

> [With cultural pluralism] the outlines of a possible great and truly democratic commonwealth become discernible. Its form would be that of the federal republic; its substance a democracy of nationalities, cooperating voluntarily and autonomously through common institutions in the enterprise of self-realization through the perfection of men according to their kind. The common language of the commonwealth, the language of its great tradition, would be English, but each nationality would have for its emotional and involuntary life its own peculiar dialect or speech, its own individual and inevitable esthetic and intellectual forms. The political and economic life of the commonwealth is a single unit and serves as the foundation

and background for the realization of the distinctive individuality of each nation that composes it and of the pooling of these in a harmony above them all. Thus "American civilization" may come to mean . . . a multiplicity in a unity, an orchestration of mankind.[24]

Lest it be feared that the nurturance of ethnic differences must inevitably lead to an inequality of privilege and power, Kallen continues:

> Female and male, Indian, Negro and White, Irishman, Scotchman and Englishman, German and Spaniard and Frenchman, Italian and Swede and Pole, Hindu and Chinaman, butcher, baker and candlestick maker, workingman and gentleman, rich man and poor man, Jew and Quaker and Unitarian and Congregationalist and Presbyterian and Catholic—they are all different from each other, and different as they are, all equal to each other.[25]

It is to this dream of difference that the writer appeals. And it is to such an ideology that social welfare should attend. Probably the most passionate and eloquent advocate of this point of view was a former social worker who later became Commissioner of Indian Affairs. His concern was with humanity and he agonized over the irreparable loss to the world that comes from the homogenization of peoples. The forces of the melting pot, he contends, imply

> that through polite "engineerings of consent," or if need be through brute force, there shall come about a dead manipulable flatness of human life in the United States and in the rest of the world; that the individual isolate, "freed" from grouphood, culture and home, an atomized "go-getter," shall become—each individual—one among three billion interchangeable grains of sand in an unstructured sandheap of the world.[26]

---

[22] Again, a full discussion of this alternative is found in Gordon, *op. cit.*

[23] Israel Zangwill, from his drama *The Melting Pot* (1908), as quoted in *ibid.*, p. 120.

[24] Horace M. Kallen, "Democracy vs. the Melting Pot," *The Nation* (1915), as quoted in *ibid.*, pp. 142–143.

[25] *Ibid.*, p. 146.

[26] John Collier, "Divergent Views on Pluralism and the American Indian," in Roger Owen, James

Social welfare, historically, has taken an ambivalent position between the melting pot and the pluralistic society; the settlement house movement was a striking example of that ambivalence.[27] But no matter—the settlement house movement is dying; sectarian agencies are dying. Perhaps with some reluctance, we seem to be stoking the fires of the melting pot.

This is really what is being done. What would be the outcome of a truly successful Economic Opportunity Act? What is the intent of Head Start programs? To what is urban renewal going to lead? The writer is not against equal opportunity, income redistribution, education, open housing, or the elimination of slums—these programs ought to be implemented immediately and heavy taxation imposed to achieve them. But the country and people in need are done a hideous disservice if these programs are designed along the lines of their prototypes—if job training, Head Start, and urban renewal lead to the homogenization of people into a vast ocean of white-collar suburbia.

ETHNICITY IS DESIRABLE

Let there be no misunderstanding. The pluralistic utopia of Collier or of Kallen has nothing in common with *apartheid*. Nor is it a reversion to the farce of the old separate-but-equal doctrine. The difference is fundamental: it revolves around the issue of individual choice. Whereas *apartheid* grows out of an enforced ethnicity, cultural pluralism depends on a voluntary ethnicity. *Apartheid* is terror-stricken in the face of differences; it builds walls around its enclaves and requires armed men to police its barriers. A vision of cultural pluralism thrives on differences; the membranes of Collier's enclaves are permeable.

Deetz, and Anthony Fisher, eds., *The North American Indians* (New York: Macmillan Co., 1967), p. 685.

[27] This ambiguity as to the ultimate mission of the settlement house movement can be found in Jane Addams, *Twenty Years at Hull House* (New York: Macmillan Co., 1910).

But if individuals are to opt for the choice of maintaining their ethnic identity, the choice must be a viable one. And it is precisely that lack of choice to which attention is being called here. In some perverse way, the choice exists but the price is dear. In order to keep out of the melting pot, the price is either poverty and stigma or antagonistic militance. It is indecent to say to an individual: "You must either homogenize yourself or you must remain poor or you must become an angry man."

This vision of cultural pluralism has its problems. The most tormenting one is trying to maximize what some think are two negatively correlated goods, the goods of individual autonomy and of ethnic integrity. But these are not necessarily contentious values. Martin Luther King was immersed in black culture and yet he was not narrow; Freud was a thorough Jew and yet his perspective was rather large. U Thant is Burmese as well as Secretary-General of the United Nations. Culture is not the enemy of personality; indeed, it is the ally of selfhood. It is likely a prerequisite of the full personality.

But if we, as social workers and as citizens, buy this idea of cultural pluralism, it means that we must radically revise our programs and policies. We would, for example, think much differently about the nature of public education. We would entertain the possibility of parochial schools and neighborhood schools with curricula and teachers selected by local parents rather than by state boards and financed by public funds. Surely this rankles, but perhaps we are ingenious enough to construct an educational system that accommodates to both parochial interest and the interest of the general public. We could hardly do worse than what has been done.

Further, we would—as cultural pluralists—react quite differently to the Panther cry for black policing of black neighborhoods. We would have to rewrite as well as refinance the Economic Opportunity Act of 1964. Job training would be not only for General Motors or Metropolitan Life or

IBM: it would also be for indigenously owned and operated industry and craft. White America stole the black man's music; it ought, at least, to return the record companies to him.

And so we think of black schools and black police and black commerce—and we steer a difficult course between *apartheid* and Black Nationalism. But in a very real sense the programmatic aspects of cultural pluralism are self-evident—they are built into the ideology. For social workers it means, at long last, that we work in behalf of clients (the advocacy role), we visit them only when we are invited, we let them use us to get things that *they* want, whether money, housing, jobs, or treatment. Above all, it means that we interact as equals—different perhaps, but still equal. And it means that we do not see them as culturally deprived (what a demeaning term!), educationally disadvantaged (education for what?), matriarchal (with a snicker of superior manhood), or injured, damaged, or helpless.

THE GREAT EXPERIMENT

Let social workers begin to think of these things—of philanthropy and paternalism and clinicalism and the melting pot and cultural pluralism. If we opt for the desirability of ethnicity, we are then obligated to construct institutions and mechanisms that would allow for the flourishing of ethnic groups while at the same time allowing for a decent standard of living and the opportunity to enter the mainstream. It may be impossible; it may be that the seductions of Levittown and television and instant dinners are too great to withstand; it may be that pluralism is unworkable. But we do not know, we have never seriously tried it, and before it is too late, before we all become as "three billion interchangeable grains of sand," perhaps we ought to undertake the great experiment.

164

Saul D. Alinsky

OF MEANS AND ENDS

The *real* question has always been,
"Does this *particular* end justify
this *particular* means?"

Life and how you live it is the story of means
and ends. The *end* is what you want, and the
means is how you get it. Whenever we think
about social change, the question of what and
how, or means and ends, always arises. The
man of action views the issue of means and
ends in pragmatic and strategic terms. He has
no other problem; he thinks only of his actual
resources and the possibilities of various choices
of action. He asks of ends only whether they are
achievable and worth the cost; of means, only
whether they will work.

He is not trapped in the mental maze induced
by that perennial, meaningless, abstract question, "Does the end justify the means?" He
knows intuitively that the real and only question
regarding the ethics of means and ends is,
and always has been, "Does *this particular* end
justify *this particular* means?" The application of
this question to the issue of .action quickly
dispels the fog and semantical overcast that is
preventing or delaying takeoff into action.

He knows that the first principle of action is
the justification of the act. If he is sophisticated,
he will know that the day-to-day tactics will be
more concerned with the issue of limited means
justifying selected, limited ends; of dramatizing
the importance of minor ends so as to induce
and sustain action. If he is experienced, he will
also know, long before the dust of battle has
settled, that not only will unforeseen and un-
planned means enter the scene, but that the

Saul D. Alinsky, "Of Means and Ends," *Union
Seminary Quarterly Review*, Vol. XXII, No. 2 (January, 1967). Reprinted by permission of the author.
Saul D. Alinsky is Executive Director of the Industrial Areas Foundation in Chicago. This article
was one of four Auburn Extension Lectures, which
he delivered at Union October, 1966, and will be
included in his book *Rules for Revolution*, to be
published by Random House.

UNION SEMINARY QUARTERLY REVIEW, 1967, Vol. 22, No. 2,
pp. 199-208.

ends will also shift and change. If he is wise,
he will also know that life is a story of means
and not of ends, that ends when they are
achieved become means to other "ends."

He will understand Goethe's statement that
"conscience is the virtue of observers and not
of agents of action," that in action one does
not always enjoy the luxury of a decision which
is consistent both with one's individual conscience and the good of mankind. The choice
must always be for the latter. Action is for mass
salvation and not for the individual's idea of
his own personal salvation. He who sacrifices
the mass good for his personal conscience has
a perverted conception of what is meant by
"personal salvation."

THE ETHICS OF INACTION

It is the men of inaction, the Do-Nothings, who
pile up the heaps of discussion and literature
on the ethics of means and ends, which with
rare exception is conspicuous for its dearth of
insight and comprehension and its general steril-
ity. The backgrounds of these Do-Nothings have
rarely included the battlefields of experience in
the perpetual struggle of life and change. They
have not been involved in the kinds of conflicts
in which the consequences of defeat could be
personally disastrous. They are strangers to the
burdens and problems of operational responsibility and the unceasing pressure for immediate
decisions. They are passionately committed to a
mystical objectivity where passions are suspect.
They assume a nonexistent situation where men
dispassionately and with reason draw and devise
means and ends as if on a navigational chart
prior to setting sail on the seas of action. To
them, the following statement by Alfred North
Whitehead would seem to apply to another
planet: "We cannot think first and act after-
wards. From the moment of birth we are immersed in action and can only fitfully guide it

by taking thought." They usually carry the mark of Cain on their tongues and can be recognized by one of two verbal brands: "We agree with the ends but not the means" or, "This is not the time." *The means-and-end moralists, or non-doers, always wind up on their ends without any means.* These Do-Nothings become the nadir of immorality and vividly revive Edmund Burke's statement, "Evil only triumphs when good men do nothing."

They are constantly obsessed with the ethics of the means used by the Have-Nots against the Haves and should search themselves for their real political position. In actual fact they are passive allies of the Haves, and their judgment of the ethical nature of the means being used by the Have-Nots stems from this *de facto* political position. Those who parrot the chant that they agree with the objectives but not with the means are in the facts of life part of the Haves or the status quo, and in their hearts they do not agree with the ends, let alone the means.

They are the ones Jacques Maritain referred to in his statement, "The fear of soiling ourselves by entering the context of history is not virtue, but a way of escaping virtue." These non-doers were the ones who chose not to fight the Nazis in the only way they could have been fought; they were the ones who drew their window blinds to shut out the shameful spectacle of Jews and political prisoners being dragged through the streets; they were the ones who privately deplored the horror of it all—and did nothing. This is the nadir of immorality. *The most unethical of all means is the non-use of any means.* It is this species of the political innocent who so vehemently and militantly participated in that classically idealistic debate at the old League of Nations on the ethical differences between defensive and offensive weapons. Their position indicates little, if any, conception of the world as it is. Their fears of action drive them to refuge in an ethic so divorced from the politics of life that it can apply only to angels and not to men. The standards of judgment must be rooted in the whys and wherefores of life as it is lived—the world as it is and not our wished-for fantasy of the world as it should be.

ELEVEN ETHICAL RULES

I present here a series of rules pertaining to the ethics of means and ends.

First, one's concern with the ethics of means and ends varies inversely with the degree of one's personal vested interest in the issue. When we are not directly concerned, our morality overflows; for as La Rochefoucauld put it, "We all have strength enough to endure the misfortunes of others." Accompanying this rule is the parallel one that *one's concern with the ethics of means and ends varies inversely with one's distance from the scene of conflict.*

The second rule of the ethics of means and ends is that the judgment of the ethics of means is and has been dependent upon the political position of those sitting in judgment. If you actively opposed the Nazi occupation, joined the underground resistance movement, then you adopted the means of assassination, terror, property destruction, the bombing of tunnels and trains, kidnapping, and the willingness to sacrifice innocent hostages to the end of defeating the Nazis. All those who opposed the Nazi conquerers regarded the underground resistance as a secret army of selfless patriotic idealists, courageous beyond expectation and willing to sacrifice their lives to their moral principles, convictions, and beliefs. Conversely, to the occupation authorities these people were lawless terrorists, murderers, saboteurs, assassins, believers that the end justified the means, and utterly unethical according to the mystical rules of war. Any foreign occupation would so ethically judge its opposition. However, in such conflict neither protagonist is concerned with any considerations except victory. It is life or death.

To us the Declaration of Independence is a glorious document and an affirmation of human rights. To the British, on the other hand, it was a statement notorious for its deceit by omission. In the Declaration of Independence the Bill of Particulars attesting to the reasons for the Revolution cited all of the injustices of which the colonists felt that England had been guilty but listed none of the benefits. There was no mention of the food which the colonies had received from the British Empire during times of famine, medicine during times of disease, soldiers during times of war with the Indians and other foes, as well as many other forms of direct and indirect aid which contributed to the survival of the colonies. Neither was there notice of the growing number of allies and friends in the British House of Commons and the hope for imminent remedial legislation to correct the inequities under which the colonies suffered.

Jefferson, Franklin, and others were honorable men, but they knew that the Declaration of Independence was a call to war. They also knew that a listing of many of the constructive benefits of the British Empire to the colonists would have so diluted the urgency of the call to arms for the Revolution as to have been self-defeating. The result might well have been a document attesting to the fact that justice weighted down the scale at least 60 percent on our side and only 40 percent on their side; and that because of that 20 percent difference (or really 10 percent) we were going to have a revolution. To expect a man to leave his wife, his children, his home, to leave his crops standing in the field, and to pick up a gun and join the Revolutionary Army for a 10 or 20 percent difference in the balance of human justice was to defy common sense.

The Declaration of Independence, as a declaration of war, had to be what it was, a 100 percent statement of the justice of the cause of the colonists and a 100 percent denunciation of the role of the British government as evil and unjust. Our cause had to be all shining white justice, allied with the angels, while theirs had to be all black evil, tied to the devil; in no war has the enemy or the cause ever been gray. Therefore, from the point of view of politics the omission was justified; from the British position it was deliberate deceit.

History is made up of "moral" judgments based on politics. We condemned Lenin's acceptance of money from the Germans in 1917 but were discreetly silent while our Colonel William B. Thompson in the same year contributed a million dollars to the anti-Bolsheviks in Russia. As allies of the Soviets in World War II we praised and cheered Communist guerrilla tactics when the Russians used them against the Nazis during the Nazi invasion of the Soviet Union. We denounce the same tactics when they are used by Communist forces in different parts of the world against us.

The opposition's means, used against us, are always immoral, and our means are always ethical and rooted in the highest of human values. George Bernard Shaw, in his play *Man and Superman*, perceptively pointed out the variations in ethical definitions by virtue of where you stand. In the conversation between Mendoza and Tanner:

Mendoza: I am a brigand; I live by robbing the rich.
Tanner: I am a gentleman; I live by robbing the poor. Shake hands.

The third rule of the ethics of means and ends is that in war the end justifies almost any means. Agreements on the Geneva rules on treatment of prisoners or use of nuclear weapons are observed only because the enemy or his potential allies may retaliate.

Winston Churchill's remarks to his private secretary a few hours before the Nazis invaded the Soviet Union graphically point out the politics of means and ends in war. Informed of this imminent turn of events, Churchill's secretary inquired how he, the leading British anti-Communist, could reconcile himself to being on the same side as the Soviets. Would not Churchill find it embarrassing and difficult to ask his government to support the Communists? Churchill's reply was clear and unequivocal: "Not at all. I have only one purpose, the destruction of Hitler, and my life is much simplified thereby. If Hitler invaded Hell I would make at least a favorable reference to the Devil in the House of Commons."

In the Civil War President Lincoln did not hesitate to suspend the writ of habeas corpus and to ignore the directive of the Chief Justice of the United States. Again, when Lincoln was convinced that the use of military commissions to try civilians was necessary, he brushed aside the illegality of this action with the statement that it was "indispensable to the public safety." He believed that the civil courts were powerless to cope with the insurrectionist activities of civilians. "Must I shoot a simple-minded soldier boy who deserts, while I must not touch a hair of a wily agitator who induces him to desert? . . ."

The fourth rule of the ethics of means and ends is that judgment must be made in the context of the times in which the action occurred and not from any other chronological vantage point. The Boston Massacre is a case in point.

British atrocities alone, however, were not sufficient to convince the people that murder had been done on the night of March 5: There was a death bed confession of Patrick Carr, that the townspeople had been the aggressors and that the soldiers had fired in self defense. This unlooked for recantation from one of the martyrs who was dying in the odor of sanctity with which Sam Adams had vested them sent a wave of alarm through the patriot ranks. But Adams blasted Carr's testimony in the eyes of all pious New Englanders by pointing out that he was an Irish "papist" who had probably died in the confession of the Roman Catholic Church. After Sam Adams had finished with Patrick Carr even Tories did not dare quote him to prove Bostonians were responsible for the Massacre.[1]

To the British this was a false, rotten use of bigotry and an immoral means characteristic of the Revolutionaries, or the Sons of Liberty. To the Sons of Liberty and to the patriots, Sam Adams' action was brilliant strategy and a God-sent lifesaver. Today we may look back and regard Adams' action in the same light as the British did, but we should remember that we are not today involved in a revolution against the British Empire.

Ethical standards must be elastic to stretch with the times. In politics, the ethics of means and ends can be understood by the rules suggested here. History is made up of many examples, such as our position on freedom of the high seas in 1812 and 1917 contrasted with the 1962 blockade of Cuba, or our alliance in 1942 with the Soviet Union against Germany and Japan and the reversal in alignments in less than a decade.

Lincoln's previously mentioned suspension of habeas corpus, his defiance of a directive of the Chief Justice of the United States, and the illegal use of military commissions to try civilians

were actions done by the same man who fifteen years earlier had said:

> Let me not be understood as saying that there are no bad laws, or that grievances may not arise for the redress of which no legal provisions have been made. I mean to say no such thing. *But I do mean to say, that although bad laws, if they exist should be repealed, still, while they continue in force, for the sake of example, they should be religiously observed.*[2]

This was the same Lincoln, who a few years prior to his signing the Emancipation Proclamation, stated in his First Inaugural Address:

> I do but quote from one of those speeches when I declared that "I have no purpose, directly or indirectly, to interfere with the institution of slavery in the States where it exists. I believe I have no lawful right to do so, and I have no inclination to do so." Those who nominated and elected me did so with full knowledge that I made this and many similar declarations and have never recanted them.

Those who would be critical of the ethics of Lincoln's reversal of positions have a strangely unreal picture of a static, unchanging world, where one remains firm and committed to certain so-called principles or positions. In the politics of human life, consistency is not a virtue. It is, in fact, nonexistent. To be consistent means "standing still or not moving." Men must change with the times or die.

The change in Jefferson's orientation when he became President is pertinent to this point. Jefferson had incessantly attacked President Washington for using national self-interest as the point of departure for all decisions. He castigated the President as narrow and selfish and argued that decisions should be made on a world-interest basis to encourage the spread of the ideas of the American Revolution; he said that Washington's adherence to the criteria of national self-interest was a betrayal of the American Revolution. However, from the first moment when Jefferson assumed the presidency of the United States, his every decision was dictated by national self-interest.

The fifth rule of the ethics of means and

---

[1]John C. Miller, *Sam Adams: Pioneer in Propaganda* (Boston: Little, Brown and Co., 1936).

[2]Abraham Lincoln, "The Perpetuation of Our Political Institutions," address before the Young Men's Lyceum, Springfield, Illinois, Jan. 27, 1837; italics added.

ends is that concern with ethics increases with the number of means available and vice versa. To the man of action the first criterion in determining which means to employ is to assess what means are available. The reviewing and selection of available means is done on a straight utilitarian basis: Will it work? A means which will not work is not a means; it is nonsense. The question of moral factors may enter when one is making a choice among equally effective alternative means. But if one lacks the luxury of a choice and is possessed of only one means, then the ethical question will never arise; automatically the lone means becomes endowed with a moral spirit. Its defense lies in that eternal cry of mankind from the very beginning, "What else could I do?" Inversely, the secure position in which one possesses the choice of a number of effective and powerful means is always accompanied by that ethical concern and serenity of conscience, so admirably described by Mark Twain as "the calm confidence of a Christian holding four aces."

The sixth rule of the ethics of means and ends is that the less important the end to be desired the more one can afford to engage in ethical evaluations of means.

The seventh rule of the ethics of means and ends is that generally success or failure is a mighty determinant of ethics. The judgment of history leans heavily on the outcome of success or failure; it spells the difference between the traitor and the patriotic hero. As Sir John Harrington aptly pointed out, "Treason doth never prosper; what's the reason? Why, if it prosper, none dare call it treason."

The eighth rule of the ethics of means and ends is that the morality of a means depends upon whether the means is being employed at a time of imminent defeat or imminent victory. The same means employed where victory seems sure may be defined as immoral, whereas if it had been used in desperate circumstances to avert defeat, the question of morality would never arise. In short, ethics are determined by whether one is losing or winning. From the beginning of time killing has always been regarded as justifiable if committed in self-defense. Let us confront this principle with the great-

est example of the ethics of means now plaguing the world's attention. Did the United States have the moral right to use the atomic bomb at Hiroshima? When we dropped the atomic bomb, the United States was assured of victory. In the Pacific Japan had suffered an unbroken succession of defeats. Now we were in Okinawa with an air base from which we could bomb the enemy around the clock. The Japanese air force was decimated, as was their navy. Victory had come in Europe, which released the entire European air force, navy, and army for use in the Pacific. Russia was moving to be in on the kill for a cut in the spoils. Defeat for Japan was an absolute certainty and the only question was how and when the final coup de grâce would be administered. For familiar reasons we dropped the bomb and triggered off a universal debate on the morality of the use of this means for the end of finishing the war.

I submit that if the atomic bomb had been developed shortly after Pearl Harbor, when we stood defenseless—when most of our Pacific fleet was at the bottom of the sea, when the nation was fearful of invasion on the Pacific coast, when we were committed as well to the war in Europe—then the use of the bomb at that time on Japan would have been universally heralded as a just retribution of hail, fire, and brimstone upon an unscrupulous enemy that had violated all the rules of fair play and was now poised at our jugular. Then the use of the bomb would have been hailed as proof that good inevitably triumphs over evil. The questions of the ethics of the use of the bomb would never have arisen at that time, and the character of the present debate would have been very different. Those who would disagree with this assertion have no memory of the state of the world at that time. They are either fools or liars or both.

In other words, the difference between the use of a means to an end, to wit, the dropping of the atomic bomb at a time of imminent defeat, or in a time of certain victory, would have had more than a major bearing upon the ethical question of means and ends; in actual fact it would have been decisive for the ethical question. Mankind has always drawn the ethical line at self-defense, and it has always sanctioned the taking of life in these circumstances.

The ninth rule of the ethics of means and ends is that any means which is effective is automatically judged by the opposition as being unethical. One of our greatest revolutionary heroes was Francis Marion of South Carolina, who became immortalized in Amercan history as "the Swamp Fox." Marion was an outright revolutionary guerrilla, and he and his men operated in all of the traditions and with all of the tactics commonly associated with the present-day guerrillas. Cornwallis and the regular British army found their plans and operations harried and disorganized by Marion's guerrilla tactics. Infuriated by the effectiveness of his operations and incapable of handling or coping with them, the British denounced him as a criminal and charged that he did not engage in warfare "like a gentleman" or "a Christian." He was subjected to an unremitting denunciation about his lack of ethics and morality and his use of guerilla means to the end of winning the Revolution.

The tenth rule of the ethics of means and ends is that you do what you can with what you have and clothe it with moral garments. In the field of action the first question that arises in the determination of means to be employed for particular ends is: *What means are available?* This requires an assessment of whatever strengths or resources are present and can be used. It involves a sifting of the multiple factors that combine in creating the circumstances at any given time and an adjustment of the popular views to the popular climate. Questions of chronology, of how much time is necessary or available, must be considered. Does the opposition possess the power to the degree that it can suspend or change the laws? Does its control of police power extend to the point where legal and orderly change is impossible? If it is a revolution, then are weapons available for this purpose? Availability of means determines whether you will be underground or above ground; whether you will move quickly or slowly; whether you will move for extensive changes or limited adjustments; whether you will move by passive resistance or active resistance; or whether you will move at all.[3]

_____
[3]The absence of any means might drive one to

A naked illustration of this point is to be found in Trotsky's summary of Lenin's famous *April Thesis,* issued shortly after Lenin's return from exile. Lenin pointed out:

The task of the Bolsheviks is to overthrow the Imperialist Government. But this government rests upon the support of the Social Revolutionaries and Mensheviks, who in turn are supported by the trustfulness of the masses of people. We are in the minority. In these circumstances there can be no talk of violence on our side.

The essence of Lenin's speeches during this period was: "They have the guns, and therefore we are for peace and for reformation through the ballot. When we have the guns, then it will be through the bullet." And it was.

Mahatma Gandhi and the development of passive resistance in India present a striking example of the selection of means. Here, too, we see the inevitable alchemy of time upon moral equivalents as a consequence of changing circumstances and positions respecting power patterns of Gandhi and his followers from the Have-Nots to the Haves with the natural shift of desired ends from *to get* to *to keep.*

Gandhi is viewed by the world as the epitome of the highest moral position with respect to means and ends. We can assume that there are those who would believe that if Gandhi had lived the invasion of Goa, or any armed invasion, would never have occurred. Similarly, the politically naive would not have believed that the great apostle of nonviolence, Nehru, would ever have countenanced the invasion of Goa, for it was Nehru who stated in 1955:

What are the basic elements of our policy in regard to Goa? First, there must be peaceful methods. This is essential unless we give up the roots of all our policies and all our behavior. . . . We rule out nonpeaceful methods entirely.

Gandhi was a man committed to nonviolence and ostensibly to the love of mankind, including his enemies. His end was the independence of India from foreign domination, and his means was that of passive resistance. History, and religious and moral opinion, have so enshrined

martyrdom in the hope that this would be a catalyst in starting a chain reaction culminating in a mass movement. Here a simple ethical statement is used as a means to power.

Gandhi in this sacred matrix that in many quarters it borders on the blasphemous to question whether this entire procedure or means of passive resistance was not simply the only intelligent, realistic, expedient program that Gandhi had at his disposal; or whether the "morality" that surrounded this policy of passive resistance was not to a large degree a rationale to cloak a pragmatic program with a desired and essential moral cover.

Let us examine this case. First, Gandhi, like any other leader in the field of social action, was compelled to examine the means at hand. If he had had guns, he might well have used them in an armed revolution against the British, which would have been in keeping with the traditions of revolutions for freedom through force. Gandhi did not have the guns, and if he had had the guns, he would not have had the people to use the guns. In his autobiography he records his astonishment at the passivity and submissiveness of his people in not retaliating or having any desire for revenge against the British.

As I proceeded further with my inquiry into the atrocities that had been committed on the people, I came across tales of Government's tyranny and the arbitrary despotism of its officers such as I was hardly prepared for, and they filled me with deep pain. What surprised me then, and what still continues to fill me with surprise, was the fact that a province that had furnished the largest number of soldiers to the British Government during the war, should have taken all these brutal excesses lying down.

Gandhi's astonishment at the people having "taken all these brutal excesses lying down" is a rather odd reaction on the part of one already committed to *satyagraha,* the spirit of passive resistance.

Gandhi and his associates repeatedly deplored their people's seeming inability for organized, effective, violent resistance against injustice and tyranny. His own experience was corroborated by an unbroken series of reiterations from all the leaders of India that India could not act in physical warfare against her enemies. Many reasons were given, including that of weakness, lack of arms, having been beaten into submission, and other arguments of a similar nature. Pundit Jawaharlal Nehru

described the Hindese of those days as "a demoralized, timid, and hopeless mass bullied and crushed by every dominant interest and incapable of resistance."[4]

Faced with this situation, we revert for the moment to Gandhi's assessment and review of the means available to him. It has been stated that if he had had the guns he might have used them. This statement is based on the Declaration of Independence of Mahatma Gandhi issued on January 26, 1930, where he discussed "the fourfold disaster to our country." His fourth indictment against the British reads:

Spiritually, compulsory disarmament has made us unmanly, and the presence of an alien army of occupation, employed with deadly effect to crush in us the spirit of resistance, has made us think we cannot look after ourselves or put up a defense against foreign aggression, or even defend our homes and families. . . .

These words more than suggest that if Gandhi had had the weapons for violent resistance and the people to use them this means would *not* have been as unreservedly rejected as the world would like to think! On the same point, we might note that after India had secured independence, when Nehru was faced with a dispute with Pakistan over Kashmir, he did not hesitate to use armed force. Now the power arrangements had changed. India now had the guns and the trained army to use these weapons.[5]

---

[4]Interview with the Prime Minister, Jawaharlal Nehru, by Norman Cousins, *Saturday Review,* May 27, 1961.

[5]Reinhold Niebuhr, "British Experience and American Power," *Christianity and Crisis,* XVI (1956), p. 57.

"The defiance of the United Nations by India on the Kashmir issue has gone comparatively unobserved. It will be remembered that Kashmir, a disputed territory, claimed by both Muslim Pakistan and Hindu India, has a predominately Muslim population but a Hindu ruler. To determine the future political orientation of the area, the United Nations ordered a plebiscite. Meanwhile, both India and Pakistan refused to move their troops from the zones which each had previously occupied. Finally, Nehru took the law into his own hands and annexed the larger part of Kashmir, which he had shrewdly integrated into the Indian economy. The Security Council, with only Russia abstaining, unanimously called upon him to obey the United Nations directive, but the Indian government refused. Clearly, Nehru does not want a plebiscite now for it would

Any suggestion that Gandhi would not have approved the use of violence is negated by Nehru's own statement:

It was a terrible time. When the news reached me about Kashmir I knew I would have to act at once—with force. Yet I was greatly troubled in mind and spirit because I knew we might have to face a war—so soon after having achieved our independence through a philosophy of nonviolence. It was horrible to think of. Yet I acted. Gandhi said nothing to indicate his disapproval. It was a great relief, I must say. If Gandhi, the vigorous, nonviolent, didn't demur, it made my job a lot easier. This strengthened my view *that Gandhi could be adaptable.*[6]

Confronted with the issue of what means he could employ against the British, we come to the other criterion previously mentioned: that the kind of means selected and how they can be used is significantly dependent upon the face of the enemy, or the character of the opposition. Gandhi's opposition not only made the effective use of passive resistance possible but practically invited it. His enemy was a British administration characterized by an old aristocratic liberal tradition and way of life. This administration granted a good deal of freedom to its colonials and always had operated on a pattern of utilizing, absorbing, seducing, or destroying through flattery, bribery, or corruption the revolutionary leaders who arose from the colonial ranks. This was the kind of opposition which would tolerate and ultimately capitulate before the selected tactic of passive resistance.

Gandhi's passive resistance would never have had a chance against a totalitarian state such as the Nazis'. It is doubtful whether under those circumstances the idea of passive resistance would even have occurred to Gandhi. It has been pointed out that Gandhi, who was born in 1869, never saw or understood totalitarianism and defined his opposition completely in terms of the character of the British government and what it represented. George Orwell in his essay "Reflection on Gandhi" made some pertinent observations on this point:

He believed in "arousing the world," which is only possible if the world gets a chance to hear what you are doing. It is difficult to see how Gandhi's methods could be applied in a country where opponents of the regime disappear in the middle of the night and are never heard of again. Without a free press and the right of assembly it is impossible, not merely to appeal to outside opinion, but to bring a mass movement into being, or even to make your intentions known to your adversary.

From a pragmatic point of view passive resistance was not only possible but was the most effective means that could have .been selected in India for the end of ridding India of British control. Being a genius as an organizer, Gandhi knew that the major negative in the situation had to be converted into the leading positive. In short, knowing that one could not expect violent action from this large mass of torpid passivity, he organized the inertia; he gave it a goal so that it became purposeful. Its wide familiarity with *Dharna* made passive resistance no stranger to the Hindese. What Gandhi did, in over-simplified terms, was to say, "Look, you are all sitting there anyway—so instead of sitting there, why don't you sit over here, and while you're sitting, say 'Independence Now'!"

This raises another question about the morality of means and ends. We have already noted that in essence mankind divides itself into three groups: the Have-Nots, the Have-a-Little-and-Want-Mores, and the Haves. The purpose of the Haves is to keep what they have. Therefore, the Haves want to maintain the status quo, and the Have-Nots want to change it. The Haves usually establish the kinds of laws and judges who maintain the status quo. The result has been that Have-Nots, from the beginning of time, have been compelled to appeal to "a law higher than man-made law." This has permitted the use of means which, according to the established

surely go against India, though he vaguely promises a plebiscite for the future.

"Morally, the incident puts Nehru in a rather bad light. . . . When India's vital interests were at stake, Nehru forgot lofty sentiments, sacrificed admirers in the *New Statesman* and *Nation*, and subjected himself to the charge of inconsistency.

"This policy is either Machiavellian or statesmanlike, according to your point of view. Our conscience may gag at it but on the other hand, those eminently moral men, Prime Minister Gladstone of another day and Secretary Dulles of our day, could offer many parallels of policy for Mr. Nehru, though one may doubt either statesman could offer a coherent analysis of the mixture of modus which entered into the policy. That is an achievement beyond the competence of very moral men."

[6]Cousins, *op. cit.;* italics added.

laws, are frequently illegal and nearly always unethical. At this point the Have-Nots support the morality of their means on the basis of this "law higher than man-made law" and their "natural rights." The Haves develop their own morality to justify their means of repression and all other means employed to maintain the status quo. When the Have-Nots achieve success and become the Havès, they are then in the position of trying to keep what they have, and their means and morality shift with their change of location in the power pattern.

This was clear when, eight months after securing their independence, the India National Congress outlawed passive resistance. It was one thing for them to use the means of passive resistance against the previous Haves, but now in power they were going to insure that this means would not be used against them! They were no longer appealing as Have-Nots to laws higher than man-made law. Now that they were making the laws, they were on the side of man-made laws! We need not even mention Goa, except to note that only the naiveté of the quixotic practitioners of the ethics of means and ends could have been so taken by surprise. There was a similar reaction in the case of the hunger strikes used so effectively by Mahatma Gandhi, as evidenced by this statement from Nehru: "The government will not be influenced by hunger strikes. . . . To tell the truth I didn't approve of fasting as a political weapon even when Gandhi practiced it."[7]

We see this illustrated with Sam Adams, the firebrand radical of the American Revolution, who was foremost in proclaiming the right of revolution. However, following the success of the American Revolution, and now that the revolutionaries were in power, it was the same Sam Adams who was foremost in demanding the execution of those Americans who participated in Shay's Rebellion, charging that no one had a right to engage in revolution against us!

Moral rationalization is indispensable at all times of action, whether to justify the selection or the use of ends or of means. Machiavelli's blindness to the necessity of moral clothing to all acts and motives in his statement, "Politics has no relation to Morals,"[8] was his major weakness. All great leaders—including the cited examples of Churchill, Gandhi, Lincoln, and Jefferson—always invoked "moral principles" to cover naked self-interest in the clothing of "freedom," "equality of mankind," "a law higher than man-made law," and so on. This even held under circumstances of national crises when it was universally assumed that the end justified any means. *All effective actions require the passport of morality.*

The examples are everywhere, whether past or present. The recent use of passive resistance in the South against segregation was typical. Violence in the South would have been suicidal; political pressure was then impossible; the only recourse was economic pressure with a few fringe activities. Legally blocked by state laws, they were compelled like all Have-Nots from time immemorial to appeal to "a law higher than man-made law." Rousseau noted the obvious: that "law" is a very good thing for men with property and a very bad thing for men without property." Passive resistance remained one of the few means available to anti-segregationist forces until they had secured the voting franchise in fact. Furthermore, passive resistance was also a good defensive tactic, since it curtailed the opportunities for use of the power resources of the status quo, who possessed the means and will for forcible repression. Passive resistance was chosen for the same reason that all tactics are selected, pragmatism. But it assumes the necessary moral and religious adornments.

However, when passive resistance becomes massive and threatening, we may expect violence. Southern Negroes have no tradition of *Dharna,* and they are close enough to their Northern compatriots that contrasting conditions between the North and the South are visible as well as a constant spur. Add to this the fact that the Southern poor whites do not operate by British tradition but on a pattern of generations of violence, and the future does not argue for making a special religion of nonviolence instead of its being what it has been, the best tactic for its time and place. As more effective means become available, the Negro civil rights

---

[7]Cousins, *op. cit.*

[8]Niccolo Machiavelli, *The Prince,* chap. 17.

movement will divest itself of these decorations and substitute a new moral philosophy in keeping with its new means and opportunities. The explanation will be, as it always has been, that "times have changed." This is happening today.

The eleventh rule of the ethics of means and ends is to phrase goals in general terms like "Liberty, Equality, Fraternity," "Of the Common Welfare," "Pursuit of Happiness," or "Bread and Peace." Whitman put it this way: "The goal once named cannot be countermanded." It has been previously noted that the wise man of action knows that frequently, in the stream of action of means towards ends, whole new and unexpected ends are among the major results of the action. From a Civil War fought as a means exclusively for the preservation of the Union came the end of slavery.

Relevant to this point, it must be remembered that history is made up of actions for one end resulting in other ends. Repeatedly, scientific discoveries have resulted from experimental research committed to ends or objectives having little relationship with the discoveries. Work on a seemingly minor practical program has resulted in feedbacks of major creative ideas. Flugel notes:

In psychology, too, we have no right to be astonished if, while dealing with a means (e.g. the cure of a neurotic symptom, the discovery of more efficient ways of learning, or the relief of industrial fatigue) we find that we have modified our attitude toward the end (acquired some new insight into the nature of mental health, the role of education, or the place of work in human life.)[9]

THE ENEMIES OF CHANGE

The mental merry-go-round and shadow boxing in the area of means and ends is exemplified by those who are the observers and not the actors in the battlefields of life. We see this in Koestler's *The Yogi and the Commissar,* where Koestler begins with the basic fallacy of an arbitrary demarcation between *expediency* and *morality;* between the Yogi, for whom the end never justifies the means, and the Commissar, for whom the end always justifies the means. Koestler attempts to extricate himself from this self-constructed straitjacket by proposing that the end justifies the means only within narrow limits. Here Koestler, even on an academic confrontation with action, was compelled to take the first step in the course of compromise on the road to action and power. The questions of how "narrow" the limits are and who defines the "narrow" limits open the door to the premises discussed here. The kind of personal safety and security sought by the advocates of the sanctity of means and ends lies in the womb of Yogism or the monastery, and even there it is darkened by the repudiation of that moral principle that they are their brothers' keepers.

Bertrand Russell, in his *Human Society in Ethics and Politics,* observed:

Morality is so much concerned with means that it seems almost immoral to consider anything solely in relation to its intrinsic worth. But obviously nothing has any value as a means unless that to which it is a means has value on its own account. It follows that intrinsic value is logically prior to value as means.[10]

The means and ends moralist must be seen for what he is, a supporter of the status quo and an enemy of change; his inaction is action in support of the prevailing authorities and practices.

We have repeatedly noted that judgment of the ethics of means and ends is dependent upon the particular political position of the judge at that particular time and in the particular circumstances then operating. Means and ends are so qualitatively interrelated that the question of the ends justifying the means is unreal nonsense. The true question has never been the proverbial one, "Does the end justify the means?" but always has been and is "Does *this particular* end justify *this particular* means?"

[9]J. C. Flugel, *Man, Morals and Society* (London: Duckworth, 1955), p. 13.

[10]Bertrand Russell, *Human Society in Ethics and Politics* (N. Y.: Simon & Schuster, 1955), p. 42.